THE MAUDSLEY
Maudsley Monographs

MAUDSLEY MONOGRAPHS

HENRY MAUDSLEY, from whom the series of monographs takes its name, was the founder of The Maudsley Hospital and the most prominent English psychiatrist of his generation. The Maudsley Hospital was united with the Bethlem Royal Hospital in 1948 and its medical school, renamed the Institute of Psychiatry at the same time, became a constituent part of the British Postgraduate Medical Federation. It is now a school of King's College, London, and entrusted with the duty of advancing psychiatry by teaching and research. The South London & Maudsley NHS Trust, together with the Institute of Psychiatry, are jointly known as The Maudsley.

The monograph series reports high quality empirical work on a single topic of relevance to mental health, carried out at the Maudsley. This can be by single or multiple authors. Some of the monographs are directly concerned with clinical problems; others, are in scientific fields of direct or indirect relevance to mental health and that are cultivated for the furtherance of psychiatry.

Maudsley Monographs number forty-four

Social Inequalities and the Distribution of the Common Mental Disorders

Edited by

David Melzer
Clinical Senior Research Associate, Department of Public Health and Primary Care, University of Cambridge, UK

Tom Fryers
Visiting Professor of Public Mental Health, Department of Psychiatry, University of Leicester, UK

Rachel Jenkins
Director, WHO Collaborating Centre, Institute of Psychiatry, London, UK

Routledge
Taylor & Francis Group
LONDON AND NEW YORK

First published 2004 by Psychology Press Ltd

2 Park Square, Milton Park, Abingdon, Oxon OX14 4RN
711 Third Avenue, New York, NY 10017, USA

Routledge is an imprint of the Taylor & Francis Group, an informa business

First issued in paperback 2016

Typeset in Times by Mayhew Typesetting, Rhayader, Powys

Cover design by Lisa Dynan

British Library Cataloguing in Publication Data
A catalogue record for this book is available from the British Library

Library of Congress Cataloging-in-Publication Data
Social inequalities and the distribution of the common mental disorders / editors, David Melzer, Tom Fryers, Rachel Jenkins.
p. ; cm. – (Maudsley monographs, ISSN 0076-5465 ; no. 44)
"October 2002."
Includes bibliographical references and index.

1. Psychiatric epidemiology–Great Britain. 2. Social medicine–Great Britain. 3. Poor–Mental health–Great Britain.
[DNLM: 1. Neurotic Disorders–epidemiology–Great Britain. 2. Socioeconomic Factors–Great Britain. WM 170 S678 2004]
I. Melzer, David. II. Fryers, Tom. III. Jenkins, Rachel. IV. Series.
RC455.2.E64S626 2004
362.2'0422'0941–dc21

2003013932

ISBN 978-1-138-87196-0 (pbk)
ISBN 978-1-84169-385-9 (hbk)

Contents

List of contributors

David Melzer, Clinical Senior Research Associate, Department of Public Health and Primary Care, University of Cambridge, Cambridge CB2 2SR, UK.

Tom Fryers, Visiting Professor of Public Mental Health, Department of Psychiatry, University of Leicester, University Road, Leicester LE1 7RH, UK.

Rachel Jenkins, Director, WHO Collaborating Centre, Institute of Psychiatry, De Crespigny Park, Denmark Hill, London SE5 8AF, UK.

Brenda McWilliams, Research Associate, Department of Public Health and Primary Care, University of Cambridge, Cambridge CB2 2SR, UK.

Ajit Shah, Honorary Senior Lecturer and Consultant Psychiatrist, West London Mental Health NHS Trust, Uxbridge Road, Southall, Middlesex UB1 3EU, UK.

SUMMARY

Social inequalities and the distribution of the common mental disorders

David Melzer, Tom Fryers and Rachel Jenkins

Address for correspondence: Dr David Melzer, Department of Public Health and Primary Care, Institute of Public Health, Forvie Site, Robinson Way, Cambridge CB2 2SR, UK. Email: dm214@medschl.cam.ac.uk

KEY POINTS

(1) Links between social class and psychiatric disorder have been unclear: while the first national Psychiatric Morbidity Survey of Great Britain reported a strong association between occupational social class and the common (neurotic) mental disorders, the 1998 Health Survey of England found no link between class and psychiatric symptom scores.

(2) Report 1 re-examines large recent studies from developed countries to clarify the nature of links between the common mental disorders and social position, measured by occupational social class, education, material circumstances, or employment.

(3) We identified nine large, well-conducted studies from the UK, North America, Holland, and Australia, with good markers of mental disorders and social position. Of these, eight showed an association between one or more markers of less privileged social position and higher prevalence of the common mental disorders. No study showed a contrary trend with any indicator.

(4) Occupational social class was the least consistent marker for higher prevalence rates.

(5) Incompatible methods made estimation of effect sizes across studies invalid. We therefore analysed the first national Psychiatric Morbidity Survey to quantify associations for the British population, to identify the most specific markers, and to include measures of disability arising from the common mental disorders (Report 2).

(6) Having less education and being unemployed or economically inactive were the most consistent independent social position makers. However, people with more specific markers, such as having two or more physical illnesses, were at six times higher risk of disabling mental disorder, and those having had two or more recent adverse life events were at more than three times higher risk. Less strong risk factors were present for being a lone parent or perceiving a severe lack of social support.

(7) Within comprehensive programmes to reduce the burden of these conditions, it may be possible to target efforts to reduce mental health inequalities on relatively small and specific high-risk groups with disabling disorders. Targeting broad groups or geographical areas defined by social class is likely to be inefficient.

(8) There is evidence that ethnic minority groups experience common mental disorders at least as commonly as the general population (Report 3), and some groups may experience more. The dramatic differences in prevalence reported from clinical settings for some groups and some disorders are not evident in population surveys for the common disorders. Research thus far has been insufficient to provide unequivocal guidelines for policy, but the additional problems faced by ethnic minorities need to be specifically addressed in programmes to identify and treat common mental disorders, at all levels.

Social inequalities are established features of the distribution of physical disease in the UK and many other developed countries[1;2] and efforts to reduce these inequalities are a national priority. Severe "psychotic" mental illnesses are also distributed very unequally by social position; they are often highly disabling to sufferers, but are relatively rare. However, the majority of the burden of mental illness in the community arises from the less severe but more numerous "neurotic" conditions, dominated by anxiety, depression, or a combination of both, now called the "common mental disorders".

For the common disorders, the links with social position in the general population have been less clear: for example, of two recent large-scale government-commissioned studies covering mental health in the UK, one found occupational social class to be the strongest risk factor while the other showed no association.[3;4] Similarly, in a review of studies internationally at the end of the 1980s, Dohrenwend[5] reported that findings were inconsistent.

The reviews reported in this volume were undertaken to:

- provide a systematic review of the published evidence on the links between the range of conventional markers of social position and the common mental disorders in the general population, in developed countries (Report 1);
- quantify the strength of associations linking social position and common mental disorders, with analyses of the most detailed available British mental health data (Report 2);
- provide a systematic review of published evidence on ethnicity and the common mental disorders in Britain (Report 3).

The ultimate purpose of this work is to contribute to the evidence base for targeting mental disorders in efforts to reduce morbidity and social inequalities in the UK.

Report 1: A systematic literature review (principal author Tom Fryers)

Before about 1980, population surveys had no validated, systematic instruments to identify disorders, but since then several have been developed. Because of the inherent ambiguities of both mental disorder and social position, large populations are necessary to provide detailed analysis that can be interpreted with some confidence. It is also necessary to have data linking mental disorder and indicators of social position in individuals, although the analysis is of population frequencies. In addition, studies must be limited to developed economies if they are to have relevance to UK policy.

Therefore the following criteria were used to identify studies for inclusion in the review:

- Community-based studies (general household populations).
- Populations encompassing a broad spectrum of social class variation.
- Samples of 3000 or more adults of working age.
- Methods of identification of mental disorder by validated standard instruments.
- Social position identified by explicit, standard markers.
- A diagnostic range encompassing the common mental disorders.
- Individual data linking mental health measures and social indicators; i.e., not area studies.
- Relevance to UK policy development; studies from established market economies.
- Fieldwork undertaken since 1980.
- Published output on the key areas of interest.

A wide range of searches was undertaken to identify all eligible studies. The international research databases were searched, with limited effectiveness due to the broadness of the study focus. A wide variety of key words was used, followed by review of abstracts, follow-up of cross references, and direct enquiry of researchers and research units. Books or reports published by research institutes or government departments were also covered, a necessary source of detailed information on large-scale population surveys. From this a database of almost 1000 references was established, of published work broadly related to inequalities in mental health. This is available to future researchers.

Nine large-scale studies fulfilling our criteria were identified, and for each of these, the published work was examined independently by two researchers, in respect of the validity and reliability of their methods, and their findings regarding social position differentials in the prevalence of the common mental disorders. Four studies were from the UK, two from the USA, and one each from Canada, Australia, and The Netherlands. (Note: A recent large-scale national survey in Germany[7] provisionally gives similar positive associations with education, unemployment, and a social class index, with no negative ones.)

Findings

A number of methodological challenges arose in reviewing these studies. Measuring psychiatric symptoms and disorder is difficult, and although the studies all used recognised instruments with some published validation, there were several different ones in use, and they were not always used in the same way. The results are not, therefore, immediately comparable; no quantitative meta-analysis was possible because categories of disorder, indicators of social position, and presentation of statistics were generally diverse. It is not clear how to relate measures of symptoms experienced by individuals to measures of disorders identified by different instruments with somewhat different criteria. There are also limitations imposed by low response rates, varying between 54% and 80%.

Social position, and therefore social disadvantage, is also diversely recorded with indicators that necessarily overlap and interact. Poverty, education, housing, occupation, employment, social status, and social engagement are still the key concerns for which "social class" or "socio-economic status" are merely proxies or indicators. Additional factors that are already known to be important include childhood experience, physical illness, life events, working situations, and social networks. These are barely encompassed by the large-scale cross-sectional studies here reviewed, which cannot inform us on direction of causation, but there is information to be gained from the UK birth cohort studies and a number of other studies commented on in the report. They are also addressed in the second part of this review based upon further analysis of the UK national Psychiatric Morbidity Survey.

Nevertheless, it is possible to bring the evidence on social inequalities in these nine studies together in certain general ways to inform policy. We have concentrated on those categories that most nearly approximate to the common mental disorders, or form a major part of them. Thus all affective disorders; all depressive disorders, dysthymia, and all anxiety disorders, have mostly been the groups drawn into the comparison. Similarly, it is possible to examine in most studies three major indicators of social position: education, employment, and material circumstances, as well as the broader indicator of occupational social status.

Education was measured either as the time of completing full-time education or the qualifications achieved. Although such measures are culture-specific, it is possible to compare the lowest and highest groups in each study population. Employment status has concentrated in most cases on comparing the unemployed and seeking work with either all others of working age, or all those employed. Material circumstances are more varied, encompassing income, wealth as financial or other assets, and housing status. Again, the best comparisons tend to be between the lowest and highest social group in each case. British studies tend to use the Registrar General's Occupational Social Classes, which give some consistency in spite of the problems of application, especially to women, but other countries generally have nothing comparable.

In spite of these many inconsistencies in the data, it has proved possible to analyse these nine studies together, and to draw general conclusions. For each study, the associations between the frequency of common mental disorders in the population and particular indicators of social position have been subjected to statistical tests of significance, and the report quotes the odds ratios for each relationship wherever possible.

Of the nine core population-based studies with adequate measures of mental health and indicators of social disadvantage, *eight provide evidence of an association between less privileged social position and higher prevalence of the common mental disorders*, on at least one of the available indicators (Table S.1). The one study showing no clear relationships on any measure had the lowest response rate for its mental health measure (54%), and this may have limited its capacity to demonstrate associations. For some individual indicators in particular studies, no clear trend was evident, but *no study showed a contrary trend with any indicator.*

TABLE S.1
Number of included studies reporting associations with higher rates of the common mental disorders, by dimensions of less privileged social position

	Less education	*Unemployment*	*Lower income or material circumstances*	*Low social status*
Total reporting	5	7	6	6
Positive association				
Men and women separately	2	3*	2	2
Men and women combined (separate data not given)	2	3	4	1
Total positive	4	6	6	3
No clear association	1	1	0	3
Inverse association	0	0	0	0

* In one study, positive only for men; women equivocal.

Taking a higher prevalence of disorder in less privileged groups (unadjusted for other aspects of social position) as "positive" associations then, in relation to those studies reporting these associations:

- less education was "positive" in four out of five studies;
- unemployment showed positive associations in six out of seven studies, although in one study the association was positive only for men;
- low income, wealth, assets, or markers of material standard of living were positive in all six studies;
- less privileged occupational social class was positive in three studies out of six;
- no studies showed an inverse relationship.

While counting numbers of positive studies gives some sense of the consistency of findings, it does not convey the degree to which prevalence is increased in less privileged groups. In general, compared to the most privileged groups, the most deprived groups seldom had more than a doubling in prevalence of neurotic disorder (or a subset of these, e.g., mood disorders). For example, measures of education reported in different studies have more consistency than most of the other markers of social position. The odds ratios from reporting studies included the following:

- In Britain, those with no educational qualifications had an odds ratio of less than 1.3 compared to those with A levels, for recent neurotic disorder in the first national Psychiatric Morbidity Survey.
- In Australia, those who did not complete secondary school had an odds ratio of 1.53 compared to those with post-school qualifications, for affective disorders.
- In the US, those with 0 to 11 years of education had an odds ratio of 1.3 for mood disorder in the past 12 months, compared to those with 17 or more years of education.
- In The Netherlands, those with 0 to 11 years of education had an odds ratio of 1.55 (95% CI 1.22–1.98) for mood disorders compared to those with 16 or more years of education.

The lack of comparability in the measures of disorder and relative education in this and other examples illustrates the point that mathematical pooling of results across these studies would be invalid. Instead, this project undertook analyses of the most detailed British study (the first national Psychiatric Morbidity Survey) to explore effect sizes, establishing whether markers were independent of each other and incorporate measures of disability into the identification of cases. Results of this work are presented in Report 2 and summarised below.

Conclusions

This simple overview suggests some robustness of findings despite the many methodological limitations of a review of such diverse studies. The more precise indicators relating to education, employment, and material circumstances are better than the generalised indicator of occupational social class, but there is remarkable consistency in the broad evidence. From the evidence of the nine large-scale population-based studies carried out during the last 20 years, common mental disorders are significantly more frequent in socially disadvantaged populations, and the evidence is strongest when material indicators of social position, education, or unemployment are used to define the disadvantaged groups.

Report 2: Quantifying associations between social position and the common mental disorders in Britain (principal author David Melzer)

The review of published studies set out above provides a powerful overview of the evidence linking the common mental disorders with the traditional indicators of social disadvantage. However, the lack of comparability in the measures of disorder and relative social position made assessment of effect sizes difficult and mathematical pooling of results across these studies invalid. Instead, this project undertook analyses of the most detailed British study (the first national Psychiatric Morbidity Survey) to:

- estimate effect sizes;
- establish whether social position markers were independent of each other;
- incorporate measures of disability into the identification of cases.

The common mental disorders often cause considerable distress, but only a proportion of "cases" identified in epidemiological studies experience disability, i.e., difficulty or inability in carrying out normal activities. While most "cases" would benefit from intervention of some kind, those who have disability are a priority group in efforts to reduce the burden of these disorders. The first UK national Psychiatric Morbidity Survey of Great Britain[3] provided the most detailed data relating to the common mental disorders and disability of relevance to UK policy making.

The first UK national Psychiatric Morbidity Survey of Great Britain[3] interviewed a representative household sample of over 10,000 people aged 16–64 years. The survey employed the Clinical Interview Schedule (revised version) to define the presence of mental disorder, identifying both neurotic symptoms and neurotic disorders during the week before interview. Case definitions used for all disorders would justify some form of clinical monitoring or active treatment in primary care. Of the neurotic disorder group 63% had symptoms with an average duration of 6 months or more. In this statistical analysis of those with "neurotic disorder" we added the dimension of functional limitations or disabilities. Those with "limiting neurotic disorder" reported that "their mental symptoms stopped them doing things". Those with "disabling neurotic disorder" reported *in addition* difficulty in doing at least one "activity of daily living".

Of the general population aged 16 to 64, 15.5% had neurotic disorder, 8.3% had limiting neurotic disorder, and 3.4% had disabling neurotic disorder. These categories of common mental disorders are each composed mainly of people with depression and/or anxiety disorders. As predicted by the WHO Global Burden of Disease estimates[6] neurotic disorder made a large contribution to all reported disability in the survey: for example, 38% of those with more severe disabilities (difficulties with three or more activities of daily living) had a limiting neurotic disorder. Women have a greater risk of neurotic disorder than men, but risks were equal for disabling neurotic disorder.

Each of the available markers of less privileged social position was associated with higher prevalence rates of the common mental disorders on their own. In multivariate models adjusting for gender and age, and the competing markers (Table S.2) the "surviving" independent markers were:

- being unemployed or economically inactive;
- poorer material circumstances (housing tenure and lack of car ownership);
- less education (having left full-time schooling before age 16).

Note that odds greater than 2 were present, linking disabling disorder with being economically inactive or unemployed.

Occupational social class was not a significant marker, after adjustment of the other factors.

In comprehensive models including specific factors linked to the common disorders, adjusted for the factors in Table S.2, the strongest associations were having:

- two or more physical disorders—with an odds ratio of over 6 for disorder with disability;
- being economically inactive or having had two or more adverse life events—with odds ratios of 3 or more for disorder with disability.

Social position markers that remained independently significant in these models included having left full-time education at age 15 or younger and being unemployed.

TABLE S.2
Age- and sex-adjusted odds ratios for common mental disorders and disabling disorders, by markers of social position, from multivariate logistic regression analysis

Variable and comparison category		*Common mental disorder OR (95% CI)*	*Disabling disorder OR (95% CI)*
Type of accommodation			
vs Detached house	Flat, bedsit or other	1.31 (1.08–1.59)*	1.42 (0.96–2.10)
	Terraced	1.19 (0.97–1.44)	1.40 (0.95–2.08)
	Semi-detached	0.95 (0.78–1.16)	1.25 (0.84–1.84)
Housing tenure			
vs Owned	Rent other	1.31 (1.08–1.59)*	1.22 (0.68–2.20)
	Rent from LA or HA	1.46 (1.20–1.78)*	1.60 (1.08–2.37)*
	Mortgage	1.17 (0.96–1.43)	1.23 (0.83–1.83)
Car or van ownership			
vs 2+ cars	None	1.46 (1.20–1.78)*	1.80 (1.22–2.67)*
	One	1.20 (0.98–1.46)	1.27 (0.86–1.88)
Age left school			
vs 16 years plus	Up to 15 (including no education)	1.32 (1.09–1.61)*	1.72 (1.41–2.09)*
Work status			
vs Working full time	Economically inactive	1.68 (1.38–2.05)*	4.26 (2.88–6.31)**
	Unemployed	2.16 (1.78–2.63)**	2.97 (2.01–4.40)**
	Working part time	1.20 (0.98–1.46)	1.13 (0.76–1.67)
Occupational social class			
vs Groups I+II	Never worked	0.57 (0.31–1.02)	0.76 (0.35–1.67)
	IV+V	0.93 (0.77–1.13)	1.07 (0.72–1.59)
	III M	0.97 (0.80–1.18)	0.91 (0.75–1.11)
	III NM	1.17 (0.96–1.43)	1.13 (0.76–1.67)

*statistically significant odds at $p < 0.5$, ** odds greater than 2.0.

Odds for disorder in the major ethnic groups did not reach statistical significance. Lone parents, those with physical diseases involving two or more disease systems, and those who were unemployed, together made up 20% of the population but contributed 51% of those with disabling common mental disorder. Only 35% of all those with disorder had spoken to their general practitioner about mental health problems during the previous year, in 1993. In the high-risk groups identified above, between 44% and 56% had spoken to a GP about such problems.

Discussion

The work presented above was based largely on cross-sectional data, and it is thus impossible to clarify from most of the studies examined whether less privileged material circumstances cause the common mental disorders, or vice versa. As discussed in the systematic review, the wider evidence does provide some support for a causal link, with deprived circumstances causing the disorders. It is important, however, that the direction of causality in the link between neurotic disorder and inequality is fully clarified, with a longitudinal study.

A second major limitation of this analysis is that certain important potential risks were absent from the available data, including, for example, carer status (carers have high rates of depression), and history of abuse.

The lone parent group raises concern partly because the children of lone parents suffering from a common mental disorder can be adversely affected. In the survey, 3% of children were in this category, although this may be an underestimate. There was a sizeable increase during the 1990s in the percentage of households headed by a lone parent.

Report 3: Ethnicity and the common mental disorders (principal author Ajit Shah)

Psychiatric morbidity is a major source of ill health, social disability, and use of health and social services. The epidemiology of common mental disorders in younger adults from ethnic minority groups has been sparsely studied in the UK, but the proportion of ethnic minority individuals is increasing. This review focuses on population-based studies of common mental disorders in ethnic minority groups in the UK, where large-scale surveys can assist policy development by providing information on prevalence, social consequences, aetiology, and implications for health and social services.

Methods

The review focuses on population-based studies of common mental disorders in ethnic minority groups with the following characteristics:

- Community-based studies in the UK including an ethnic minority population.
- Age-group to include 16–64 years.
- A diagnostic range encompassing the common mental disorders.
- Use of standardised screening and diagnostic instruments to identify the common mental disorders.
- A clear definition of ethnicity.

- Published data on the common mental disorders related to ethnicity.
- Studies conducted in the last 15 years (so that they are of current relevance).

So few studies have been done that limiting sample size would have left little to consider and some ethnic groups unrepresented.

Results

Definitions of ethnicity and methods of ascertaining ethnicity varied, and ethnic groups were often amalgamated into heterogeneous categories without any clear rationale other than small numbers. Sample size was often small and confidence intervals were consequently wide. Comparison groups were inadequately defined or absent, or were unrepresentative of the population due to the sampling method used. Some sampling methods, such as postal surveys, were inappropriate to populations with high levels of illiteracy, leading to low response rates.

Instruments used to detect common mental disorders were only partially evaluated and were often based on unwarranted assumptions that instruments effective in one ethnic group or one setting (e.g., primary care or hospitals), would be effective in other groups or settings (e.g., community). Special issues of ethnic minorities, such as language and literacy, were not always accommodated, and details of analysis were often not reported. Different methods and presentation of results thus made direct comparison difficult, but some general conclusions emerged.

There was no clear evidence that the prevalence of common mental disorders in any ethnic minority group studied was lower than in the general population; the available evidence suggests that it was at least similar, and in some ethnic groups may be higher. In particular, the prevalence of the common mental disorders, particularly depression, may be higher in Caribbean and African groups compared to the white population, anxiety may be more frequent in Irish-born populations, and phobias more common in Asian and Oriental groups.

A number of probable risk factors for the common mental disorders in ethnic minority groups were identified, though not confirmed by multiple studies:

- absence of a full-time worker in the household;
- unemployment, low standard of living, financial difficulties;
- migration before the age of 11;
- being a lone parent;
- victimisation, personal attacks, racial harassment;
- problems with the police;

- discrimination in housing and employment;
- absence of a confidante, absence of parents in law, social isolation, small primary group, and perceived lack of social support.

One study found that the common mental disorders were more prevalent among ethnic minority people who lived in areas of low density of their own ethnic group, suggesting that living in areas of high density of their own group may have a protective effect.

Although all ethnic minority groups had higher GP consultation rates than Whites, those with common mental disorders generally appear to have lower rates of treatment. In particular, members of Caribbean and African groups appear to receive fewer anti-depressants and minor tranquillisers, and use therapists, social workers, and alternative healers less frequently than White and South Asian groups.

Discussion

The common mental disorders in ethnic minority populations in the UK have been subject to very little study. The few population studies available are very varied in method and presentation, and some have such small numbers or adopt such heterogeneous categories that little of consequence can be drawn from them. The results reviewed have been found in one or more studies but none can be said to have been established with reasonable certainty by multiple studies. However, the broadest generalisation can be made that these studies collectively suggest that common mental disorders are generally at least as common in all ethnic minority groups as in the indigenous population, and maybe more so in some. The dramatic differences in prevalence of some disorders for specific groups suggested by studies from clinical settings are not evident in the population-level studies reviewed. Probable risk factors identified in the literature need further research to clarify their status. It seems probable that, in spite of high general-practice consultation rates, identification and treatment rates are relatively low.

Overall conclusions across Reports 1 to 3

(1) The common mental disorders (including depression, anxiety, and certain other psychiatric syndromes) are linked to markers of lower social position. There is limited evidence that lower social position is involved in producing this excess of common mental disorder in relatively deprived groups.

(2) The excess of common mental disorders is *not* well described by occupational social class in the general population. More specific

relevant social position markers include unemployment or economic inactivity, poorer material circumstances, and less education.

(3) The large contribution of the common disorders to morbidity and disability in working-age adults justifies priority being given to addressing mental health inequalities within social and economic policy. Comprehensive care initiatives are also needed, including improvement in access to effective diagnosis and treatment, especially at the primary healthcare level.

(4) There are very high-risk sub-groups for more severe (disabling) disorders, including those who are unemployed or economically inactive, those with two or more physical illness or physical disabilities, and single parents. There is a need to evaluate efforts to reduce mental health inequalities by targeting such groups within comprehensive programmes to reduce the burden of these conditions.

(5) There is evidence that the common mental disorders are at least as prevalent in ethnic minorities as in the general population, and in some cases perhaps more prevalent. However, the dramatic differences in prevalence reported from clinical settings for some groups and disorders are not evident in population surveys for the common disorders. Research up to now has been insufficient and inadequate to provide unequivocal guidelines for policy, but the additional problems of ethnic minorities need to be specifically addressed in programmes to identify and treat the common mental disorders at all levels.

(6) The research relating mental ill-health to socio-economic status has already produced a wealth of useful evidence. However, general conclusions useful to policy makers are to some extent prejudiced by the use of a wide variety of different measures, which produce incompatible analyses. Efforts should be made to standardise and validate a small range of instruments and indicators, for use in future studies.

Acknowledgements

We thank Professor Terry Brugha for his invaluable input on the survey instruments and diagnostic issues. We acknowledge the help of The Data Archive, University of Essex, for supplying material relating to the National Survey of Psychiatric Morbidity.

This work was undertaken by the University of Cambridge who received funding from the Department of Health; the views expressed in this publication are those of the authors and not necessarily those of the Department of Health.

Notes

1. Acheson D. *Independent Inquiry into Inequalities in Health.* London: The Stationery Office, 1998.
2. Marmot M, Wilkinson R. *Social Determinants of Health.* Oxford: Oxford University Press, 1999.
3. Meltzer H, Gill B, Petticrew M, Hinds K. *The Prevalence of Psychiatric Morbidity among Adults Living in Private Households. 1.* London: ONS, 1995.
4. Erens B, Primatesta P (Eds). *Health Survey for England: Cardiovascular Disease 1998.* London: The Stationery Office, 1999.
5. Dohrenwend BP. Socio-economic status (SES) and psychiatric disorders: Are the issues still compelling? *Social Psychiatry and Psychiatric Epidemiology* 1990;**25**:41–7.
6. Murray C, Lopez AD. *The Global Burden of Disease.* Harvard: Harvard School of Public Health, 1996.
7. Wittchen HU, Carter RM, Pfister H, Montgomery SA, Kessler RC. Disabilities and quality of life in pure and comorbid generalized anxiety disorder and major depression in a national survey. *International Clinical Psychopharmacology* 2000;**15**(6):319–28.

REPORT ONE

A systematic literature review

Tom Fryers, David Melzer, Brenda McWilliams and Rachel Jenkins

Address for correspondence: Dr David Melzer, Institute of Public Health, Forvie Site, Robinson Way, Cambridge CB2 2SR, UK. Email: dm214@medschl.cam.ac.uk

We thank Professor Terry Brugha for his invaluable input on the survey instruments and diagnostic issues.

This work was undertaken by the University of Cambridge who received funding from the Department of Health; the views expressed in this publication are those of the authors and not necessarily those of the Department of Health.

Contents: Report one

List of tables and figure: Report one

TABLES

FIGURE

1.1 INTRODUCTION

Social inequalities are established features of the distribution of physical disease in the UK and many other developed countries.[1;2] In most physical diseases, a clear trend of poorer health is evident with each step down the hierarchy of social position, defined either by lower social status or by poorer material circumstances. This stepwise trend across social classes was present throughout the 20th century and only a handful of clinical conditions show a distribution that does not follow this pattern.

By contrast, the nature of links between social position and mental illness in the general population has appeared less clear. For example, while the first national Survey of Psychiatric Morbidity in Great Britain[3] reported a strong association between social class and the common (neurotic) mental disorders, the 1998 Health Survey for England found no link between social class and psychiatric symptom scores.[4] In a 1990 review, Dohrenwend[5] commented on the inconsistency in findings relating mental disorders to socio-economic status, at that time. In addition, surveys showing that the related concept of "stress" is more commonly reported by people in more privileged social classes have added to the apparent confusion.[6;7]

This lack of clarity in the evidence on social inequalities and mental health is problematic, as mental disorders are major causes of disability, especially in adults of working age. The "Global Burden of Disease" study[8] for the World Health Organization and the World Bank estimated that mental illness is responsible for 38% of all years lived with a disability in women and 25% in men in the established market economies.

In July 1997, the UK Government commissioned an independent inquiry into "Inequalities and Health".[1] Unfortunately, this inquiry gave relatively little attention to mental health. However, in 1998 the Department of Health commissioned this review of current evidence on mental health and social inequalities. The review includes three major components:

- A systematic review of recent large-scale epidemiological studies containing data on the common mental disorders and inequalities in social position, in developed countries (Report 1).
- A further analysis of the 1993 National Survey of Psychiatric Morbidity of the general adult population, to quantify the associations for British policy making (Report 2).
- A literature review of epidemiological research relating to ethnic differences in the frequency of common mental disorders (Report 3).

In Report 1 we review the evidence now available from large-scale population-based surveys, supplemented where appropriate with evidence from other relevant research.

1.1.1 Scope of the review

The severe "psychotic" mental illnesses are often highly disabling to sufferers, but they are also relatively rare in general populations. The link between economic deprivation and the psychotic conditions is very well established, including from the first UK national Household Psychiatric Survey of people with these conditions in Great Britain in 1993.[9]

The majority of the burden of mental illness arises from the less severe but far more numerous "neurotic" conditions, dominated by anxiety and depression, separately or together, which are now called the "common mental disorders". It is this latter category that provides the focus for this report. The literature on "stress" has not been included; the complexities of definition and measurement render interpretation very difficult and there is no direct or clear relationship to the common mental disorders.

The notion of inequalities in health includes very many dimensions, and unfortunately it is not possible to consider all aspects together. In this review, we have not focused on the following specific issues:

- Gender differentials—because a recent comprehensive review has been published by WHO.[10] However, gender differences are so fundamental that it is inevitable that reference to gender frequently appears in the report.
- Ethnic or race differences—because this requires different though overlapping issues to be addressed, which generally do not arise within the large-scale population studies addressing social position, and because most studies are from the USA and findings cannot readily be translated into a UK context. There are some data available, however, particularly from the fourth British National Survey of ethnic minorities, which provide recent population-level evidence on the links between ethnicity and mental health in Britain,[11] so this[12;13] is made the subject of a separate literature review (Report 3).
- Populations with special needs, such as homeless people or prisoners—the Office for National Statistics has published recent psychiatric surveys on these sub-populations which provide ample evidence of high prevalence rates of psychiatric illness.
- Inequalities in use, access and quality of services—because they represent a rather different set of issues from studies of the population frequency of disorders.

1.1.2 Mechanisms of disadvantage

There are many ways in which disadvantages in mental health may differentially occur within general populations, any of which may affect the expression, identification, and distribution of the common mental disorders, and which may need to be considered in interpreting epidemiological data. Inequality and inequity might occur in the distribution of:

- mental illness (MI) or mental health problems (MHP);
- personal and social factors causing MI and MHP;
- personal and social factors that increase resistance to MI and MHP;
- personal and social factors that facilitate recovery;
- personal and social factors that handicap individuals with MI or MHP;
- and/or access to services that help to prevent MI;
- and/or access to services that limit morbidity in duration or severity;
- and/or access to services that diminish social disadvantage.

The primary objective of the review was to establish whether less privileged general population groups have higher prevalence rates of the common mental disorders and, therefore, to examine the evidence for differential distribution of the common mental disorders according to markers of social position. Having achieved that aim, the limited information available to clarify the causal mechanism(s) is also discussed.

There is a very large literature of small-scale studies that are difficult to interpret in relation to population prevalence, because of small numbers, study groups not representative of large-scale populations, non-standard or non-validated measures of either mental disorders or social position, or absence of appropriate analyses to inform this issue. The main review, therefore, was based entirely on data from large-scale community surveys with validated measures of psychiatric symptoms and mental disorders, and relevant indicators of social class, socio-economic status, or social disadvantage. However, there is some discussion of additional evidence drawn from other studies.

1.1.3 Outline of Report 1

In the sections that follow, we will describe:

- The strategy and methods of the review, including the inclusion criteria used to select the well-conducted studies of links between social position and the common mental disorders (Section 1.2). Summaries of the studies meeting inclusion criteria (Section 1.2.5). (Rejected and additional studies that provide some evidence on specific issues are summarised in Appendix A.)
- Issues involved in identifying "cases" and recording psychiatric symptoms in epidemiological surveys, and interpreting the results, including details of the diagnostic instruments used in the studies reviewed (Section 1.3).

- Issues relating to the measurement of social position, and the overlapping nature of most of the available indicators (Section 1.4).
- The results of the review, with detailed presentation of findings on each measure of social deprivation (Section 1.5).
- Conclusions and recommendations (Section 1.6).

1.2 REVIEW STRATEGY AND METHODS AND PRELIMINARY EVALUATION OF THE AVAILABLE EVIDENCE

The earliest population-based psychiatric surveys had no systematic instruments to identify disorders, and even later, research varied in what was intended to be measured by the various instruments under development.[14] This review has therefore focused upon those large-scale population surveys undertaken after 1980, by which time validated instruments were beginning to appear and to be applied to detecting common mental disorders in large representative populations.

An initial scoping search of the research literature indicated a broad and varied use of the concept and term "inequalities", with studies and papers addressing many different, overlapping issues, often without standardised definition. A principal group is of those addressing the obviously related issues of social class (or socio-economic status/socio-economic group), income differentials and material resources, education, and employment. Others address issues of stressful environments, life event experiences, or life-styles in adulthood, or similar issues in childhood including genetic factors. Others address gender or ethnic differentials, and yet others address disadvantages in society for people with psychiatric disorders and their carers, including differential access to or quality of care.

Not all of these could be comprehensively encompassed in one review, although none can be entirely avoided in discussion of the principal group of indicators of social status. The main exclusions are explained below.

1.2.1 Inclusion criteria

For the reasons set out above, the focus became clearly defined in terms of the common mental disorders and social class or socio-economic status, perhaps better called "social position". This necessarily included the connected issues of income and material resources, education, and employment. Other issues could not be wholly excluded, of course, but would be dealt with in this context as they arose within broader studies of social position, with those apparently of some importance given some detail.

The following criteria were adopted for identifying studies to be included in the main systematic review:

- Community-based studies (general household populations).
- Samples of at least 3000 people.
- Populations encompassing a broad spectrum of social class variations.
- Social position indicated by explicit, standard markers.
- Methods of identification of the common mental illnesses by validated standard instruments or measures.
- A diagnostic range encompassing the common mental disorders.
- Individual data linking mental health measures and social indicators; i.e. not area studies.
- Relevant to the UK policy context—studies from developed countries/established market economies: Western Europe, North America, Australia, New Zealand (no relevant studies from Japan were identified).
- Studies undertaken in the last 20 years (fieldwork 1980 and after).
- Published output on the key areas of interest.

1.2.2 Issues not included in the review

The major mental disorders, mostly psychoses, were not the subject of our review. However, they were usually encompassed by the large-scale studies we have reviewed, so that they are included in some of the descriptions of the studies later in this section. There are also occasional references to findings in Section 1.5 where there is a particular point of interest.

"Stress" has often been investigated and was sometimes encompassed by the large-scale surveys included in this review. However, self-reported "stress" cannot be construed as representing psychiatric symptoms, and even less "mental disorder". It is conceptualised in a variety of ways often confusing objective stressors, subjective experience of those stressors, and the physical and psychological responses to or sequellae of those experiences. It is generally the subject of a very different body of literature from psychiatric symptoms and common mental disorders, and is addressed in this review only where it arises as part of the description of the major surveys later in this section.

Because aspects of social difference and disadvantage are so many and varied—though overlapping and inter-relating—it is impossible to focus on all of them in one review, and it is necessary to be selective. Of the several known important factors likely to reveal mental health differentials, gender was the most obvious, as, whatever else is the focus of study, gender differences almost always appear and must be taken into account. However, it has recently been comprehensively reviewed on behalf of, and published by, the World Health Organization.[15]

For ethnic and race differences, most studies providing evidence that can be interpreted in terms of social-economic status and other related variables were conducted in the USA, and it is unlikely that findings can validly be translated into a UK context. UK studies have often focused on psychotic illness or differentials in admission to hospital and receipt of treatment, which are not the major concerns of this review.[16] The fourth British National Survey of Ethnic Minorities has provided recent population-based evidence on the links between ethnicity and mental disorders in the UK,[11] and there is some other relevant evidence.[12;13] It is an area of substantial current interest, therefore a parallel review of the relevant literature appears as Report 3 of this publication.[17]

Homeless groups have been subjected to a great deal of research, and there can be no doubt about the high prevalence rates for mental illness among them,[18] but most published studies are exclusively of groups of homeless people, without full community control populations. In this case too, many are from the USA where cultural differences make application to the UK very difficult.

Inequalities in use, access, and quality of services have not been included per se, because they represent a rather different set of issues from studies of population frequency of disorders. However, the issues sometimes arise in the context of the studies of distribution. Moreover, we are unlikely to find internationally applicable data. As an illustration of this, published comparisons of NCS data on treatment rates in the USA with the Canadian Ontario Health Survey of 1990 suggested that lower rates in the USA were related to financial barriers. This is supported by the finding that in the USA those in the highest income group were most likely to receive psychiatric care, and almost entirely from the specialist sector, while in Canada those in the lowest income group were most likely to receive psychiatric care, both from specialist and generalist sectors.[19–21]

1.2.3 Search strategy

The available international research databases offer huge potential for reviewing the literature, but they are not equally effective in all areas. For precisely defined, commonly used categories of medical disorder, they can provide an efficient source of appropriate information from a focused set of published papers. However, broader, more ambiguous, less clinical, and less commonly used categories can prove resistant to the most persistent search. "Inequalities" and "mental health" or "common mental disorders" inevitably proved problematic. For example, a search in MEDLINE using the MESH terms "mental disorders" and "prevalence" yielded 16,627 citations in March 2001, far too many to process. A search using the terms "Neurotic disorders" and "prevalence" yielded 154 papers, and "Neurotic disorders" and "incidence" yielded 150. When combined there were 162 separate papers, which after screening yielded 22 studies for checking. However, on examination, only one of these studies met the inclusion criteria. It is apparent that many well-known and relevant epidemiological studies were missed by this MESH heading search, despite the "catch-all" nature of the terms used.

In addition, the research databases do not include books or reports published by research institutes or government departments, a likely source of detailed information on large-scale population surveys. The search strategy ultimately adopted for this poorly defined and ill-standardised field was, therefore, necessarily broad. A wide range of searches were undertaken using EMBASE and MEDLINE international databases, in medical, psychological, sociological, and other journals, largely in English. Search terms included:

- psychiatry, psychiatric symptoms/disorder/illness, mental disorder/illness, emotional disorder/illness, mental health;
- epidemiology, frequency, prevalence, incidence, community/population surveys;
- social class/status, socio-economic class/status, income, wealth, material resources, education, employment, occupation;
- inequality, inequity, disadvantage, poverty.

These searches led to the identification of several large-scale studies matching the inclusion criteria, together with a wide range of other related research. It was then possible to:

- follow-up cross-references in publications addressing the key issues, to identify other relevant studies and published reviews, using author searches;
- make direct enquiry of certain authors, research group leaders, and researchers known to be experienced in the field, for relevant publications, additional authors, and unpublished or informally published reports;
- review large numbers of abstracts, and obtain copies of selected full papers, where relevant, from journals, libraries, the British Library, authors, and research institutions;
- make requests to various institutions for unpublished reports of methodological details of major surveys;
- discuss with a number of experienced researchers and prominent authors in the field in the UK and the USA.

From this, a large database of almost 1000 references was established, of published work broadly related to or relevant to inequalities in mental health. Most are papers published in the last 10 years and almost all include abstracts. This should be a useful starting point for future projects, and the database is to be made available to any future researchers.

Within this large collection of literature, we identified all the studies that fulfilled our inclusion criteria. Given our focus on large-scale well-conducted population studies, we believe that it is unlikely that our search strategies failed to identify any relevant study. For each of these major studies, the published work was examined in respect of:

- the validity and reliability of their methods;
- their findings regarding socio-economic status differentials in the prevalence of the common mental disorders.

A standard form was developed for summarising study characteristics, method details, and findings for each study considered for inclusion in the review. The data extraction was carried out by one of the authors (Tom Fryers) and independently by another author (Brenda McWilliams). This task did not prove easy: sources of method detail are often difficult to track down, and may be available only within unpublished reports from research units, government departments or other agencies, from which they may be very difficult to extract.

1.2.4 Preliminary assessment of findings

There were few studies revealed in the literature search which did not require substantial qualification before being used. There was no possibility of combining data in any form of meta-analysis, and the hope of considering all the major studies available as a single coherent body of work could be only partially fulfilled. There has been so little standardisation of measures of both psychiatric disorder and social position that straight comparison and collective consideration were barely possible.

Some studies addressed mental health issues rather tangentially. Some large-scale studies, including mental health amongst other aspects of health, have produced few published papers addressing mental health issues. However, some other issues, such as the longitudinal relationship of previous childhood characteristics and experiences to subsequent adult psychiatric disorder, may be of interest in the context of socio-economic differences, because childhood conditions, events and experiences are themselves unequally distributed by socio-economic group, and thus may be worth drawing to attention and commenting upon.

1.2.5 Cross-sectional psychiatric surveys included in the review

Table 1.1 summarises the main methodological features of the cross-sectional studies that met the inclusion criteria. Studies not meeting the criteria, but nevertheless providing some relevant evidence are summarised in Appendix A. A description of each of the studies included in the main analysis is set out below, together with some discussion of the individual findings. The results of studies are presented quantitatively in Section 1.5, grouped by each major measure of social position. It should be remembered that few studies shared the same instruments and means of collection of data, and few analyses in the literature use exactly the same diagnostic categories and indicators of social status. In some cases, the cross-sectional studies also had a longitudinal component. The second UK national Household Psychiatric Survey of 2000 has not yet published analyses relating specifically to markers of social position. It is not included in the tables or in comparisons, but a short description of what is already available in given in Section 1.2.5.3.

1.2.5.1 Health Survey for England, 1993–98

In response to the national "Health of the Nation" strategy in the UK, an annual sample survey was started in 1991 of adults aged 16 and over in England comprising structured interviews and clinical tests. From 1993 to 1999, with the exception of 1996, the survey included the General Health Questionnaire, 12-question version (GHQ-12),[22] which was designed to identify common mental disorders, together with two additional questions about stress. Data on perceived social support, occupation, income, material standard of living, and employment have also been recorded. In 1993, 16,569 interviews were completed; in 1998, the latest year for which a report is available, 15,908 interviews were completed with people aged 16 or over, a response rate of 74% of sampled households, and 92% of adults within these households.[4;23] According to one report, the EQ-5D European questionnaire, which includes a section on anxiety and depression, has also been used.[24]

Using GHQ-12, a score of 4 or more was considered "positive"; that is, likely to have a psychiatric disorder diagnosable by a clinician. In 1998, this was recorded for 13% of men and 18% of women, and there was little variation from 1993 to 1998. Frequencies correlated highly with perceived lack of social support, and both recent acute sickness and long-standing illness. There was variation but no clear pattern of GHQ-12 results with age, although long-standing illness, recorded on average by 40% of men and 41% of women, increased steadily with age.[25]

There has been limited analysis by occupational social class; from 1993, men in social classes I and II, and women in social class II reported the highest stress levels, controlled for age. People with a "high work pace" reported more stress affecting their health. Social classes I and II were more likely to have a high pace at work, but very much less likely to have little variety and low control than manual social classes. In 1998, there were

TABLE 1.1
Details of the cross-sectional and limited follow-up studies that met the inclusion criteria for the review

							Measures included in published mental health results				
	Year	*Type of study*	*Population sampled*	*Size of sample (achieved)*	*Response rate*	*Mental health instrument*	*Social status*	*Employment status*	*Income and material standard of living*	*Education*	*Comments*
UK Surveys											
Annual Health Surveys for England	1993, repeated annually	Population survey	All adults in England, children from 1995	16,569 (in 1993)	76% for full interview, 66% for nurse tests (1993)	GHQ-12, cut-off 4+	Occupational social class	Yes	Yes, including housing	–	GHQ results published for 1993 and 1995, summary results for 1998
National Survey of Psychiatric Morbidity in Great Britain (household sample)	1993	Population survey	All adults in England, Wales, and Scotland (excluding Highland and Islands)	10,108	80%	Clinical Interview Schedule (revised)	Occupational social class	Yes	Yes, including housing tenure and type, and car ownership	Years of, qualifications	
Health and Lifestyle Survey	1984–85	Population survey	Adults 18+, England, Wales, Scotland	9,003	73% for interview, 54% for self-completed questionnaire	GHQ-30 (+ a malaise measure)	Occupational social class (of head of household)	Yes	Housing tenure and income	Yes	
Health and Lifestyle Survey – follow-up	1991–92	Follow-up of 1984–85 respondents	Adults 18+, England, Wales, Scotland	5,352	59% of those interviewed in 1984–85 were re-interviewed	GHQ-30 (+ a malaise measure)	Occupational social class (of head of household)	Yes	Housing tenure and income	Yes	

British Household Panel Survey	1991–92	Population survey, with follow-up after one year	Adults aged 16+, households in Great Britain, south of Caledonian Canal	10,264	74% of 7488 households	GHQ-12, cut-off 3+	Occupational social class (personal and head of household)	Yes	Yes, including housing	–	Used combined indicator of material standards of living
Other Countries											
National Comorbidity Study (USA)	1990–92	Population survey	Continental US residents, adults 15 to 54	8098	83%	Composite Inter-national Diagnostic Interview	–	Yes	Yes	Yes	
Epidemiologic Catchment Area Program (USA)	1980–83	Population survey in five sites in USA	Age 18+, not institutional residents	approx. 15,000 (3000 per site)	68% to 80%	Diagnostic Interview Schedule	Socio-economic status Nam-Powers index	Yes	Yes	Yes	
Australian National Mental Health Survey	1997	Population survey	Australian population aged 18+	10,641	78%	Composite Inter-national Diagnostic Interview	–	Yes	–	Yes	
Edmonton Survey of Psychiatric Disorders (Canada)	1983–86	Population survey	Adult (all ages) population of Edmonton City, Alberta, Canada	3258	73%	Diagnostic Interview Schedule; GHQ-30	–	Yes	–	–	
Netherlands Mental Health Survey and Incidence Study (NEMESIS)	1996	Population survey with follow-up at 1 and 3 years	Adults 18–64 resident in The Netherlands	7147	64%	Composite International Diagnostic Interview; GHQ-12	–	Yes	Yes	Yes	

Details of rejected studies are set out in Appendix B.

variations in high GHQ score frequencies by occupational social class, in which classes IV and V showed more high scorers than classes I and II in both men and women, but the overall pattern including social classes III non-manual and III manual was not considered significant.[4]

However, GHQ-12 scores of 4 or more have shown marked and significant consistent decreases with increasing equivalised household income, especially among men, but weaker in women. In 1998, the age-standardised proportion of men scoring 4 or more increased from 9% in the highest income quintile to 20% in the lowest income quintile. Severe lack of social support was highly correlated with high GHQ-12 scores. This reduced the odds ratios to non-significance for high GHQ scores in women of low income. There is some lack of clarity in the relationships analysed: GHQ high scores and severe lack of social support were strongly related; severe lack of social support was strongly related to occupational social class, but GHQ high scores were not clearly or strongly related to social class.[4]

Summary GHQ-12 statistics for 1994 to 1996 are available, analysed by type of area, although the areas do not necessarily imply clearly defined social class differentiation. Of six categories, four—"mining and industrial", "urban", "mature", and "prosperous"—had frequencies of GHQ-12 scores of 4 or more, very close to the average for all England, except for a small excess for women in "mature" communities. However, of the other two, "Inner London" had significantly more, and "rural" communities significantly less than the all England average for both men and women. In 1998, Inner London areas had significantly higher frequencies than other area types.[4]

1.2.5.2 The first national Survey of Psychiatric Morbidity in Great Britain, 1993

Out of a representative sample of over 15,000 households in Great Britain, over 12,000 adults aged 16–64 were selected for the first national Household Psychiatric Survey and over 10,000 interviewed in 1993, a response rate of 80%.[3] The Clinical Interview Schedule–Revised (CIS-R) was administered by trained lay interviewers and scores were converted by computer algorithms to ICD-10 diagnostic categories. A score of 12 or more was taken as the threshold for "likely to have a neurotic disorder". In addition the Psychosis Screening Questionnaire, developed specifically for the survey, identified people with "possible psychosis" who were to be followed-up with a SCAN (Schedules for Clinical Assessment in Neuropsychiatry) interview by a clinician. There was a separate alcohol and drug schedule. Data on occupational social class, income, material standard of living, housing status, education and employment were all available.[26]

Women had more than men of each neurotic disorder in the week before interview, with a prevalence of 19.5% and 12% for neurotic disorders in total, respectively. There was a clear gradient in occupational social class for women, about 15% for social classes I–II, to 25% for social classes IV–V, but this gradient more or less disappeared after adjustment for age, family unit, car access, housing tenure, education, and economic activity. For men, all classes were similar at 12–14%, except for social class I with only 6%, a relationship that remained after adjustment.[27] Unemployed men and women revealed much higher rates of neurotic disorder than those employed, and unemployment was the factor most strongly associated with symptom prevalence. Rates for economically inactive women were mid-way, but economically inactive men were not much different from those unemployed.

Housing tenure, house type, and ownership of car or van all show clear gradients for both probable neurotic disorders and individual symptoms. These may all be pointing to the same group of relatively disadvantaged people in terms of standard of living, but this is not revealed by conventional occupational social class distributions. Probable neurosis was more common in urban than rural areas. Those with least education or qualifications had the highest rates of probable neurosis for both men and women, but this was not sustained when adjusted for other socio-demographic variables.

Functional psychosis showed extremely high figures in social class V in both sexes, but very low in social class I only for men. Frequencies for functional psychosis were strongly related to employment status, the highest being unemployed. The lowest-status groups in housing tenure and type had the highest rates of functional psychosis in both men and women. Urban frequencies of functional psychosis were always higher than rural frequencies.[26;28]

1.2.5.3 The second national Survey of Psychiatric Morbidity in Great Britain, 2000

The second UK national Household Psychiatric Survey of 2000 largely followed the pattern and methods of the first survey, but also included adults aged from 65 to 74.[29] Over 8800 interviews were conducted (response rate 69%) using the CIS-R among other questionnaires, and the SCAN if "possible psychosis" was indicated. There were separate alcohol, drug, and personality disorder schedules, and similar personal data were collected to the previous survey.

As in 1993, in the week prior to interview, the prevalence of neurotic disorder was higher in women (19.4%) than in men (13.5%) and this was true for all categories of disorder except panic. Comparing figures for ages 16–64 with 1993 (slightly adjusted since the original publications), women were slightly higher (20.2%; 19.9%) and men were significantly higher

(14.4%; 12.6%), especially in the 45–54 age group where the increase was from 12.6% in 1993 to 17.6% in 2000.

Prevalence analysis by markers of social inequality is not yet available, but data already published indicate some continuing gradient with occupational social class. Men with neurotic disorder were more likely to have no educational qualifications than those without, but there were no significant differences for women. There appears to be some change since 1993 in the relationship with employment, perhaps related to the substantial fall in general unemployment in the UK since 1993. In the 2000 survey, unemployment was not associated with higher prevalence of neurotic disorder, but there were only small numbers of respondents who were unemployed. Being economically inactive, however, was far more common among those with any neurotic disorder (39%) than those without (28%). Those with a neurotic disorder were far more likely to be renting their home (26%) than those without (15%), and conversely, much less likely to be outright home-owners (15%) than those without a neurotic disorder (25%).

Those with possible psychosis were even more likely to be of low occupational social class, to have poor educational qualifications, to be economically inactive, and to live in rented accommodation.

As far as available data permit us to judge, the general indications regarding social inequalities in the common mental disorders are similar to the first survey.

Functional psychosis showed extremely high figures in social class V in both sexes, but very low in social class I only for men. Frequencies for functional psychosis were strongly related to employment status, the highest being unemployed. The lowest-status groups in housing tenure and type had the highest rates of functional psychosis in both men and women. Urban frequencies of functional psychosis were always higher than rural frequencies.[29]

1.2.5.4 The Health and Lifestyle Survey (HALS), 1984–85 and 1991–92

Two home visits were paid to a sample of residents of Great Britain aged 18 years or over, first for an hour-long interview, involving 9003 people, and second for an examination by a nurse, achieving 82.4% of the interviewed sample, and including tests of cognitive function, that is, memory, reasoning, and reaction time. The GHQ-30 was used and 6572 were completed. A score of 5 or more was treated as positive, but the prevalence was so high that the researchers considered it an unrealistic estimate for real illness, and contemplated using a higher cut-off point. They noted that scores were continuously varied for both men and women.[30] The Eysenck Personality Inventory (EPI) and the Framingham Type-A Personality Scale were also used.

For socio-economic indicators, the survey recorded the occupation of the head of the household, but also collected data on income, housing tenure, and education. Although the original sample had not been designed for follow-up, and no regular contact had been kept, a 7-year follow-up traced and re-interviewed 5352 people (59% of the original sample), using similar measures of mental status.[31]

Self-reported "ever had depression" was, "like all other indicators of ill-health", distributed in a social class gradient with no sharp steps.[32] In men, the highest GHQ-30 scores were in occupational social classes I–II, in the age group 18–39. The lowest were in social classes IV–V, in age group 65 and over. In women, the highest GHQ-30 scores were in occupational social classes IV–V, in the age group 65 and over, the lowest in social classes I–II, also in the age group 65 and over. The researchers considered these results to be "difficult to interpret".[30] High scores in 1984–85 were closely correlated with high scores at follow-up in 1991–92. High scores in 1991–92 were not clearly related to unemployment, but in 1984–85 there had been approximately double the frequency of GHQ high scores in unemployed compared to employed men in two separate age groups. People divorcing between 1984–85 and 1991–92 had had the highest scores in 1984–85. Living alone and being over age 65 was associated with high scores. The EPI scores for neuroticism and extroversion proved unreliable.[30]

There was an association of high frequencies of GHQ-30 scores of 5 or more with life events, especially if these events were recalled by the subject as "stressful". One stressful life event doubled the frequency of GHQ-30 scores of 5 or more, but the possibility of recall bias makes this unreliable.[30]

Particularly interesting was the finding that GHQ-30 scores of 5 or more in 1984–85 were associated with significantly increased all-cause mortality after 7 years, the association remaining after adjustment for age, sex, social class, smoking behaviour, and limiting long-standing illness, and after removing "un-natural" deaths which might have been specifically related to psychiatric disorder. Smoking was, of course, independently associated with higher mortality, but was also associated with GHQ-30 scores of 5 or more. There was an approximately linear relationship between the risk of dying and the number of symptoms on the GHQ-30, especially for men.[31]

Cox, Huppert, and Whichelow[33] examined the prevalence of GHQ-30 "cases" (scoring above the threshold of 5 or more) in men according to changes in employment status between baseline and 7-year follow-up. Unfortunately, the very interesting results are not significant, because there were so few men with different employment status after 7 years.

There were interesting regional differences in distribution of GHQ-30 results. Scores of 5 or more gave a mean prevalence of 31%, but with significant north–south differences with the exception of Greater London. Four southern regions had a range of 26.8–30.1; four northern regions a range of 32.8–36.9. Standardised prevalence ratios (SPRs) followed standardised mortality ratios (SMRs) closely for these two regional groupings, though not all individual regions had exactly the same ranking. This north–south difference varied by occupational social class: social classes I–II showed none, but the greatest difference was in social classes IIINM–IIIM, that is, greater than social classes IV–V. However, when adjusted for several factors known to be associated with psychiatric morbidity, there was no statistical significance in the north–south difference. The two major factors contributing to this were occupational social class and living environment.[34]

1.2.5.5 The British Household Panel Survey (BHPS), 1991–92

The BHPS was designed as a cohort study from a 1991 cross-sectional sample of all households in Great Britain south of the Caledonian Canal, interviewing all adults aged 16 and over in the sample households, to be followed up after 1 year. Of a selected sample of 7488 eligible households, 5511 were contacted, producing 10,264 individual subjects. Weightings were used in the analyses to adjust for various known and suspected sources of bias in the sample. The GHQ-12 was used, a score of 3 or more being considered "positive", and 9064 adults, 88% of subjects, completed it. Occupation of subject, parents, and head of household were recorded, together with employment data.[35]

Various measures of material standard of living were combined to produce an indicator for analysis. The principal five elements were: income below the bottom quintile for the region of residence; not currently saving from income; living in rented accommodation; having no access to a car or van; living in property with one major or two minor structural problems.[36] Two elements rejected in this analysis as not independent variables after logistic regression were included in other analyses: fewer than four household appliances; and overcrowding of more than an average of two persons per bedroom.[37]

The overall prevalence of "common mental disorders", defined as a score of 3 or more on the GHQ-12, was 24.6%, which many would consider unrealistically high as a measure of defined "illness". It is notable that the Health Survey for England from 1993 took the view that the threshold for "probable psychiatric disorder" should be a score of 4 or more on the GHQ-12. Others have proposed additional measures of disability or disadvantage related to the symptoms recorded. This prevalence provided a gradient with occupational social class of either subject or head of household, but not of parents. This gradient disappeared in men after adjusting for material standard of living, but was still true for women of all ages. Older men, those aged 56–75, also retained an association with occupational social class and GHQ-12 scores.[36]

Material standard of living, indicated by the five elements described above, was reported in one analysis to be the strongest association with GHQ-12 scores of 3 or more, in both men and women, even when adjusted for occupational social class and other variables, and was true, therefore, for all social class groups. Physical illness was associated with GHQ-12 scores of 3 or more, but material standard of living remained associated with GHQ-12 scores even after adjustment for physical illness.[36] However, a different analysis reported that material standard of living, using an indicator including the two additional components described above, was associated only with maintenance and not onset of common mental disorders as measured by the GHQ-12. "Subjective financial strain", indicated by one question with three categories of answer, was correlated with onset of symptoms.[37]

Comparing data from the baseline survey and the 1-year follow-up, unemployment was also associated with maintenance but not onset of symptoms recorded by the GHQ-12, which, however, decreased in those gaining employment in the year, and increased in those losing employment in the year, unless for retirement or looking after the family. Scores also decreased for those getting married, and increased for those divorcing or separating during the year.

Occupational social class was highly correlated with both GHQ-12 (3+) and self-assessed health, themselves highly correlated at one interview and in changes between interviews.[35]

1.2.5.6 USA National Comorbidity Study (NCS), 1990–92

The NCS took a national representative sample of 8098 of the USA population for a cross-sectional study. It used a structured psychiatric interview—the composite international diagnostic interview (CIDI)—a further development of the diagnostic interview schedule (DIS) used in the Epidemiologic Catchment Area (ECA). It also recorded income, assets, education, occupation, and employment. A diagnosis of psychosis (28.4% of respondents answered at least one question indicating possible psychosis) was validated by physician interviews and proved extremely unreliable.[38] Similarly "generalised anxiety disorder" tested against SCID (Structured Clinical Interview for DSM-IV) clinical interviews had very low validity even within the same interview, and even less 19–26 months later.[39] Regier et al.[40] commented that higher thresholds and/or additional impairment, disability, or duration criteria are required for epidemiological surveys, if those truly requiring treatment are to be identified.

Strong and graded associations were found for the life-time prevalence and 12-month prevalence of most disorders with income and education. Odds ratios (ORs) were stronger and more consistent for income, where the lowest group had the highest OR for both life-time and 12-month disorder in the psychiatric diagnostic categories "any affective", "any anxiety", "any substance abuse", "any disorder", and "three or more disorders". Similarly the highest group always had the lowest prevalence, the other income groups lying between. The categories "any anxiety" and "three or more disorders" were most prevalent in the least educated group, and the most educated group had the least prevalence of all diagnostic categories.[41]

For depression, major illness was related particularly to low income, minor and moderate illness to education.[42] There were also high rates of all the above diagnostic categories for those unemployed and not seeking work up to age 54, except for "any anxiety" which was highest in housewives.[41] The data argue for depression to be a continuum rather than discrete categories.[43]

Within economically active men, frequencies of early onset disorder or any disorder within the previous 12 months of interview were far higher among those currently not working. Early onset anxiety disorders (mostly girls) and conduct disorders (mostly boys) were strongly associated with not finishing school or college, and were also related to socio-economic status (SES). Early onset disorders were also highly correlated with later disorder, poor education, non-marriage, and not working.[44]

Parental psychiatric disorder showed a strong association with current depression, anxiety disorder, alcohol or other drug abuse, and anti-social personality disorder in the adult subject. Childhood adversity had only a weak association except for anti-social personality disorder. Major depression, generalised anxiety disorder, and alcohol abuse tended to be specific in family repetition, but other drug abuse was related to any disorder in parents.[45] Could this be a period effect?

Comparisons are available for NCS data and the 1993 to 1996 ECA follow-up in East Baltimore.[46] Income was a strong negative correlate of 12-month prevalence of the three common disorders in the USA, mood disorders, anxiety disorders, and substance abuse disorders, especially anxiety disorders. Similarly correlated was wealth, either as assets possessed or income from capital. These are possibly mediated by lack of material and social resources or increased exposure to stressful life events and noxious environments, with increased vulnerability and less resistance. Education also correlated negatively.

Occupational grades showed no clear pattern—USA occupational categories may not represent culturally, experientially, or environmentally consistent groups, or share anything with categories in the UK or elsewhere. Jobs with high demand but low control were related to alcohol disorder but only in the supervisor grade, which stands between management and workers. Because occupational status seemed relatively immaterial in the USA, researchers perceived an additional problem of multiple indices such as the Nam-Powers index used in the ECA, which combine it with income and education that do seem important. Perhaps status in the USA is perceived far more to relate to capital and income than job type. However, an NCS study of work days lost or cut because of psychiatric disorder shows a clear occupational group gradient for most specific disorders, "pure affective disorder" having the greatest impact.[47]

Published comparisons with the Ontario Health Survey, 1990, are somewhat confusing and apparently contradictory, but suggest that Ontario's better treatment rates for those with depression, though still not high, were related to financial barriers in the USA. This is supported by findings, for all disorders, that in the USA those in the highest income group are most likely to receive care, and from the specialist sector, whereas in Ontario the poorest group is most likely to receive care, from both generalist and specialist sectors. The authors conclude that Ontario's universal healthcare insurance coverage has improved access for the poor, but still most people who need treatment don't get it.[19–21]

Summaries by Dohrenwend and Schwartz[48] claim that NCS results show life-time and 12-month frequencies related strongly to income and education for most specific psychiatric disorders. Because life-time frequencies show a stronger correlation, they suggest that there may be factors affecting duration as well as incidence. There is also increasing multiple diagnosis ("comorbidity") with low income and education.

1.2.5.7 USA Epidemiologic Catchment Area Program (ECA), 1980–83

Between 1980 and 1983 five very different areas of the United States were sampled with some subsidiary sampling variation between areas. Some areas were also followed-up later. About 3000 people were involved in each site, with over-sampling of the elderly.[49] The areas were not very representative of the USA in total, and various weightings, of disputed validity, were used in analysis.[50] The Diagnostic Interview Schedule (DIS) was used by trained lay interviewers to identify categories of mental disorder described in DSM-III, diagnosis depending upon recall of subjects. Validity of diagnoses was acknowledged to be a problem.[38] Occupation, education, income, material standard of living, housing type, and area were recorded. In analysis, socio-economic status (SES) was often indicated by a "Nam-Powers" index similar to that previously used in the Mid-town Manhattan Study[51;52], combining income, education, and occupation data, then divided into distribution quartiles.[53]

There was a follow-up of the ECA Baltimore sample in 1993 to 1996, interviewing subjects three times in a year. This is considered in comparison with the NCS above. The results with regard to social class or SES are somewhat confusing, partly because of differences between different areas, and partly because different papers present data in different ways, sometimes in apparent conflict.

Generally the Nam-Powers index gave a clear gradient for phobias, panic disorders, and obsessive-compulsive disorders, and for anxiety disorders in total.[53] There were ethnic differences, but these disappeared, except for cognitive impairment as measured by the Mini Mental State Examination (MMSE), when adjusted for age, gender, marital status, and SES. The odds ratio (OR) for the lowest SES group having any disorder derived from the DIS was about 2.5 compared to the highest SES group. For schizophrenia the OR was 8.1. One of the strongest correlates of anxiety disorder was SES, which was also inversely related to violent behaviour, anti-social disorder, and cognitive impairment.[54]

Horwath and Weissman[55] summarise that there was no association between SES and major depression in the ECA study, although rates were higher among the unemployed, and bipolar illness was higher among the least well educated. The New Haven area found current rates higher in lower SES groups, and life-time rates higher in upper SES groups, possibly due to longer duration in lower SES groups. However, there was also evidence of higher rates of reporting in less educated, financially strained, unemployed, and those employed in low status jobs. Symptoms of major depression were more common in urban than in rural areas, not fully explained by differences in education. Depression was associated with higher education in the Piedmont area,[56] but with lower education in New Haven.[57]

In New Haven, after various adjustments, poverty, home-bound status related to physical illness, and low levels of social contact remained strong associations of depression of first onset. Social isolation modifies the effects of poverty and home-bound status. These authors believe that much of the effect of poverty may be mediated through social isolation (not necessarily living alone, which was not correlated), and that increased risks of depression in the elderly are strongly related to increases in physical illness, correlated with low income, education, and unemployment.[57] Over all areas, people in poverty, as defined by USA Federal guidelines, had twice the risk of others of having any Axis I DSM-III disorder, and this was matched for most specific disorders, independent of age, gender, race, or previous history of disorder.[58]

It is relevant to note that early-onset alcohol abuse tended to reduce educational achievement, the status of occupations engaged, and personal income in subsequent adult years, which may have important implications for associations with mental illness later.[59;60]

1.2.5.8 Edmonton Survey of Psychiatric Disorders (1983–86)

A sample survey of Edmonton private households (one adult from each) was conducted over more than 3 years. A response rate of 73% gave 3258 adults aged 18 or over, including 11% aged 65 and over. This means that only 2899 were aged 18–64. Instruments included DIS and GHQ-30, together with the Life Events Scale (LES).[61] Six-month prevalence rates for any core disorders (including substance abuse) were 17.1%; 18.9% for men and 15.3% for women. Men had significantly more alcohol and other substance abuse; women had significantly more mood and anxiety disorders.[62]

There is apparently no published analysis of data related specifically to social status and it is not clear from the literature available if income, education, or occupation data were collected. There is an analysis of unemployment based on a DIS question. Having a life-time history of any DSM-III disorder increased the odds of being unemployed (defined as more than 20% of the last five years unemployed while seeking employment; that is excluding those not seeking employment, including the retired) by 2.8 times (OR 2.8). The strongest associations were with anorexia (OR 15.6), anti-social personality disorder (PD) (OR 6.2), schizophrenia (OR 3.8), and substance-use disorders (OR 3.0). GHQ scores showed that those currently unemployed and not seeking work were likely to have higher symptom scores (OR 2.0).[63]

Life events were associated with major depressive episode and generalised anxiety disorder, especially if both were present.[64]

1.2.5.9 The Netherlands Mental Health Survey and Incidence Study (NEMESIS), 1996

This cross-sectional survey of the whole of the Netherlands was designed to provide a cohort for follow-up in 1 and 3 years (and possibly later). It used a multi-stage sampling procedure based on municipalities and private households, one individual aged 18–64 being chosen from each household. The study identified 11,140 eligible households from which 7147 individuals (64.2%) were interviewed. In terms of the Dutch population, there appeared to be under-representation of the age group 18–24 years. The CIDI was used to record life-time experience of DSM-III disorders, plus SCID when answers indicated the possibility of psychosis. Those who refused the CIDI were asked to complete the GHQ-12 (43.6% of non-responders did) to compare their mental health profile with responders; it appeared to be not significantly different by this measure. The short-form general health questionnaire (SF-36) was also used for disability, and the MMSE for cognitive function. The study recorded family income, analysed in quartiles, and the average net income per person within each family;

years of education, and unemployment.[65] The 1-year follow-up captured 5618 adults, 79.4% of the cohort.[66]

Life-time occurrence of at least one DSM-III disorder was 41.2%; 1-year prevalence was 23.3%. Men had more alcohol and other drug disorders; women had more anxiety and depressive disorders. The three most common disorders, anxiety, depression, and alcohol, were often present together. The frequencies for "all anxiety disorders" were: life-time 19.3%; 1-year 12.4%; 1-month 9.7%.

In relation to education, there were significant excess prevalences in those groups with very poor education for both mood and anxiety disorders. Similarly there were significantly more of both diagnostic groups in the bottom quartile of income, and also the middle 50% compared to the wealthiest quartile. There were significantly higher frequencies in all employment groups compared with those described as "employed".[65]

In the only analysis yet available on the 1-year follow-up, major depression showed no significant variation by education, but a very significant variation by employment for "dysthymia" and "generalised and other anxiety disorders". Potential risk factors for poor outcome after 1 year of major depression were clinical features, gender, unemployment, and two or more negative life events; however, these last three were not quite statistically significant, given the small numbers involved.[67]

1.2.5.10 Australian National Mental Health Survey, 1997

In 1997, a representative sample of 13,624 private dwellings in Australia, (excluding institutions, hospitals, homes, hostels, prisons, and remote areas, therefore excluding many Aborigines) produced 10,641 adults (aged 18 or over), no more than one from each household, who agreed to be interviewed, a response rate of 78%. The CIDI was used to create ICD-10 and DSM-IV diagnoses, a five-item screen for psychosis, the MMSE for cognitive defect, and the SF-12 for disability. Other questions related to demographic, socio-economic, health, and health service issues. The initial reports did not give detailed methodology, nor did they present analyses by occupational social class or related factors except for employment status and education. Analyses available up to now exclude those with "probable psychosis" or "probable cognitive defect".

Unemployed groups showed higher than average mental disorders as detected by the CIDI.[68] The relationship with educational qualifications (not completing secondary school, secondary school completion, post-school qualifications) was mixed, and different for men and women. However, for both sexes together the lowest-qualified group had higher prevalences of anxiety and affective disorders.

A very recent paper[69] gives more detail, and shows statistically significant ($p = 0.05$) ORs for "any affective disorder" and "any anxiety disorder" in both short-term and long-term unemployed compared with those employed. It also shows significant ORs for both diagnostic groups in those who were not educated beyond high school, and for "any anxiety disorder" also in those with vocational qualifications only, compared to those with university degrees. No income data are presented. Although the categories used do not appear very discriminating, the general trend is the same as in other studies: the social groups with the lowest status and resources show the highest frequency of disorders.

1.2.6 Surveys providing cohort evidence

Studies of cross-sectional evidence of associations with the common mental disorders in adulthood cannot establish whether psychological problems or the social disadvantages occurred first. Cohort studies starting with adults also suffer from this problem, and only studies following-up children from early in their lives can provide decisive evidence on this point. The British birth cohorts were the only general population-based cohorts identified as relevant for this review.

1.2.6.1 The 1946 birth cohort

The 1946 cohort[70] studied all births in Great Britain in one week of 1946 with an original cohort of 13,687. A sub-sample of these has been kept in touch with throughout the ensuing years, and formal follow-up studies have been done at several ages, notably at 15, 26, 36, and 43; at age 43, in 1991, 5362 were followed-up.[71]

At age 15, measures included the Maudsley Personality Inventory, "behaviour habits" such as nail-biting, stammering, and thumb-sucking, general behaviour ratings at school, and records of delinquency. At age 26, measures included only self-recorded treatment as a psychiatric in-patient, and consultation with any doctor for "psychiatric or nervous problems", so no reliable diagnostic groupings were available. At age 36 a short Present State Examination (PSE) was administered by trained nurses, achieving 3293 assessments. At age 43, the Psychiatric Symptom Frequency Scale (PSF) was given and tests of memory and cognitive function. All hospital admission reports were checked in the NHS.[72;73]

Occupations were recorded for parents, and for subjects as adults. Housing status, financial hardship in childhood and employment status as adults were recorded, as well as educational achievement of both parents and subject.

In general, there was remarkably little evidence for strong associations of particular experiences and characteristics of childhood with adult psychiatric disorder. The strongest predictor to emerge was anti-social behaviour in girls, especially in adolescence, associated with adult anxiety and depression. "Overall, early environment did not seem to hold great significance for adult disorder, although multiple disadvantages had a cumulative effect. There was little evidence of early benefits being protective."[74] This is interesting in the light of evidence of disadvantages accumulating in certain low-status groups in society, whether measured by wealth, income, housing tenure, unemployment, or occupational status. But there was no evidence of neurosis in men having any association with parental occupational social class, and the association of neurosis in women was weak.

At age 36, for men, PSE scores for neurosis were unrelated to occupational social class of either father or self. For women, PSE scores were strongly associated with both father's and own occupational social class, but only in comparing the lowest category (in or previously in unskilled manual work) with all others. Children at home made no difference.[72] These results applied to mean PSE scores, "case-ness" and affective symptoms in particular, but there were some doubts about the validity of PSE scores in these circumstances.

For women only, the frequency of affective symptoms was associated with poor educational test results at age 36, and PSE "case-ness" was strongly associated with educational achievement when divided simply into "O-level and above" (10.9% cases) and "less than O-level" (65% cases).

Renting a house rather than owning one was associated with affective symptoms, higher mean scores, and frequency of "case-ness" in both sexes, but the latter only applied to women when children were present in the home.

Personal income was not related to scores, but household income, which might be more relevant, was unknown. In response to one question, people recording "financial hardship" in the previous 12 months, showed very high symptom levels. This group included many single parents, unemployed men and wives of unemployed men, so financial hardship recorded in this way certainly overlaps with several other factors. It could "explain" a high proportion of the associations with housing tenure, employment and presence of children in the home[72] (Table 1.2).

Employed men had lower rates than others. Especially high were men unemployed and not seeking work, but numbers were small and they were mostly men with chronic sickness or disability. For unemployed men, but only if seeking work, higher scores were associated with longer periods of unemployment. Husband's unemployment was strongly associated with high scores in married women.[72]

In conclusion, for neurosis, occupational social class of subject or parents was barely associated, and education weakly associated, but unemployment

TABLE 1.2
The 1946 birth cohort at age 36: PSE scores and "cases" by indicators of material hardship

	Mean PSE score		*"Cases"*		
	%	*p*	*%*	*p*	*n*
Housing tenure					
men—owner occupiers	1.7		2.8		1224
renting/others	2.1	0.037	6.8	0.001	412
women—owner occupiers	2.78		7.1		1243
renting/others	3.84	0.001	13.2	0.001	410
Financial hardship					
Men—none	1.63		2.9		1390
had to go without	2.73	0.001	8.4	0.001	250
women—none	2.65		7		1393
had to go without	5.12	0.001	17.3	0.001	260

Source:[72] (Tables 2 and 3).

was an important factor, not fully explained by financial hardship. Combining factors, the highest PSE scores were in men not fully employed, from the lowest occupational social class, and renting their home. However, renting was not significant if "financial hardship" was brought into the analysis. Financial hardship was also important in women.

For schizophrenia, there was no evidence of association with occupational social class of parents during the subject's childhood, in spite of associations with some early developmental factors (walking and talking later; more speech problems; low test scores for age) which might be expected to be more common in lower-class homes.[75] Multiple disadvantage in childhood summarised by a "childhood adversity score" was associated with higher PSE scores at age 36. Parental divorce or separation was associated with higher PSF scores at age 43, but only in single, divorced, or remarried women.[73] The social class distribution of multiple disadvantage was not clarified.

Because this is a cohort study, results may not be applicable to later cohorts even in the British population.

1.2.6.2 1958 birth cohort

The original cohort in this study was of 17,414 babies born in one week in 1958. 12,537 were effectively followed up in 1981 at age 23, and 11,407 in 1991 at age 33. At age 23 they were asked to report specialist consultations for psychological problems since the age of 16, through several questions. The Malaise Inventory (MI) was administered at both age 23 and age 33.

At birth, the father's occupation and education were recorded, together with the family's economic situation. At 23 and 33 income, housing tenure, educational achievement, and own occupation and employment were recorded.[76]

MI scores and having sought specialist help both showed a steady gradient by own occupational social class, the MI having the steeper gradient. Odds ratios (ORs) for MI scores were reduced if controlled for (especially) occupational social class of father at birth, housing tenure at age 11, behaviour score at 16, and educational qualifications. ORs for psychological problems needing help were reduced only by behaviour at 16 and adult unemployment.[77]

Three different methods of analysis gave similar results for social class differences, suggesting robustness of the results. Father's occupational social class revealed minimal differences in MI scores. At age 23 and 33, own occupational social class (IV/V compared with I/II) showed significant differences for both MI scores and self-reported health. From age 23 to 33, MI score differences diminished in men and increased in women, whereas self-rated health differences increased for both men and women. There is generally an association between self-rated health and MI scores. Educational qualifications gave the greatest inequalities in both MI scores and psychological problems in men and women at ages 23 and 33. Unemployment up to age 23 was associated with higher scores, not explained by social class of family of origin. Having small children at home was a factor in women.[76]

Although parental occupational social class was not very significant in itself, it is closely associated with many important features of childhood and earlier adult life associated with subsequent high MI scores. These include poorer economic conditions in childhood and adulthood, less social support, lower educational qualifications, less secure employment, and more psycho-social job stress. But high MI scores, especially indicative of depression, were also associated with parental divorce, pre-marital pregnancy, low own occupational social class, poor emotional support in adulthood, and high rates of adverse life events.

The conclusion is that early factors may not determine psychological health inequalities, but increase the risks of experiencing later causal factors and, perhaps, increasing the deleterious effects of those later factors. Parental divorce in childhood or even in young adulthood, especially when combined with own divorce, was a powerful factor increasing MI scores.[78;79]

Falling social status between ages 23 and 33, as indicated by housing tenure, was associated with increased MI scores in men and the least decline in MI scores in women (most notable if divorced) compared with people who were status-stable or upwardly mobile as indicated by housing status. The upwardly mobile showed the greatest decline in MI scores in women.[80]

MI scores were only weakly correlated with having sought medical help for symptoms of depression and anxiety between ages 23 and 33. Occupational social class at birth showed virtually no correlations. Educational qualifications were correlated, with degree level the lowest, O or A level intermediate, and less than O level the highest MI scores. Unemployment correlated with depression and anxiety, but this was mostly related to recent unemployment, especially for those with no previous history of depression at age 23. Accumulated unemployment was only associated with MI scores in those with a previous history of depression at 23.[81]

Because this is a cohort study, results may not be applicable to later cohorts even in the British population.

1.2.6.3 The 1970 birth cohort

The 1970 British Cohort study recorded all those born in one week in April 1970 in the UK, but Northern Ireland births were never followed-up. The scope of successive enquiries has increased and at age 26 it encompassed physical, educational, social, and economic development. In 1975 and 1980 the cohort was augmented with immigrants to Britain born in the same week. The last documented follow-up was 1996.

The Malaise Inventory was used in the 1996 follow-up of the cohort aged 26 years, but no studies of its distribution appear to have been published yet.[82]

1.2.7 Issues arising from the included studies

The literature on the links between the common mental disorders and the many markers of social position is vast. In this review, we have focused on the relatively few large, population-based studies. Multiple strategies were used to identify these studies, and nine have been assessed as meeting inclusion criteria. Appendix A contains details of studies that did not meet inclusion criteria but provide some additional relevant information.

In examining the included studies, four major issues are apparent:

- inconsistencies in the definition of mental disorders;
- issues relating to concepts and measurement of social position;
- the varying degrees to which these issues have been examined in the published output from studies;
- cross-cultural interpretation of results.

1.2.7.1 Definition of common mental disorders

A 1990 literature review[83] identified 17 different definitions of severe and persistent mental illness used by 13 authors to estimate need and formulate service programmes. When applied to a representative sample of 222 current patients of a Philadelphia service, these various definitions gave estimates varying from 4% to 88%! This problem is confirmed by our own search: many different definitions of mental illness or mental health problems or psychiatric symptoms are used and several identification instruments. In Section 1.3, we discuss the definition and measures of psychological symptoms and illness status in more detail.

1.2.7.2 Concepts of social position

Definitions of social class or socio-economic position also vary greatly, and many studies of social class also include employment, housing, income, education, and other markers. These are all clearly interdependent variables.

Whatever classification system is used, "social class" is only an indicator taxonomy; it is the associations and determinants of social position that might actually be important factors, and sometimes these will not follow expectations, nor can they be assumed to be the same in every community. In these studies, social position is often defined by occupational status, a system threatened by high levels of unemployment, job flexibility, part-time working, increasing participation in higher education, and the changing roles of women in employment. It seems clear that it needs to be unpacked in order to identify more precise indicators of disadvantage or possible causal factors related to income, material assets, education, employment, adult situation, and childhood experience.

Classification systems based on occupation have always been at best inadequate and at worst useless for women—conventionally, married women were allocated their husband's occupational class, which assumed a shared culture or that the husband's culture dominated in its effects on or indications of health. Increasingly over the last 50 years, women have had occupations of their own, whether married or not, and can be classified personally, but it is doubtful if, throughout the whole community, women's occupations have the same meaning as men's in terms of status or health-related characteristics. For example, many women, for practical reasons, work part-time in low-paid jobs that do not reflect their background, education or abilities.

There is also an age issue inherent in occupation-based systems. Young adults have not had time to achieve their career potential; it is likely that many would have jobs in a higher social class in later years. It might be argued that some would be expected to modify their attitudes, life-style, and behaviour in line with their changing status, income, and assets, but others would already, as young people, share those attributes of their seniors. It is merely another illustration of the ambiguity of occupational social class when examined in detail; nevertheless, however surprisingly, as a broad and very general indicator of social difference, it has proved useful.

Section 1.4 contains a detailed discussion of conceptual issues relating to social class, and an analysis of the measures used in the studies assessed for inclusion in the review.

1.2.7.3 Degree of research attention

Findings need to be assessed carefully in the light of the literature as a whole. For example, unemployment is commonly found associated with mental illness, but it is commonly looked for. It is possible that another association demonstrated only in one paper is more important, but has been seldom studied. Working conditions and work characteristics may be more important in their association with mental illness than occupational status used to categorise social class, but there are few large-scale studies.

It was not possible to reanalyse the original survey data from the relevant studies systematically to explore results on all the measures of interest.

1.2.7.4 Cross-cultural interpretations

Findings also need to be judged in terms of generalisability between countries and cultures; for example, major differences between the USA and the UK in health service funding, structure, and distribution, and attitudes and expectations in health, healthcare, work, welfare, and so on, make it difficult to apply research findings in this field from one country to another. Of course, it is also true that there are widely varying cultures within countries, and interpretations of data which imply the need for policy developments will have to be particularly sensitive to this issue.

1.3 MEASURING PSYCHIATRIC DISORDER IN POPULATIONS

1.3.1 Introduction and concepts

It is impossible to read the literature on inequalities in mental health without facing the problems of concept, definition, and measurement of mental disorder. It is fundamental to epidemiological investigation that there are clearly defined entities to measure, and reasonably accurate and reliable measures to identify them in populations. With regard to mental function and dysfunction, pathologies cannot be visualised and examined; there are no "gold standards" for "case" identification. Underlying these problems is the even more fundamental issue of conceptualisation of mental conditions.

Two key issues are explored below:

(1) The identification of clinical entities or diseases, and the drawing of boundaries between "illness" and "normal" psychological distress.
(2) The validity of sub-dividing the common mental disorders into specific syndromes.

1.3.2 Identifying clinical entities in surveys

With regard to clinical entities, mental health surveys pose a very basic question:

- Are we identifying definable clinical entities to which an illness model may reasonably be applied, which can, therefore, be susceptible to medical intervention, which might offer hope of cure or amelioration

or

- Are we recording psychological and emotional experiences that are so common as to be considered an inevitable part of life, and, therefore, "normal", given the challenges and exigencies of human life and the imperfections of human beings?

However, this question is too simple. Putting aside functional psychoses as, arguably, discrete illnesses, the psychological and emotional symptoms referred to are distributed throughout the population in a gradation of severity and combination, and the "entities" clinicians use are the product of arbitrarily drawn thresholds, similar to the labelling of "hypertension" at certain levels of blood pressure.

Moreover, in individuals there is temporal variation in relation to changing circumstances, and individuals will, therefore, from time to time, cross the various thresholds applied, and thus become defined as "ill" depending on the classification system or instruments applied. The circumstances or events that push them over a threshold might be considered a cause of the illness, but may not be the most important of several or many causal factors accumulating in the life of the individual concerned.

Most of the research considered here is concerned with both symptoms and thresholds in varying degrees. But instruments vary, thresholds vary even on the same instrument, and the treatment of symptoms varies, so that simple comparison with other studies is prejudiced. There is a tendency for research reports to treat their own chosen thresholds as representing clearly defined entities, and some instruments, such as the CIDI, are apparently used mainly to generate diagnoses, though acknowledging that these are not fully clinically validated.[68] Inevitably in relatively short journal papers, the issues are often not discussed.

Measuring accumulated symptoms and identifying possible clinical "cases" are both legitimate objectives, but the implications for policy options and priorities might be different. The relatively rare serious psychotic illnesses throw up few cases in mass surveys (the USA ECA identified 144 people with schizophrenia out of a sample of about 9500[52]), and may require second stages for verification, as in the UK National Survey. Further research is probably better approached with case-control studies.

However, even using essentially arbitrary thresholds for "case-ness", clinical categories less dramatic and much more common than functional psychoses can be usefully identified, and people offered a range of standardised health service responses in treatment, care, and rehabilitation. They can confer all the benefits of recognised sickness models in the family and community, although this is seriously constrained in practice by public attitudes to mental disorder in all societies. Unfortunately, standard diagnostic systems have serious limitations. They have generally been developed out of hospital and specialist experience and categories are generally based on hospital populations not community samples. Many of the categories are only partly validated syndromes, and psychological symptoms that do not readily coalesce into standard diagnostic categories may nevertheless be serious enough to cause substantial suffering, functional disability, social disadvantage, and family disruption.

Such symptoms, most commonly anxiety and depression, can be conceived as the mental equivalent of physically generated pain, extreme discomfort, and functional disability. They often present to medical services, especially primary healthcare, where they may be accompanied by many other symptoms. If identified, they can often be ameliorated with a variety of treatments. Their origins may be difficult to clarify, but they are frequently of long duration. Although similar experiences in other people may be of short duration and may be susceptible to relief from the family or non-medical support in the community,[84] there is evidence of very large numbers in the community who could benefit from medical help, and very many who do not get it.[19;85]

This could also be reflected in Dohrenwend's[14] interpretation of screening measures used in early population psychiatric surveys before the development of appropriate structured interview schedules. They appear to record aspects of "non-specific distress" (which Dohrenwend calls "demoralisation"), which could be a response to, for example, chronic physical illness, recent stressful life events, coping with psychotic symptoms, or being in a low-status social position. In other words, they may represent "normal" reactions to stressful experiences, affected also by personality features, previous experience, and personal social support. At some point these responses develop into a dysfunctional state that may legitimately be called illness, depending on definitions used, but essentially independent of functional psychosis. In examining this, Dohrenwend and colleagues[86] found this non-specific distress occurred with about equal frequency in the presence or absence of diagnosable psychiatric disorder.

Thus, measuring numbers of symptoms or measuring "case-ness" are likely both to follow the same pattern in populations. From epidemiological studies of other aspects of health such as high blood pressure, population means of continuously distributed variables tend to be closely related to the proportion of "cases" however defined within the distribution. This has been shown to apply to the GHQ.[87;88]

1.3.2.1 *Taxonomy of mental conditions*

The development of standard taxonomies in recent years, particularly ICD-9/10 and DSM-III/IV, has been very important in clarifying diagnosis and focusing treatment, but the detail of current systems can be misleading. In particular, the discrimination of many categories of depression and anxiety, the commonest range of both symptoms and disorders, may well be spurious; they might be better understood as a continuum of symptom clusters that are experienced differently by different people according to their varying vulnerabilities, and do not necessarily imply different causal factors or different treatment needs.[84;89]

There is evidence from these large-scale studies that supports such a view.[43;45] The fact that anxiety and depression can be separated on factor analysis of instruments such as the GHQ-30, does not argue against this.[90] Patients may be able to discriminate their different symptoms as anxiety or depression, but they may still represent variable personal responses to the same general conditions and experiences. There is, of course, much other literature that supports the separation of bipolar illness, major depression, and other specific categories of serious illness.

The problem is not confined to anxiety and depression, although the issue may not be so clear for neuroses in general. Since pathology is usually unknown, and causes are largely uncertain, differentiation of many sub-categories is essentially speculative. This could be important, as both treatment and research strategies will differ according to the interpretation of multiple symptoms. The assumptions that appear to be expressed constantly in the NCS literature by reference to "comorbidity", and even to "comorbid persons" may be misleading; it may be that the observed symptoms represent coherent, but not yet understood, clusters of experiences and responses to many causes, rather than several separate discrete syndromes.[91–93] A similar problem presents with the Australian National Mental Health Survey, which like the NCS used the CIDI, where anxiety and depression are presented as separate categories and their combination as "comorbidity".[68]

"Comorbid" may mean no more than having symptoms that fall into more than one DSM-III/IV or ICD-9/10 category, and does not imply that the "morbidity" represents separate, understood, pathological processes. Nevertheless, the NCS emphasis on the multiplicity of symptoms revealed by many people, which are not satisfactorily contained within one DSM-III category, is a very positive contribution. This is not to deny the importance of discrete diagnostic categories and the observation of comorbidity when justified, but it raises again the possibility that, for example, "depression", "alcohol abuse", "social phobias", and "simple phobias", the commonest four categories in the NCS results, may have common origins in some people.[92]

The context of large-scale epidemiological surveys is important. Enumerating the relatively uncommon but most readily identified major, serious syndromes, especially those generally termed psychoses, is not usually the principal aim, as numbers are too small for satisfactory statistical analysis when the many other factors—age, gender, socio-economic variables, etc.—are taken into account. So the main focus is the neuroses, ("minor mental illness" or the "common mental disorders") and psychological symptoms. However, these are least susceptible to clear definition and standardised, reliable identification, and there is no doubt that prevalence figures in such circumstances will depend on the criteria for "case-ness", or, rather, because questionnaires are generally screening instruments, the specificity and sensitivity of the screen.

For example, in the UK, the British Household Panel Survey (BHPS) used the GHQ-12, accepting a score of 3 or more as positive, that is, indicating a likelihood of this being confirmed as a "case" if subjected to clinical examination. Their overall prevalence was 25%.[36] The Health Survey for England (HSE), also used the GHQ-12, but a positive response required a score of 4 or more. This obtained consistent prevalences of about 16%.[4;7] Of course the probability of a score of 4 indicating a "case" is more than that of a score of 3, and, of course, the proportion will necessarily be less.

Similarly, in the UK Health and Lifestyle Survey (HALS), short-period prevalence figures of 25% for men and 30% for women obtained from the GHQ-30 were not considered by the authors to represent real "illness" rates,[30] and in the USA, figures of 28–29% of the adult population deriving from more detailed instruments, the DIS and CIDI, used in the ECA and NCS surveys, were interpreted as not representing treatable psychiatric disorder. These researchers considered it necessary to use "additional symptom threshold, impairment or disability, and duration criteria" in future surveys.[40] But validity of the screening instruments was an acknowledged problem.[38]

However, it is worth noting that, although these issues prejudice prevalence estimates for healthcare resourcing, they do not necessarily prejudice associations with other factors, including those encompassed by social class or socio-economic status. Thus the relativities of socio-economic status may be preserved at different levels of symptom or syndrome identification.

1.3.2.2 Objectivity and validity in surveys

Because there are few objective signs of neuroses on short observation, and because most surveys are reliant on questionnaires answered only by the subject, it is pertinent to ask both to what degree positive answers represent objective phenomena, and to what extent objectivity is desirable or possible. The more complex instruments such as CIDI aspire to objective, or at least standardised and reproducible, results, even though validity remains problematic when tested against full clinical examination.[38] Many include, as well as current symptoms, questions about previous experience of psychological symptoms, often over the past year, and sometimes over the past adult life-time. This can be neither examined nor verified; although questionnaire design and interviewer techniques have been developed to improve recall,[94] there is no evidence that recall is accurate for more than a few weeks. "Life-time" prevalence figures dependent on such studies are necessarily extremely suspect.[20;43]

Several studies have shown a close correlation between positive results on the psychological instrument used and answers to a simple question called "self-reported health"—for example, "Do you consider that your health is generally excellent, good, fair or poor?".[25;35;76] No one would consider this sufficient—it does not identify even the general body systems affecting subjective health, but it might argue, at least, for simplicity in approach rather than complexity. Since we are concerned with a range of feelings and thoughts, perhaps subjective experience should be overtly the main focus. It is, after all, subjective experience of, for example, depression and anxiety, that provokes people into seeking medical help, or, for that matter, attempting suicide.

Understandably, this fosters unease in clinicians and researchers alike; are people to be considered ill just because they say they are? Fortunately, the situation is not quite like this; subjects are not merely volunteering their feelings in an unstructured way, nor are they volunteering themselves for interview. Both sampling and interviewing procedures have become very sophisticated. Instruments used in large-scale surveys have been, to some extent, tried and tested, and, though they are far from perfect in identifying "clinical cases", they offer a considerable degree of consistency across different populations and different groups within populations. Research interviewers are highly trained to deliver a standard interview in a controlled way. A great deal of research effort has been put into testing and improving the validity and reliability of instruments. Even subjective responses reveal common patterns, trends, and associations, not least with indicators of socio-economic status.

1.3.3 Definitions and methods of identification of psychiatric disorder

It was not one of the objectives of this literature review to examine in detail the technical validity and reliability of the various instruments used in surveys; this would be an additional major task. But some comment cannot be avoided. Dohrenwend[14] observed that before about 1980, studies were hampered by very inadequate instruments, and, indeed, concepts and taxonomies, which did not render diagnoses. He believed that they all tended to measure aspects of the same phenomenon, even though they were not clear about what it was. He interpreted it as "non-specific distress", which he preferred to call "demoralisation". Although such measures "are interesting in their own right, they are often very imperfectly related to diagnosable mental disorders" (p.197). However, they may be closer to later symptom lists and the type of questionnaire represented by the various versions of the GHQ.

There is a fundamental conflict in this context. It is necessary to have as near perfect standardisation of measurement as possible for epidemiological work, but clinical diagnosis, against which instruments are validated, has always been subject to the vagaries of clinical judgement by individual doctors.[95] Much of the history of development of survey instruments has been trying to work out a satisfactory compromise of this inherent conflict. It is particularly obvious in psychiatry because of the lack of objective pathology or biochemical markers of illness, and the ambiguity of discrimination between normal behaviours, reactions, and experiences, and deviance or illness. Diagnosis often requires information from people other than the patient who may lack insight or be confused or deluded. Clinical diagnosis by specialists has itself become much more standardised, not least because of the development of extensively validated structured interviews for their use, but this is still a big issue wherever objectives include the identification of established diagnostic categories. It does not pose the same problem where the main focus is on the distribution of symptoms of psychological distress or disturbance in the population.

There are many instruments that have been subject to a great many validation studies. There are no "gold standards" for validation of psychiatric diagnostic entities; no biochemistry, no radiology, no sophisticated imaging. And many of the categories in DSM-IV or ICD-10 are not epidemiologically validated as distinct entities. Yet studies have shown substantial consistency and reliability for experienced clinical judgement after thorough examination using standard categories in DSM-IV or ICD-10. So, although validation of both interview-based and self-report-based survey results still poses problems, most well-established instruments show good internal consistency, temporal stability, and inter-interviewer reliability.

Finally, we should be alert to the varieties of epidemiological measures used by different instruments or in different surveys. Incidence is rarely possible, but is sometimes addressed in cohort studies. Prevalence may be described as point prevalence but data may have been collected over a long period of time from the whole sample. Within the instruments used, data on psychiatric symptoms or disorders may relate to the previous week, month, year or any previous time, so analyses may present week prevalence, month prevalence, year prevalence, or lifetime prevalence, which last should always be related to specific age-groups. These various measures are not readily compared.

1.3.3.1 The General Health Questionnaire (GHQ)

The General Health Questionnaire (GHQ) was developed primarily to assist general medical practitioners in detecting psychiatric disorders in their practice, following research showing large numbers of people consulting GPs to have unrecognised and therefore untreated mental health problems.[84;96] The GHQ has had many versions, with 12, 30, 36, or 60 questions, and has been used in many population surveys as well as practice populations. Although the weight of opinion now seems to favour the shortest version, GHQ-12, as offering virtually as reliable results as the others in a much shorter time, some surveys have used the GHQ-30, which poses problems for comparison.

The GHQ has been subject to extensive validation in a wide variety of settings in many countries, for which studies were collated by Goldberg et al.[22] Median values for sensitivity of 83.7% and specificity of 79% look very acceptable, but the range was very broad, and the validity of the very varied clinical standards against which it was tested was often in doubt. In their own very large-scale international validity study, Goldberg and his colleagues obtained mean sensitivity of 76.3% and specificity of 83.4% with a much more limited range of results from individual centres. However, the optimal threshold for "case-ness" was very varied. From HALS data, Cox et al.[32] claimed the GHQ-30 to be fairly sensitive but very non-specific.

One possible limitation of the GHQ in predicting "case-ness" is its exclusive concentration on current or recent symptoms or changes, which creates uncertainty as to the period of assessment prior to the interview[97] and limits its capacity to uncover long-standing symptoms or illness.[98] This is because chronic symptoms would elicit no response regarding recent changes. This would argue for one or more additional criteria to identify them and any limitations on daily life imposed by them. This has been done for the GHQ-30 using data from the HALS study, creating the C-GHQ-30. The conventional scoring was then compared with that of the C-GHQ-30.[90] In the major recent UK surveys using the GHQ-12, the BHPS and the Annual Health Survey for England, other data have been available from the broader questionnaire administered, so it is theoretically possible to explore this in analysis as though it were the C-GHQ. Anderson et al.[99] have done this for the BHPS data. However, the C-GHQ answers have been scored differently from the GHQ, and Goldberg et al.,[22] in their recent review of validity, claim, on the basis of various quoted studies, that this has been shown to have no advantage.

A problem that emerges from the literature is the different threshold used to record a positive response, or a "probable case"—for the GHQ-12 there are examples of 2 or more, 3 or more, or 4 or more, which necessarily give very different population frequencies. The "best threshold" varied in the various validation studies reviewed by Goldberg et al.,[22] although the variation was small when the standard was either the CIS or the PSE. However, all options, 2 or more, 3 or more, and 4 or more, should be available from large-scale survey data, now stored and made widely available, and it should be possible eventually to analyse them all in exactly the same ways. The same problem arises with the GHQ-30. In the HALS, Huppert and Whittington[30] found that the threshold recommended by validation studies in general practice produced prevalence figures of 25% for men and 30% for women, and considered that the threshold for community studies may need to be different. Again, the data are available to show the distribution of frequencies by threshold. There are obvious problems in comparing data from different versions of the GHQ, but there are also ways of translating or harmonising them.

The GHQ-30 has been subject to factor analysis, creating apparently satisfactory sub-scores, or various scales representing anxiety, feelings of incompetence, depression, difficulty in coping, and social dysfunction.[90] A scaled version designed after factor analysis, the GHQ-28, differs from the others in not having the whole of the GHQ-12 embedded within it. A quarter of the items are concerned with severe depression, and another quarter with somatic symptoms, so the GHQ-28 may not be so suitable for general population samples. Recent validation of both these versions has shown that the GHQ-12 is just as good for predicting "case-ness" as the GHQ-28, which should only be used if separate sub-scores are required. The clinical standard was established using the primary care version of the CIDI (CIDI-PC) which can generate diagnoses according to either ICD-10 or DSM-IV.[22]

It was not the original intention that the GHQ should produce clear diagnostic categories, but rather that it would screen people as having "probable neurotic disorder", for further clinical examination and diagnosis. However, Goldberg himself[84] has argued that it is artificial to categorise people into "possibly disordered" or not, and it is equally possible to use the GHQ to examine the distribution of individual symptoms, and total symptom scores in populations. Since neuroses and neurotic symptoms appear to be distributed continuously throughout populations,[91] it becomes possible to assess the mental health of various sub-groups in a population in a way more satisfactory than the frequency of probable cases of diagnosable disorder. This approach receives some encouragement from the UK Health and Life-style Survey (HALS) where there were close correlations within specific population sub-groups between the prevalence of "probable cases", that is, high scorers on the GHQ, and the mean score for the whole sub-group.[99]

1.3.3.2 The Revised Clinical Interview Schedule (CIS-R)

The UK National Surveys of 1993 and 2000 used the Revised Clinical Interview Schedule (CIS-R) as a lay-administered screening instrument. The CIS was originally also developed by Goldberg and others[100] for general practice and community surveys. It includes a self-report section and a section requiring professional judgement and observation of "manifest abnormality". In the development that produced the CIS-R, this second section was abandoned, so that it could be given by trained lay interviewers, thus becoming entirely self-report based and more overtly focused on "minor mental illness". Other changes have been made to certain questions and new questions added in order to increase standardisation and to make it suitable for use by lay interviewers.

Some reliability studies have been done,[95] but recent validation studies using the SCAN/PSE10, have been disappointing, with poor diagnostic agreement,[101] and it cannot yet be said to provide valid or reliable indications of clinical diagnosis.[98] Of course, the PSE was devised for hospital populations and the CIS was intended for community populations, so they are not necessarily compatible. The not very surprising conclusion is that structured clinical assessment is much better than self-report interviews at making clinical diagnoses,[102] but, of course, this does not mean that self-report interviews cannot usefully record the distribution of symptoms in populations, which has been shown closely to parallel the frequency of "cases" in population sub-groups.[99] If this is so, they could still provide very valuable data for comparisons between socio-economic groups, and therefore information on inequalities in mental health.

1.3.3.3 The Psychiatric Symptom Frequency Scale (PSF)

This scale was developed specifically for the 1989 follow-up of the 43-year-old 1946 UK birth cohort because available alternatives were considered unsuitable for the objectives of the study.[97] The GHQ was rejected because of the unspecified time-period and the requirement to compare current symptoms with how the individual "usually feels". The Malaise Inventory was rejected because it gave poor discrimination at low severity levels with items being scored only as absent or present. The PSF, therefore, used a rating scale of five levels which indicated the frequency and period of experiencing a symptom within the previous year. Its focus is on neurotic symptoms and probable disorders involving anxiety and depression. A very broad range of response was the result, which was what the researchers wanted, permitting a variety of thresholds to be examined. Although subjected to some tests, showing, for example, good internal consistency and satisfactory "receiver operating characteristics" (ROCs), it has not been externally validated and its relationship, with regard to expected results, to other similar instruments such as the GHQ is unknown. Its characteristics were published only in 1997, and it seems to have been used so far in only one large-scale study, and that with the very unusual sample of 43-year-old adults.

1.3.3.4 The Malaise Inventory (MI)

The Malaise Inventory is a self-completion questionnaire of 24 items derived from the Cornell Medical Index recording symptoms of anxiety, depression, and possible psycho-somatic illness ranging from back-ache and indigestion to "scared to be alone" and "nervous breakdown".[103] Items are scored either present or absent and those present summed. It is intended to record psychological distress (Dohrenwend's "demoralisation") rather than classified psychiatric morbidity.[104] It was used in the 1981 and 1991 follow-up studies of the 1958 UK birth cohort, constituting over 11,000 subjects, and the 1996 follow-up of the 1970 UK birth cohort.

Most users have assumed a unitary dimension of emotional disturbance, but some have doubted the validity of somatic questions, which may have no relationship to psychological disturbance, and proposed separate ratings for psychological and somatic factors.[105] This was examined by Rodgers et al.[104] using the large 1958 birth cohort sample, although without reference to alternative measures as external validation. They concluded that internal consistency was adequate or good, and probably no weaker than other similar instruments. There was only partial discrimination between psychological and somatic sub-scales, but the latter did not constitute a satisfactory independent scale.

Statistical analysis of receiver operating characteristics (ROCs) suggested that it did discriminate quite well people with recent psychiatric morbidity recorded by separate questions about long-standing illness, hospital admissions, and medical care. Although not an original objective of the instrument, the scale appeared to operate similarly in respect of this discrimination for men and women separately, and for different socio-economic groups. It was recommended that when used across age-groups, the somatic items should be deleted because they are likely to behave differently in groups with different expectations of somatic disease.

1.3.3.5 The Present State Examination (PSE)

Throughout the 1970s and later, various structured interview schedules were developed, most notably the PSE, which aimed mainly at assisting specialist professionals in making consistent, reliable, and reproducible standard diagnoses using computer algorithms. Although originally intended for the use of expert clinicians, a version of the PSE was used by trained nurses in the 1982–83 follow-up of the 1946 UK birth cohort,[106] when 3322 individuals were interviewed of 3754 traced from the original cohort. It included about half of the original 103 items. Training, interview time, and checking made this procedure very expensive; it took 56 nurses 18 months to complete, and the results were not considered satisfactory.[97] In particular, the very skewed distribution of scores was a problem for a long-term follow-up study interested in more than clear diagnostic categories of serious psychiatric disorder, and the diagnostic groups were not discriminated by many variables collected in the study at that or previous interviews.

The researchers did not repeat the experiment, and in the next follow-up, at age 43, they used a newly constructed scale focused on anxiety and depression, called the Psychiatric Symptom Frequency Scale (PSF). In general the structured interview instruments developed for psychiatrists to improve the consistency and standardisation of their diagnostic categories are considered inappropriate to mass population surveys, except possibly as a clinical final stage of a multi-stage screening design.

1.3.3.6 The Diagnostic Interview Schedule (DIS)

The Diagnostic Interview Schedule (DIS) was developed particularly for the USA ECA programme,[107;108] and has been adopted by many others, including the Christchurch Psychiatric Epidemiology Study in New Zealand.[109] It is intended to make a diagnosis, though by a trained lay interviewer, and to identify both psychotic and neurotic illness, both recent and throughout previous adult life. However, validity, when examined, has been very variable and its external reliability has not been established.[14;50;98]

Even if it was good enough to provide useful estimates of overall population frequencies, as Robins[108] appeared to argue, it cannot be assumed that errors and biases were equally distributed through different social groups, particularly, in this context, socio-economic groups.[14]

1.3.3.7 The Composite International Diagnostic Interview (CIDI)

The Composite International Diagnostic Interview (CIDI), which was used in the USA NCS programme and the NEMESIS programme in the Netherlands, was a development of the DIS used in the ECA programme. Its continuing development has been supported by WHO and it is conceived as translating the criteria for ICD-10 categories into sets of questions that identify symptoms and their impact on day-to-day activities. A computer programme can thus generate current and life-time prevalences of (probable) specific disorders within ICD-10.[68] Kessler et al.[94] reported comparisons between the ECA and NCS results and concluded that ECA prevalences using the DIS were generally under-estimates. Although they consider CIDI results more reliable, with no evidence of over-estimating prevalences, limited clinical validity tests showed only modest results. A modified CIDI was used in the Australian National Mental Health Survey of 1997. Later research has apparently suggested that the short-form version of the CIDI proposed by WHO may be as effective as the full CIDI at making diagnoses.[110] It takes 10 minutes rather than 1 hour and might, therefore, be more practicable as a first screen.

1.3.3.8 The Hospital Anxiety and Depression Scale (HADS)

This was developed primarily as a self-report questionnaire for use in hospital psychiatry to assess and separate, as far as possible, both anxiety and depression.[89] It has been validated as to classification of anxiety disorder and depressive disorder to some extent, with good initial results,[111] and recognises long-standing symptoms or illness. Like the GHQ it can be used to study the distribution of symptoms rather than disorders, and therefore the psychological health status of a population and its subgroups. It has been used outside hospital, for example in a postal survey in the UK.[112]

It has not been anything like as much researched as the GHQ,[98] but it was subject to a small-scale comparison with the CIS.[89] There was substantial correlation between the two sub-scales of anxiety and depression, and data could not be analysed in terms of these as different constructs. The CIS, requiring clinical judgement, was superior in discriminating anxiety and depression. This was not easy to interpret, but a parallel study suggested that psychiatrists tend to be biased in favour of the distinction of anxiety and depression more than actually reported by patients.[89] The results are not conclusive, but they do support an examination of the idea that anxiety and depression are not distinct clinical and aetiological entities.[113] They also emphasise the possibility that different results might be expected from surveys according to whether they rely on self-report instruments or clinical judgements.

1.3.3.9 The Short-Form 36 (SF-36)

Originally developed to evaluate health services in the USA, the SF-36 tries to encompass the full range of positive and negative psychological experiences. Some validation has been attempted, and it appears to be able to discriminate to some extent between people with different low levels of symptoms related to, for example, physical illness, and people with higher-level symptoms that may be indicative of psychiatric disorder,[114;115] but these were in clinical settings. It has also been used in community surveys with some apparent usefulness.[116;117] A recent comparison of three UK data-sets found substantial differences in mean scores after controlling for age and gender, and concluded that population norms were needed specific to different modes of employing the SF-36, that is, for example, by post or by interview.[118]

However, it is not proven that the positive items really measure "positive mental health", or to what degree, and it is not clear that "positive" and "negative" mental health are necessarily opposite ends of the same dimension rather than different constructs.[119;120] The latter authors consider that it may be useful for general monitoring of a population in terms of both general physical and mental health, but is not very useful if precise measurements are desired of either positive or negative mental health.

There is also a Short-Form 12 (SF-12), which was used in the Australian National Mental Health Survey of 1997.[68]

1.3.3.10 EuroQoL EQ-5D

This is an international self-report health survey instrument developed through WHO, which has been tested, and used in a sample survey of 3395 residents in the UK. It includes one section on anxiety and depression. It has not yet appeared much in the literature.[24]

1.3.4 Conclusion

A limited range of instruments provides the data for this review of large-scale studies. Studies have used the GHQ-30, the GHQ-12, the CIDI, the MI, PSE, PSF, DIS, and CIS-R.

Bartlett and Coles[98] noted that the GHQ used in the Health Survey for England produced prevalence estimates for probable neurotic disorder very similar to those produced by the CIS-R in the National Household Survey, 16%. This consistency derived from two different self-report instruments in the same population at a similar period of time is highly encouraging, and we look forward to further analysis of HSE data to enable the comparability of socio-economic distributions to be assessed.

Otherwise, it is clear from the above that there are many different survey instruments already used in major studies, which have all been through a period of development and validation. Although all are as yet imperfect, several offer sufficient consistency and reliability to give confidence in results when used in well-conducted, large-scale population surveys. They still need further work, so that it is difficult to recommend particular ones, yet great strides have been made in what is a fundamentally difficult field, and we can expect even better results in the next few years. Their different characteristics pose problems for detailed comparison of survey results using different instruments, and more standardisation will, no doubt, be achieved.

For the future, it is possible that multi-stage, multiple-method schemes, as advocated by Dohrenwend,[14] will prove the only acceptable way of identifying classifiable "cases". However, the range of psychiatric symptoms experienced by populations and their sub-groups may be susceptible to much simpler determination by one well-researched scale. Both may inform the debate on socio-economic disparities. Although more standardisation of approach and instruments would be welcome, the recent history of many different approaches and instruments producing very similar general results on inequalities in mental health, suggests a certain robustness in those findings.

1.4 MEASURING SOCIAL CLASS IN POPULATIONS

Concepts of social class have played an important part in the political, social, and economic history of the last 150 years. All societies show some divisions, with differentials of power, wealth, and status, and many such were and are traditional, stable, and sanctioned by religious authority. Such were, for example, the three "estates" of mediaeval Europe, and the caste system of India. In Europe these slowly diminished in impact as populations expanded, industrialisation took hold, and large towns and cities became the norm for most people. Marx's analysis of class was essentially based on economic differentials, but Weber's triad of economic position, prestige and opportunities, and political influence, although implying that social classes were not discrete, has had much more influence in industrial nations in the last half century.[121] Western industrial society under capitalism created social classes differentiated by ownership of wealth, mediating status and, eventually, both economic and political power.[122]

Social status in contemporary societies is not rigid in the same way as traditional caste societies. Ideologies of individual progress, the "work ethic", and a conception of society as a "meritocracy", have encouraged many people to "better themselves", usually facilitated by the opportunity of education and the luck of good health. The combined effects of universal free education, the growing welfare state, the effects of two world wars, and, perhaps, the threat of revolution, have facilitated social mobility on a major scale in Britain and other Western industrialised countries. Nevertheless, there remains in every country a strong continuation of class divisions based on wealth, conveying fundamental inequalities in income, power, and status, and which are associated with differentials in life expectancy, quality of life, disease distribution, and access to services.[123;124]

However, a simple conceptualisation of society as divided economically between workers and owners never was satisfactory and is even less so now. Studies of health, for example, needed more categories than two, and also to encompass social and cultural issues. To some extent the focus on occupational status was intended to do this, on the assumption that men represented the whole family. The system known as the Registrar General's Classification of Occupations, was first devised and used in the UK in 1911. Groups of occupations in very different trades were conceived as sharing a similar status in society at large, and were also considered to share similar physical and social environments (outside the specific hazards of particular jobs) and similar cultures.

This was most likely to be true where people of similar occupational status also lived in similar areas; for example in industrial inner-city slums or council-house estates as opposed to middle-class suburbs. Thus occupational social class might be an indicator of common experiences, values, beliefs, and behaviours, all potential influences on health.[125] It may also be the best simple indicator—the alternative is education—in stable societies, of life-time earning capacity, a better measure of social class than current income.[126] Only much later were residential areas themselves examined with various measures of deprivation within them,[127;128] although studies of urban and rural differences have long been done.[129] Areas of residence might indicate social class, but so also might the perceived status of individual homes, and this has also been used. Homelessness is thrown into prominence by such considerations, but represents a rather different concept more related to social exclusion than simply to poverty or low social status. It is extremely important in relation to psychiatric disorder, however measured.[18;130]

A more subtle distinction offered differentiation within the lower occupational classes or "working classes", by personal attitudes to individual advancement, identifying a "demotic" class with low aspirations and/or limited capacities, and an "aspirant" class with ambitions and capacities to improve their status.[121] This perceived that the culture of a social group, however powerful, is not the only influence, and that there are always individuals with sufficient motivation, intelligence, or deviance to seize opportunities for social advancement and move up the status, wealth, and power scale. The danger of this is to re-create attitudes blaming all those individuals not able to do this for their social situation; there are still economic and social forces within largely capitalist societies, especially those creating mass unemployment, that many individuals cannot resist. And attitudes and motivations towards self-advancement are not easy to measure in large-scale surveys.

Employment classes, as differentiated from occupational classes, have become important for social analysis in recent decades. Occupation may have been a satisfactory basis as long as families were generally stable and the occupation of a man could stand for the whole family. But it has always held problems for married women, retired people, and those in unclassifiable occupations such as students and the armed services. With increasing women's employment, breakdown of families, and unemployment, it holds even greater problems. Employment differences at normal working ages are perceived between those in stable employment, short-term unemployment and long-term unemployment, and those never employed, although this last is not satisfactory as it encompasses, for example, both young people who have never got into work, and older married women who were never formally employed.[3;131;132] And, of course, in studying potential consequences of unemployment we have to distinguish between the state of being unemployed—for various periods of time—and the event of becoming unemployed.

However, economic occupation is important in people's lives. Although it has become less easily classified in terms of social status and common cultures, it remains a source of both satisfaction and stress. Researchers have, therefore, conceived individual work situations, the characteristics of particular jobs, and the experience of daily work, in terms of psychological responses. Instead of physical and chemical hazards of earlier generations of industry, the key factors now under scrutiny are the degree of control people have over their own work, the opportunities their work offers for exploitation and development of personal skills, the variety of tasks offered, the demands made upon them, and the time-pressures under which they work. This has obvious possible implications for mental health and psychiatric symptoms, and also for social class inequalities, because there are jobs with particular characteristics that also carry the social status differentials represented by traditional occupational social class.[23;47;133]

Recently, a new taxonomy has been commissioned: the UK National Statistics Socio-Economic Classification (NS-SEC) which is said to assign people to classes based on their occupational title and their responsibilities over others, but differentiating also between employees having service relationships or labour contracts with employers. It is also said to be designed to encompass income, housing, and consumption.

Education has also been conceived in class terms, although education has also been the means of much social mobility. It is argued that people in societies with universal free education who fail to take advantage of educational opportunities at various stages share common values, behaviours, and experiences, and constitute a distinguishable group or class. They are discriminated by either level of educational achievement, which is country-specific, or years of full-time education, which might be somewhat more readily compared internationally.[134]

In recent studies of health, "social class" in any general guise has been considered suspect, because it is no longer clear exactly what it indicates.[135] It is also difficult to compare internationally, as occupational status may have very different meanings and relationships in different countries and cultures. More basic individual factors have tended to be investigated, especially education, life-time earning capacity, current personal or household income, and material possessions. In many Western industrialised societies these are not co-extensive with traditional occupational social classes, and some argue that status, especially in the USA, is perceived more in simple terms of income and material possessions than job.[136;137]

Much early research relating particular aspects of disadvantage, especially financial disadvantage, to health or other outcomes, assumed a threshold, thus defining, in various ways, a group of "the poor" that experienced prejudiced health and low life expectancy compared with the rest of society. This has been much modified as studies have revealed differentials in health and life expectancy between all the various levels of socio-economic distribution.[138;139] New concepts have arisen of "social capital", with variation in social trust, sense of belonging to the community, and social cohesion arising out of income or other *perceived* inequality, even where there is no poverty.[88;140–142] The least well-off may feel marginalised, with little control over the conditions in which they live and therefore reduced capacity to cope with life events.[27] The homeless in modern industrial societies are a good example of such a group. Clearly these are also elements that are likely to be distributed unequally in occupational social classes, or other categories of socio-economic division.

The picture in current Western societies is no doubt very mixed, and, in most, is now cross-referenced to racial or ethnic divisions and disadvantages, as well as those of age and gender. In spite of substantial social mobility, there is evidence from mental health studies of continuing influence among adults of the social class of their family of origin, but relatively little of the effects of childhood adversity. On the other hand, income and education emerge as powerful associations in many studies. What must always be remembered in this context is the issues of causal direction and complexity. There is evidence that certain psychological characteristics of younger teenage children, and early onset of psychiatric disorder, affect the level and time of completion of education, job opportunities, income, and life-style as well as the frequency of psychiatric disorder in adulthood.[44]

With these many concepts, comparing studies is not easy, but there is no doubt of the continuing existence in Western industrial societies of serious inequalities in economic resources, status, and health.[123;124;143–145] However, any investigation of this needs defined indicators and reliable measures, and an understanding, often not made clear, of what is being measured by "social class".[146]

1.4.1 Social indicators of health status

In the UK, during the 19th century, as industrialisation changed the nature of society, differences were first seriously noted in the health status of the poor, who could generally be easily identified either by where they lived or by the job they did. Major surveys of poverty by, for example, Booth in London and Rowntree in York, created widespread interest and concern.[147] Studies of labourers, tradesmen, and the gentry by Chadwick in 1842 and studies of healthy and unhealthy districts in 1885 identified great variations in health and mortality to the disadvantage of the poor.[148] Some of the earliest concerns clearly identified noxious environments as a key factor, for example cholera in certain residential areas, and various occupational cancers in certain trades. Later, more general environmental factors were implicated, such as overcrowding in the spread of tuberculosis and other infectious diseases, and damp housing for respiratory disease. And more specific occupational toxins and industrial hazards were identified, some with a relatively long time-lag, such as the pneumoconioses.

In order to investigate the causes of ill-health among the poor, techniques were developed for classification of people into groups, which represented shared environments but also shared cultures. It was recognised very early on that behaviour was important, and that education had a profound influence on behaviour, as well as creating opportunities for better jobs and higher incomes.

Once we had escaped from Victorian attitudes that blamed the poor for their poverty and inflicted workhouse regimes on them, there was a recognition that poverty itself had a fundamental impact on health, through at least two mechanisms: capacity to buy sufficient and suitable food to constitute a good diet, and capacity to pay for medical treatment. It had an impact especially on the lives of children and the elderly, and deprivation among children, especially in the big cities, was seen to threaten the country's future population. This became a major concern, reinforced by the discovery of large-scale ill-health among young men being recruited into the army for the Boer War.

Eventually, in the UK, this led to many basic welfare provisions, gradually increasing throughout the 20th century and culminating, after 50 years and two world wars, in the five great Acts of the immediate post-Second World War government, creating family allowances, national insurance, insurance for industrial injuries, national assistance, and the National Health Service.[149]

In the decades immediately following, it was generally expected and believed that poverty had been, at least, very seriously diminished, and its effects upon health almost eliminated by the "welfare state".[140] This was supported to some extent by the greatly increased life-expectancy and increased prominence in mortality statistics of non-infectious disease that was not so obviously related to disadvantaged social circumstances. However, in the last two decades, it has become obvious that this was true only to a limited extent, and has been reversed in some respects as inequalities in incomes have increased again, and as morbidity and quality of life have been given the attention they deserve alongside mortality. A renewed concern for deprivation in children has arisen with the breakdown of conventional marriage and family structures, focusing especially on emotional deprivation and possible consequences in terms of adult psychiatric disorder.

Similarly, especially with regard to psychological health and ill-health, social isolation has become an issue as the number of children has diminished, wider families have dispersed, and single parents as well as elderly people have found it difficult to maintain effective networks of social support. In the 1980s, a further issue arose of mass unemployment and under-employment, which prejudiced social status, social engagement, and income for men and for their families. And in the background, but emerging in some of the large-scale studies, the relationship between psychological ill-health and physical ill-health is evidently important, especially with regard to limiting long-standing illness and disability.[150]

These factors are clearly often involved in "life events", the study of which in relation to psychiatric disorder has a long history.[84] Some accumulation of deleterious conditions and events underlies ideas of "chronic stress" as a possible mediator of the excess of ill-health associated with lower social class.[151] The importance of all these possible factors in this context is twofold. They might be more frequent in relation to income, education, or employment, the principal ways of indicating socio-economic status. And low income, poor education, or unemployment may limit people's capacity to cope with them.

In this very brief review the key concerns can be identified, which overlap and interact. Poverty, deprivation in childhood, education, housing, occupation, employment, social status, and social engagement are still the key concerns and those for which "social class" or "socio-economic groups" are intended to be proxies or indicators. All of them raise problems of definition and measurement.

1.4.2 Definitions and methods of measurement of socio-economic status

1.4.2.1 Occupational groups; occupational social class

In the UK, the use of occupational status as an indicator of social class was formalised first in 1911 in the Registrar General's Classification of Occupations, and decennial census supplements have been issued from 1911 to 1981. This has been updated every 10 years and modified on several occasions, but it remains the basis of most British social-class-related health studies. A key change in 1961 was the division of social class III, a large proportion of the whole, into non-manual and manual. There are similar systems of occupational classification in other industrialised countries such as the Scandinavian countries, Germany, Australia, and the USA,[47;143;146;152;153] but they cannot be assumed to be comparable.

The system of classifying jobs by level of skill and social status indicating experiential, cultural, economic, and environmental commonalities originally only applied to men in employment. Women were assumed to be the same class as their husbands—unmarried women could be classified by their own occupation or their father's, but were not a large group.

There were other problem groups too, particularly students, members of the armed forces, and retired men, although the last could be classified by their final occupation. The system assumed a fairly stable society in terms of occupational differentials, and was repeatedly updated in terms of particular jobs as they changed. With successive data on the same men, it could cope with social mobility up or down in men. There were always problems of consistency in practical use, especially with certain titles such as "engineer" used in different ways in different contexts. A more fundamental criticism is that manipulations of occupations in 1921 to ensure a linear distribution of births, infant mortality, and death rates from class I to class V have rendered the system tautological for epidemiology.[146]

The British system has generally divided jobs into six classes: I: higher professional and managerial; II: lower professional, technical, and managerial; IIIN: skilled non-manual workers and clerical workers; IIIM: skilled manual workers; IV: semi-skilled workers, labourers; V: unskilled workers. A somewhat different and more complex classification was produced after the Second World War to give more detailed socio-economic groups, which have been used in the annual General Household Survey in the UK. Although these could be collapsed into six main groups, the simplicity of the older system has kept it in general use.[144]

However, social mobility through education and entrepreneurial activity, changes in family structure and stability, changes in women's employment, social and technological changes in types of work available, instability in employment, mass unemployment, and variation in income differentials have all been characteristic of periods within the 20th century. Status is not necessarily perceived in the same way, as related especially to jobs, but also to income and possessions, housing type, and area of residence, all of which are less solidly linked together. Women must now be recognised in their own occupations, but women's pattern of occupations may not convey the same differentials as men's. Both men and women may change their jobs across status boundaries several times in a working life.

Long-term unemployment, early retirement, and even timely retirement may create low-status conditions for people with previous high-status jobs, or vice versa depending on their pension situation. In recent decades, numbers of students have risen dramatically. They include a much wider distribution of occupational social class of families of origin, and, concomitantly, graduates now work in jobs with a much wider range of occupational status and material benefits.

All this means that traditional occupational social classification systems tend to have less and less validity as indicators of common social status, economic status, experiences, cultures, and environments, and, therefore, of possible factors affecting health. In spite of this, they must still carry substantial and significant meaning, because they still reveal important differentials in morbidity and mortality, and they have not been replaced by anything else using data as simple to collect. Occupation is still probably the most convenient proxy for life-time earning capacity, and is still strongly linked to wealth, income, education, and social status.[148] Data on occupational groups have, however, become more difficult to interpret, and more precise indicators, where available, may now be more useful.

1.4.2.2 Occupation characteristics

There is a long tradition of studies of work characteristics and psychological health, mostly from the discipline of psychology, adopting several different theoretical models.[154] They are mostly concerned with non-specific psychological distress, rather than identifiable psychiatric disorder about which Kessler and Frank[47] say there is little known, although it was addressed in one study from the ECA.[155] There is also a less published tradition of job assessment in industry from the discipline of personnel management. Most published work used instruments relying on self-report.

In the Whitehall study, adopting a "job strain model" and using modified Karasek indices,[156] assessments of some job characteristics were available from personnel managers within the Civil Service. There is no validation for such assessments, but within the study they were complemented by self-report data using a questionnaire developed from The Satisfaction with Life Scale,[157] and divided, after principal components analysis, into seven dimensions of work: skill and variety; control; social support at work; job importance; job satisfaction; work pace; and conflicting demands.[133;158]

Occupational direction, control, and planning were identified as work characteristics related to socio-economic status by Link et al.[159] for investigation of depression. Also in the USA, the NCS used the Duncan Scale of occupational prestige[160] and Roos and Treiman's[161] seven measures of job conditions, which are: substantive complexity; interaction with people; interaction with things; interaction with data; motor skills; physical demands; undesirable work conditions. It can be seen that both lists of job characteristics have some face validity but that they are very different from each other.

1.4.2.3 Employment status

The basic categories are "currently employed in economic activity" and not so, but "unemployed" encompasses those looking for work, those not looking for work because of chronic sickness or disability, and those not looking for work because of retirement (at any age). It is usually also divided into periods of duration of unemployment, and a group "never employed". More sophisticated treatment of changes in employment status over time can only usually be addressed in cohort studies.

1.4.2.4 Education

Two measures are common: qualifications achieved, and length of full-time education or age of completion of full-time education. Both, but especially the former, are country specific, so international comparisons are problematic, but there is cohort variation in length of education and in educational assessment systems in all countries, which also makes comparison difficult. There is a problem arising in countries where further education may be pursued as adults after a gap, such as that provided at different levels in the UK by the Open University, or local FE Colleges, or NVQ programmes. This may complicate the system of classifying qualifications, or render questions about the completion of full-time education meaningless for certain individuals.

1.4.2.5 *Housing and area of residence*

Housing status in modern industrial societies is generally considered to reflect wealth and income, and social status, but this assumes a highly mobile society of freely choosing individuals without other serious aspirations for a home than obtaining the highest-status individual house in the highest-status location. It is not that simple, and many people are still motivated to retain traditional local or ethnic minority community ties. For some, at all economic levels, renting is a positive choice, and for some their home is not their primary claim to social status.

Individual housing has most commonly been classified in two ways—by type of house and by ownership status or tenure. Type of house may have more validity in some societies than others; in England, for example, it would be commonly assumed to convey social status, but it might not in other countries. A simple English classification would be, for example, flat or maisonette, terrace house, semi-detached, detached.[3] Homelessness sits outside this classification. In the UK National Psychiatric Morbidity Survey, the homeless were targeted in a separate survey because of issues of sampling methodology.[18]

Tenure usually distinguishes homes fully owned, homes owned with a mortgage, homes rented from Local Authorities or Housing Associations, and homes rented from private landlords.[3] The local authority valuation for council tax in the UK provides eight value bands, which might be a very useful indicator of wealth in owner-occupiers with or without a mortgage, but this does not yet appear to have been used for health-related research.

Type of neighbourhood might be a useful social indicator for individual houses, but the face validity of area classifications depends on the pattern of settlement in particular countries, particularly in relation to whatever social status differentials there are. The stability and social cohesion of neighbourhoods has certainly changed dramatically in the last 50 years in the UK, and patterns will be very different in different societies, so comparisons are problematic. For satisfactory use as indicators of social status, there must be reasonable homogeneity over quite large areas.[162]

Other features of housing conditions are also sometimes used, particularly overcrowding, for which there are usually national official definitions, but sometimes also the condition of the physical structure of the property.

1.4.2.6 *Wealth and income*

Wealth has proved more difficult to classify than income, perhaps because of difficulties in definition and measurement. Most commonly, proxies are used which indicate some levels of material possessions. This includes home ownership, dealt with above, but also having access to a car and possessing a certain number of common domestic items of equipment. One study identified income from capital as a distinct item, but it is difficult to know with what degree of accuracy and completeness such data are obtained.

Income is conceptually simpler but it is still difficult to have confidence in the data collected by self-report. Many people either do not know or refuse to say what their income or their family's income is. For example, in the USA "Health United States 1998" Chartbook "*Socio-Economic Status and Health*",[163] missing family income data for all-age analyses varied between 10% and 16%; for persons aged 70 or more it was 24%. The Whitehall study of civil servants, on the other hand, had objective sources of data for income from employment. However, many people have additional sources of income which may not be disclosed. Detailed income is not usually asked for, but only broad income bands, which does help to reduce non-response.

Individual income and household income are very different measures and data on both are not always available from the same survey. The former is often the easier to obtain, but the latter would generally be considered a better indicator of material status, especially for many women.

1.4.2.7 *Composite indicators*

To reflect the multi-dimensionality of social class, composite indicators have been developed and used, especially in the USA, by Duncan, Hollingshead, Nam-Powers, and Warner. They all pose problems of validity.[146] The Nam-Powers Socio-economic Status Score dates from 1963, and was used in the USA ECA programme.[52] It encompasses family income, personal educational achievement, and occupational status. Such composite indicators have advantages in simplifying complex data for comparison, while leaving flexibility in analysis, but they may obscure important differences in associations between the components. The advent of multivariate methods of statistical analysis have discouraged pre-determined composite indicators in favour of combining factors empirically in the analysis.[146]

1.4.3 Comparisons of measures

There have been several comparisons of measures of social class to investigate their relationships. They have generally shown occupation, education, and income to be essentially independent indicators of association with health-related variables.[146] It cannot be assumed that the same social class distributions and the "best" indicators will apply to all health outcomes. Of particular relevance to mental health, Kessler[164] compared eight epidemiological surveys to estimate the relative importance of income, education, and occupation in predicting psychological distress (symptoms rather than identifiable disorders). Each indicator was independently associated, except that the importance of income or education varied with occupational status. Liberatos et al.[146] in an excellent review, conclude that for some health outcomes the choice of measure of social class will affect the results, but for others, it probably doesn't matter. The problem is to know which is which!

1.4.4 Factors often associated with psychiatric symptoms or disorder, and socio-economic status

Some factors could be very important in identifying disadvantaged groups but do not require scales or measures, such as single-parent status or having young children at home. These will also vary with age because they represent a particular stage in life.

Social support now has available scales for standard assessment of social networks and interpersonal interactions, but many published studies use what appear to be ad hoc questions. Taylor and Seeman[165] identified three main approaches in the literature: social networks as involvement in relationships and groups; perceived social support as resources which could be tapped when required; and satisfaction with current levels of life-support from others.

Life events have also been formalised into standard questionnaires and discriminate between negative and positive, although this distinction is not always clear in practice. Some have added questions about perceptions of stress related to particular events. Negative events can be divided in various ways; for example into those threatening danger and those constituting loss.[84]

Physical illness, short- or long-term, and disability are usually a matter of self-report, sometimes backed up by healthcare system data, clinical tests, or physician examination. There are many questionnaires, long and short, often encompassing physical and psychological symptoms, health behaviour, and "activities of daily living" (ADL).[23]

ADL scales have been standardised to some extent and are available. They may be used to qualify the results of self-report psychiatric questionnaires, to create a higher degree of positive response, which includes some perceived loss of activity.[166]

1.5 RESULTS

In this section we present the results of the review. First, we summarise the quantitative results of each included cross-sectional study, presenting evidence of associations of the common mental disorders with the main markers of social position. We then discuss the small amount of longitudinal evidence that is available. The section ends with a discussion of factors, including for example coexistent physical illness, which might be linked with social position, rather than being direct markers of it.

1.5.1 Factors examined as "results" for the review

Figure 1.1 is a diagram of the markers seen as potentially associated with the prevalence of common mental disorders, given the discussion in preceding sections. Social position is seen as encompassing occupational status, education, income, and wealth, with these individual dimensions overlapping but also being somewhat weighted towards identifying independent aspects of social position. Limited data are available to inform a life-cycle view of social factors, but for our age-group of working-age adults, childhood and early influences represent this dimension.

Physical illness, life events, social networks, and other such factors are identified as known risk factors for the common mental disorders to be examined separately, while recognising that there are possible links between

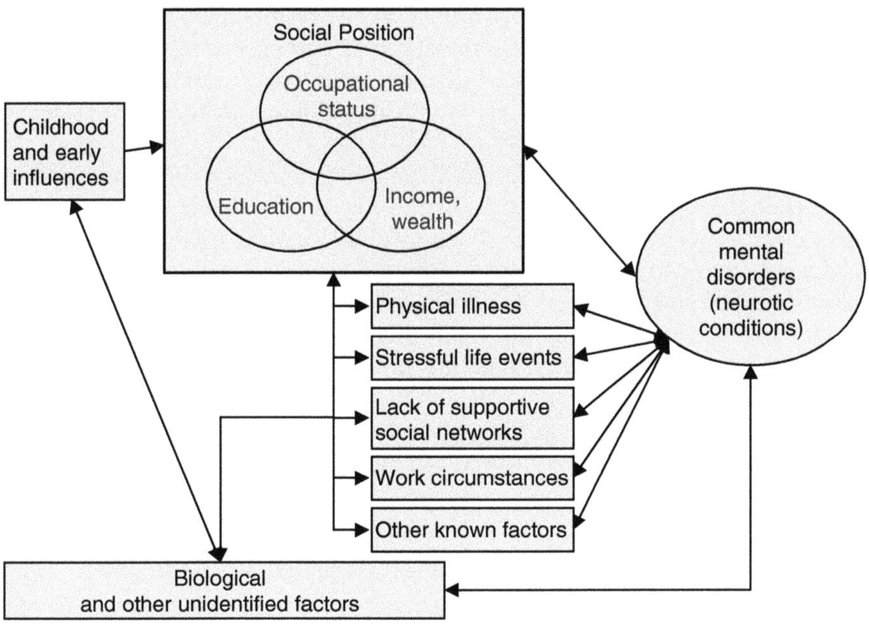

Figure 1.1. Diagram of the potential influences on prevalence rates of the common mental disorders.

these and most of the other factors in the model. Biological factors other than age are not examined, and there may be other significant risk factors for the common mental disorders that are as yet unidentified. Age and gender have both biological and social meanings.

The causal relationships between most of these factors are not necessarily simple, and therefore most linking arrows are shown as pointing both ways.

Some studies have examined prevalence rates of mental disorders for geographical areas, and have related these to markers of social class at area level. While the main review is focused on studies of individuals, some notes are provided on area-level evidence.

1.5.2 Overview of cross-sectional results

In presenting the results of the review, no attempt is made statistically to pool reported prevalence or relative risk data, because concepts, measures, and cut-off points are too varied for this to yield meaningful information (see discussion in Sections 1.3 and 1.4). In reporting results we have instead summarised the quantitative results for each study below, noting the relevant measures and cut-off points for each result.

Table 1.3 contains a global overview of the results. The table simplifies each result down to whether an association between each marker and the prevalence of the common mental disorders was present, and if so, whether the association was "positive" (i.e., with more illness in the less privileged groups) or not.

In eight of the nine included studies, there is evidence of an association between less privileged social position and higher prevalence of the common mental disorders on at least one of the available indicators. No study shows a contrary trend for any indicator, although for some individual indicators in particular studies no clear trend was evident.

The one study showing no clear relationships on any measure (the Health and Lifestyle Survey) had the lowest response rate for its mental health measure (54% of the original target sample, for a postal GHQ questionnaire), and this may have prejudiced its capacity to discriminate.

The overall results relating to the key measures of social position were as follows:

- Less education, measured either as qualifications achieved or years completed, had an overall association with higher prevalence of the common mental disorders in four of the five studies in which it was addressed, although for one of these the association was present in women only. In the fifth study, the effects varied between sites.

TABLE 1.3
Results from studies meeting inclusion criteria

	Education	*Employment status*	*Income and material standard of living*	*Occupational social status*
UK Surveys				
Annual Health Surveys for England	–	–	Progressive positive association for income in 1998 data for both men and women	No clear social class (SC) distribution for either men or women
National Survey of Psychiatric Morbidity in Great Britain (household sample)	Positive for least years of education or no qualifications for both men and women	Positive for unemployed in both men and women	Positive for income, housing type/tenure, and car ownership	Positive for women (SC I+II compared to SC IV+V); positive for men (SC I compared to all other classes)
Health and Lifestyle Survey—baseline	–	Positive for unemployment in men in both age groups	–	No clear social class distribution: mixed results by gender and age group
Health and Lifestyle Survey—follow-up	–	No clear relationship (but low response rate)	–	No clear social class distribution: mixed results by gender and age group
British Household Panel Survey	–	Unemployment associated with maintenance, not onset in 1-year follow-up; symptoms reduced on gaining employment (men and women combined)	Positive for low income and "poverty index". Positive for index of material standard of living (men and women combined)	Positive association for both men and women

Other Countries				
National Co-morbidity Study	Positive for least education (men and women combined)	Positive for unemployment (men and women combined)	Positive for income. Positive for financial assets—wealth (men and women combined)	Positive association with certain occupational groups, but social status implications unclear
Epidemiologic Catchment Area (ECA) Program	Differences between sites	–	Positive for low income in main study (men and women combined)	Not reporting occupation alone (though positive for SES indicated by Nam-Powers index—mix of income, education, and occupation—for anxiety disorders only)
Baltimore follow-up to ECA (1993–96)	No clear relationship		Positive for income but equivocal for assets	Occupation groups showed no association
Australian National Mental Health Survey	Positive for lowest qualifications, especially for women; in men only for affective disorders	Positive for unemployment in both men and women	–	–
Edmonton Survey of Psychiatric Disorders	–	No clear relationship (positive but not statistically significant)	–	–
Netherlands Mental Health Survey and Incidence Study (NEMESIS)	Positive for least education (men and women combined)	Positive for unemployment (men and women combined)	Positive for income (men and women combined)	–

"Positive" indicates association between less privileged status and the common mental disorders.

- Of the seven studies providing data on unemployment, six provided evidence for a positive association with the common mental disorders, although in one this was positive only for men, with women showing equivocal results.
- Low income was associated with high prevalence of high psychiatric symptom scores and common mental disorders in all of the six reporting studies, with high income usually associated with low frequencies. Material standard of living also emerges as important, whether indicated by tenure or type of house, access to a car, or broader measures of wealth. In every case, the poorest groups have the most psychiatric symptoms and most common mental disorders, and the wealthiest groups have the least. These individual indicators are probably not independent factors.
- Of the six included studies reporting on the association between less privileged occupational social class and mental illness, three showed a positive association and three showed no association.
- No studies showed an inverse relationship for any indicator.

This crude overview of the results requires qualification, given the many methodological concerns relating to this subject area. In the sections set out below, we present in more detail each set of quantitative results for the main indicators, and then examine the linked issues. The tables below use the same categories in each case as the original publications. Being different, the prevalence figures cannot be precisely compared, but the general trend of the data regarding social status can, in each case, be observed.

1.5.2.1 Education

Education is one of the more consistently used measures of social position across study populations, although we have only one UK survey reporting associations—the National Household Psychiatric Survey. Completion of education is undoubtedly precedent to the survey observations of mental disorder in any but the youngest adults. However, this does not necessarily imply causation in one direction, as early psychological problems indicative of later mental disorder could influence educational persistence and achievement.

1.5.2.1.1 UK National Survey. Those with least years of education (finishing at age 15 or under) or lowest qualifications (none) had the highest rates of probable neurosis.[3] The general gradient related to educational qualifications was not sustained when adjusted for other socio-demographic variables[27] (Table 1.4).

TABLE 1.4
UK National Survey: Prevalence (% and ORs—95% CIs) of neurotic disorder by gender and educational qualifications, adjusted for age and household size

	Men		*Women*	
Educational qualification	*%*	*OR (95% CI)*	*%*	*OR (95% CI)*
A level or above	10.4	1	17.6	1
GCSE grades A–C or equiv	12.9	1.27 (1.00–1.62)	17.2	0.98 (ns)
GCSE grades D–F or equiv	11.7	1.14 (ns)	20.4	1.21 (ns)
No qualifications	13.0	1.29 (1.03–1.62)	21.1	1.26 (1.06–1.49)

Source:[27] (Tables 3, 4).

1.5.2.1.2 US NCS. In the USA NCS programme, the most educated group had the lowest prevalence for all diagnostic groups; but only the categories "any anxiety" and "three or more neurotic disorders" had the highest prevalence in the least educated group.[167] Minor and moderate depression was associated with low education[43] (Table 1.5).

TABLE 1.5
NCS: Odds ratios (95% CIs) for lifetime occurrence of minor depression by education in years

Education (years)	*OR*	*95% CI*
0–11	0.75	0.58–0.97
12	0.76	ns
13–15	0.89	ns
16+	1	

Source:[43] (Table 1).

Lifetime and 12-month prevalence of both mood disorders and anxiety disorders were correlated with a poor educational record in several different analyses of the data (Table 1.6, Table 1.7).

1.5.2.1.3 US ECA. In the USA ECA programme the picture was mixed. Depression was associated with lower education in New Haven[57] but with higher education in Piedmont.[56] Similarly, the results of the Baltimore area follow-up in 1993–96 were equivocal.[46]

1.5.2.1.4 The Netherlands NEMESIS. In the Netherlands study, those with the fewest years of education had the highest prevalence rates for both mood and anxiety disorders (Table 1.8).

1.5.2.1.5 Australian National Mental Health Survey 1997. In Australia, for both sexes together, the group with post-school qualifications had lower

TABLE 1.6
NCS: 12-month prevalence and ORs (95% CIs) for mood disorders and anxiety disorders, by education in years

	Mood disorders			*Anxiety disorders*		
Education (years)	*OR (bivariate)*	*OR (multivariate)*	*95% CI*	*(bivariate)*	*OR (multivariate)*	*OR 95% CI*
0–11	1	1		1	1	
12	0.8	0.9	ns	0.8	0.8	ns
13–15	0.8	0.8	ns	0.7*	0.6	0.4–0.9
16	0.5*	0.6	0.3–0.9	0.4***	0.4	0.3–0.7
17+	0.5*	0.6	ns	0.2***	0.3	0.4–0.8 (sic)

Source:[46] (Table 1).
$*p < 0.05$, $*** p < 0.0001$.

TABLE 1.7
NCS: ORs (95% CIs) for life-time occurrence and 12-month prevalence of any affective disorder and any anxiety disorder, by education in years

	Any affective disorder				*Any anxiety disorder*			
	Life-time occurrence		*12-month prevalence*		*Life-time occurrence*		*12-month prevalence*	
Education (years)	*OR*	*95% CI*	*OR*	*95% CI*	*OR*	*95% CI*	*OR*	*95% CI*
0–11	0.98	ns	1.79	1.31–2.43	1.86	1.53–2.26	2.82	2.26–3.51
12	1		1.38	ns	1.76	1.42–2.20	2.10	1.66–2.67
13–15	1.05	ns	1.37	1.02–1.84	1.44	1.15–1.79	1.60	1.19–2.15
16+	1		1		1		1	

Source:[92] (Tables 5, 6).

TABLE 1.8
NEMESIS: 12-month prevalence (%, SE and ORs—95% CIs) controlled for age and sex for mood disorders and anxiety disorders, by education in years

	Mood disorders				*Anxiety disorders*			
Education (years)	*%*	*SE*	*OR*	*95% CI*	*%*	*SE*	*OR*	*95% CI*
0–11	9.4	0.7	1.55	1.22–1.98	17.2	0.9	2.44	1.98–3.00
12	7.7	0.5	1.16	ns	12.6	0.6	1.58	1.28–1.95
13–15	5.8	1.0	0.83	ns	10.8	1.4	1.28	ns
16+	6.5	0.6	1		7.9	0.6	1	

Source:[65] (Tables 3, 4).

12-month prevalence rates for both anxiety and affective disorders (Table 1.9). This was more prominent in women than in men. In men there was an association only for affective disorders, not for anxiety disorders.

TABLE 1.9
Australian Survey: 12-month prevalence (%) of affective disorders and anxiety disorders, by educational qualifications

Educational qualifications	*Affective disorders*	*Anxiety disorders*
Post-school qualification	4.8	8.9
Completed secondary school only	6.3	10.6
Did not complete secondary school	6.9	10.3

Source:[68] (App Table 9).

1.5.2.1.6 Additional studies. In the Whitehall II studies, employment grade seemed to predict depression better than years of education, but in the USA National Survey of Families and Households, education appeared to be the best socio-economic indicator for depression.[168]

1.5.2.2 Employment status

1.5.2.2.1 UK National Survey. In the UK National Survey, unemployed men and women had much higher rates of neurotic disorder than those employed, and unemployment was the factor most strongly associated with symptom prevalence. Rates for economically inactive (unemployed and not seeking work) women were mid-way, but economically inactive men were not much different from those unemployed (Table 1.10).

TABLE 1.10
UK National Survey: 1-week prevalence of neurotic disorder (% and unadjusted ORs—95% CIs), by employment

Employment	*%*	*Men and women OR (95% CI)*	*Men % (SE)*	*Women % (SE)*
Full-time	11.8	1	9.5 (0.6)	16.4 (1.1)
Part-time	16.0	1.42 (1.21–1.66)	11.7 (2.5)	16.8 (1.1)
Unemployed	25.9	2.59 (2.17–3.10)	20.3 (1.8)	38.1 (3.4)
Economically inactive	21.2	1.98 (1.74–2.26)	19.5 (1.8)	22.0 (1.1)

Source:[28;3]

Redundancy in the previous 6 months, as a stressful life event, was little associated with higher CIS-R scores, presumably because half of those redundant were re-employed within the same period.[166]

It is also interesting to note that frequencies for functional psychosis were strongly related to employment status, the highest being unemployed.[26;27]

1.5.2.2.2 Health and Lifestyle Survey. In the 1984–85 baseline survey, there was approximately double the frequency of GHQ high scores in unemployed compared to employed groups of men in two separate age groups covering ages 18–64[30] (Table 1.11). High scores in the 1991–92 follow-up were not clearly related to unemployment, but it should be remembered that loss to follow-up for GHQ completion was a serious problem in this study.

TABLE 1.11
HALS: Men aged 18–64 (% above GHQ-30 threshold), by employment

	Age in years	
Occupational groups	*18–29*	*30–64*
Employed	26	22
Unemployed	47	49

Source:[169] (Tables 6.5, 6.7).

Although not statistically significant because of very small numbers who had different employment status at baseline and 7-year follow-up, the results are interesting to note. There was a 23% increase in GHQ positives among the 20 men employed at baseline and unemployed 7 years later. There was a 57% decrease in GHQ positives among the 36 men unemployed at baseline and employed 7 years later. There was no change in men employed at both times. Early retirement seemed to be associated with higher scores, but timely retirement was not.[33]

1.5.2.2.3 BHPS 1-year follow-up. In the BHPS, comparing the baseline survey with the 1-year follow-up, unemployment was apparently associated with the maintenance but not the onset of symptoms recorded by the GHQ-12 (see Table 1.12). However, symptoms decreased in those gaining employment during the year, and increased in those losing employment during the year, unless for retirement or to look after the family.[35]

1.5.2.2.4 USA NCS. In the USA NCS study there were high rates for all the main diagnostic categories in those unemployed and not seeking work up to age 54.[167] Within the group of economically active men, frequencies of early onset disorder, or any disorder within the 12 months prior to the interview, were far higher among those currently not working[170] (see Table 1.13; Table 1.14).

TABLE 1.12
BHPS 12-month follow-up: Onset and maintenance of common mental disorders (unadjusted ORs and 95% CIs), by employment; men and women together

	Onset		*Maintenance*	
	OR	*95% CI*	*OR*	*95% CI*
Employed	1		1	
Unemployed	1.17	0.85–1.62	1.54	1.13–2.10

Source:[37] (Table 1).

TABLE 1.13
NCS: Lifetime occurrence of any affective or any anxiety disorder (ORs—95% CIs), by employment

	Any affective disorder		*Any anxiety disorder*	
Employment	*OR*	*95% CI*	*OR*	*95% CI*
Working	1		1	
Homemaker	2.0	1.6–2.6	3.2	2.5–4.1
Student	1.0	ns	1.2	1.0–1.5
Other	2.2	1.6–2.9	2.1	1.6–2.8

Source:[167] (Table 7.4).

TABLE 1.14
NCS: Lifetime occurrence of minor depression (ORs—95% CIs), by employment

Employment	*OR*	*95% CI*
Employed	1	
Homemaker	2.46	1.57–3.87
Students	1.28	ns
Other	2.35	1.53–3.59

Source:[43] (Table 1).

1.5.2.2.5 The Netherlands NEMESIS. As detected by the CIDI used in the NEMESIS survey, there were significantly higher prevalence rates in all other employment groups compared with those described as "employed"[65] (Table 1.15).

TABLE 1.15
NEMESIS: 12-month prevalence (ORs—95% CIs) of mood disorders and anxiety disorders, by employment, controlled for age and sex

	Mood disorders				Anxiety disorders			
Employment	*%*	*SE*	*OR*	*95% CI*	*%*	*SE*	*OR*	*95% CI*
Employed	6.0	0.4	1		10.4	0.5	1	
Homemaker	9.6	0.9	1.47	1.14–1.90	19.2	1.2	1.65	1.35–2.01
Student	7.1	1.1	1.31	ns	11.0	1.4	0.92	ns
Disabled/ unemployed	18.4	1.8	4.30	3.24–5.72	18.4	1.8	2.23	1.70–2.91
Retired/others	7.9	1.2	1.95	1.33–2.85	10.4	1.4	1.28	ns

All subjects aged 18–64.
Source:[65] (Tables 3, 4).

1.5.2.2.6 The Australian National Mental Health Survey. In the Australian National Mental Health Survey of 1997, prevalence rates of mental disorder as detected by the CIDI were highest for men and women who were unemployed. Part-time workers had higher frequencies than full-time workers. Anxiety disorders were particularly high in unemployed women, and substance abuse disorders in unemployed men[68] (see Table 1.16).

TABLE 1.16
Australian Survey: 12-month prevalence (%) of affective disorders and anxiety disorders, by employment

Employment	*Affective disorders*	*Anxiety disorders*
Full-time	4.4	7.6
Part-time	7.5	11.4
Unemployed	11.7	18.3
Not in labour force	6.1	10.4

Source:[68] (App Table 7).

A later paper gives more detail, and shows statistically significant ORs ($p = 0.05$) for "any affective disorder" and "any anxiety disorder" in both short-term and long-term unemployed groups compared with those employed[69] (Table 1.17).

1.5.2.2.7 The Edmonton Survey. In the Edmonton survey, although the prevalence of all mental disorders together gave an OR of 2.8 in relation to unemployment, associations with "dysthymia" and "anxiety disorders" were not significant.[63]

TABLE 1.17
Australian Survey: Psychiatric disorders in the previous 12 months (unadjusted ORs—95% CIs), by employment

	Any affective disorder		*Any anxiety disorder*	
Employment	*OR*	*95% CI*	*OR*	*95% CI*
Employed	1		1	
Short-term unemployed (<12 months)	2.1	1.4–3.2	2.2	1.4–3.6
Long-term unemployed (12 months and over)	2.4	1.4–4.3	2.8	1.6–5.0
Not in labour force	1.2	1.0–1.5	1.3	1.1–1.4

Source:[69] (Table 2d).

1.5.2.3 *Income and material standard of living: Housing tenure, house type, assets, and wealth*

1.5.2.3.1 Health Surveys for England. In 1998, GHQ-12 scores of 4 or more decreased consistently with increasing income, especially in men (see Table 1.18).

TABLE 1.18
HSE: GHQ-12 scores of 4 or more (ORs—95% CIs), by equivalised household income

	Men			*Women*		
Income (£)	*%*	*OR*	*95% CI*	*%*	*OR*	*95% CI*
< 7,186	20	1.53	1.12–2.09	21	1.11	0.87–1.41
–10,834	17	1.70	1.26–2.28	21	1.22	0.96–1.53
–17,890	11	1.13	0.86–1.49	18	1.09	0.88–1.34
–27,705	10	1.12	0.86–1.45	17	1.04	0.84–1.27
>27,705	9	1		17	1	

Age-standardised %.
Source:[4] (Tables 6.27, 6.31).

1.5.2.3.2 UK National Survey. The 1993 UK National Survey collected personal and household income data, but only on those scoring above the CIS-R threshold, so comparable data on the whole survey population are not available. A very limited comparative analysis using national income data from the OPCS Omnibus Survey of 1993 showed those above the CIS-R threshold to have a median weekly gross personal income of about 60% of that for the general population.[166]

In the National Survey, housing tenure, house type, and access to a car or van all showed clear gradients, with the lowest assets always being associated with the greatest frequencies of both probable neurotic disorders (see Table 1.19) and individual symptoms recorded on the CIS-R. These may all be indicating more or less the same group of disadvantaged people in terms of available assets and standard of living, which is not clearly identified by conventional occupational social class distributions. Interestingly, frequencies for functional psychosis were also highest in the poorest groups of housing tenure and house type.[26]

TABLE 1.19
UK National Survey: Prevalence (% and ORs—95% CIs) of neurotic disorder, by housing tenure and car access, adjusted for age and household size

	Men		*Women*	
	%	*OR (95% CI)*	*%*	*OR (95% CI)*
Housing tenure				
Owner	9.3	1	16.3	1
Renter	18.2	2.17 (1.79–2.64)	25.0	1.71 (1.48–1.98)
Car access				
None	19.0	2.59 (1.99–3.37)	26.0	2.25 (1.85–2.74
One	11.3	1.45 (1.11–1.78)	18.9	1.49 (1.25–1.79)
Two or more	8.3	1	13.5	1

Source:[27] (Tables 3, 4).

1.5.2.3.3 British Household Panel Survey. In the BHPS, comparing household income alone in quintiles, the middle three-fifths had more cases (OR 1.16; 1.0–1.34 95% CIs) and the lowest fifth significantly more cases (OR 1.45; 1.21–1.74 95% CIs) than the highest fifth. Using data from 1990 to 1992, two different analyses of "material standard of living" have been published, giving somewhat different results. Analysis using five elements of income, housing, and assets produced the strongest association with the frequency of GHQ-12 scores of 3 or more, even after adjustment for social class, physical illness, and other variables[36] (Table 1.20). Using an additional two elements of assets and overcrowding produced associations with the maintenance but not the onset of common mental disorders as indicated by a score of 3 or more on the GHQ-12.[37]

In the BHPS 1-year follow-up, "subjective financial strain" was apparently associated with the onset of common mental disorders. Although this factor was closely correlated with the "poverty index" used, the latter was associated with the maintenance but not the onset of common psychiatric disorders[36] (Table 1.21).

1.5.2.3.4 USA NCS. In the USA NCS study (1990 to 1992), the lowest income group had the highest prevalence of most important diagnostic categories ("any affective"; "any anxiety"; "any substance abuse"; "any

TABLE 1.20
BHPS: GHQ-12 "cases" above threshold of 3 or more (% and ORs—95% CIs), by index of low material standard of living, adjusted for several indicators of material standard of living

5-point index of low material standard of living	*% of cases*	*OR (95% CI)*
0	16.6	1
1	21.9	1.26 (1.08–1.48)
2	24.8	1.36 (1.15–1.62)
3	30.8	1.67 (1.37–2.04)
4	37.5	2.03 (1.59–2.61)
5	45.1	2.51 (1.77–3.55)

Men and women combined.
Source:[36] (Tables 2, 3).

TABLE 1.21
BHPS and follow-up: Maintenance and onset of common mental disorders (unadjusted ORs—95% CIs), by poverty score and perceived financial strain

	Onset		*Maintenance*	
	OR	95%CI	OR	95% CI
Poverty score				
0	1		1	
1	1.16	0.96–1.40	0.99	0.73–1.33
2–3	1.17	0.95–1.44	1.21	0.97–1.61
4+	1.11	0.86–1.43	1.73	1.26–2.37
Financial strain				
Living comfortably	1		1	
Just about getting by	1.25	1.07–1.45	1.56	1.25–1.95
Difficult or very difficult	1.92	1.55–2.37	2.02	1.60–2.56

Source:[37] (Table 1).

disorder"; and "three or more disorders") and the highest income group always had the lowest prevalence, with the other income groups lying between. Major depression was associated especially with low income (but minor and moderate depression with low education).[43] Summaries of NCS findings by Dohrenwend and Schwartz[48] claim that frequencies of 12-month, life-time, and multiple diagnosis are related strongly to income for most specific disorders.

Comparing NCS data with the 1993 to 1996 ECA follow-up in East Baltimore, income was a strong negative correlate of 12-month prevalence of mood disorders and, especially, anxiety disorders in both studies, as well as substance abuse disorders, the three most prevalent groups of disorder in the USA.[46]

In the NCS, not only income but also wealth, measured as assets possessed, was negatively correlated with 12-month prevalence of mood disorders and anxiety disorders, as well as substance abuse disorders. Muntaner et al.[46] suggest that underlying factors may include lack of material and social resources, or increased exposure to stressful life events and noxious environments, with increased vulnerability and reduced resistance (Table 1.22 to Table 1.25).

TABLE 1.22
NCS: 12-month prevalence (ORs—95% CIs) of mood disorders and anxiety disorders, by income

	Mood disorders			*Anxiety disorders*		
Income ($000)	*OR (bivariate)*	*OR (multivariate)*	*95% CI*	*OR (bivariate)*	*OR (multivariate)*	*95% CI*
0–19	1	1		1	1	
20–34	0.5***	0.7	ns	0.5***	0.7	0.5–0.9
35–69	0.6***	0.9	ns	0.4***	0.7	ns
70+	0.2***	0.5	ns	0.1***	0.4	0.1–0.9

Source:[46] (Table 1).
*** $p < 0.0001$.

TABLE 1.23
NCS: Lifetime occurrence and 12-month prevalence (ORs—95% CIs) of any affective disorder and any anxiety disorder, by income

	Any affective disorder				*Any anxiety disorder*			
	Lifetime occurrence		*12-month prevalence*		*Lifetime occurrence*		*12-month prevalence*	
Income ($000)	*OR*	*95% CI*	*OR*	*95% CI*	*OR*	*95% CI*	*OR*	*95% CI*
0–19	1.56	1.23–1.98	1.73	1.29–2.32	2	1.66–2.41	2.12	1.63–2.77
20–34	1.19	ns	1.13	ns	1.52	1.21–1.9	1.56	1.18–2.06
35–69	1.16	ns	1.01	ns	1.48	1.16–1.9	1.5	1.15–1.97
70+	1		1		1			

Source:[92] (Tables 5, 6).

1.5.2.3.5 USA ECA. In the New Haven area of the USA ECA programme in the early 1980s, poverty was a strong correlate of first-onset major depression even after various adjustments for other factors, but no data for the common mental disorders appear to be available. Bruce and

TABLE 1.24
NCS: Lifetime occurrence and 12-month prevalence (ORs—95% CIs) of any affective disorder and any anxiety disorder, by wealth

	Mood disorders			*Anxiety disorders*		
Wealth ($000)	*OR (bivariate)*	*OR (multivariate)*	*95% CI*	*OR (bivariate)*	*OR (multivariate)*	*95% CI*
0–9	1	1		1	1	
10–49	0.6**	0.6	0.4–0.8	0.7**	0.8	ns
50–199	0.5**	0.6	0.4–0.9	0.6**	0.7	ns
200+	0.4***	0.5	0.3–0.8	0.5***	0.7	ns

Source:[46] (Table 1).
** $p < 0.001$, *** $p < 0.0001$.

TABLE 1.25
NCS: Lifetime occurrence of minor depression (ORs—95% CIs), by income

Income ($000)	*OR*	*95% CI*
0–19	0.85	ns
20–34	0.65	0.46–0.93
35–69	0.80	ns
70+	1	

Source:[43] (Table 1).

Hoff[57] believe that the effects of poverty may be mediated through social isolation (though not living alone per se), and that the increased frequency of depression in the elderly may reflect increases in physical illness and be associated with low income. These relationships might not be the same in the UK as the USA. Over all the ECA areas, people in poverty as defined by US Federal guidelines had twice the frequency of any Axis I DSM-III disorder, and this was matched for most specific disorders, independent of age, gender, race, or previous history of disorder.[58]

In the Baltimore ECA area follow-up of 1993 to 1996, some aspects of material and financial assets were negatively correlated with 12-month prevalence of anxiety disorders, but most were equivocal.

1.5.2.3.6 The Netherlands NEMESIS. In the Netherlands study, average net income per person in the family group was divided into the highest 25%, middle 50%, and lowest 25%. Lower income was associated with higher prevalence of both mood disorders and anxiety disorders (Table 1.26).

TABLE 1.26
NEMESIS: 12-month prevalence (%, SE and ORs—95% CIs) of mood disorders and anxiety disorders, by income, controlled for age and gender

	Mood disorders				Anxiety disorders			
Income	*%*	*SE*	*OR*	*95% CI*	*%*	*SE*	*OR*	*95% CI*
Top 25%	5.4	0.6	1		8	0.7	1	
Next 50%	7.7	0.5	1.29	1.02–1.64	12.9	0.6	1.48	1.22–1.79
Lowest 25%	9.6	0.7	1.56	1.20–2.03	15.6	0.9	1.77	1.43–2.21

Source:[65] (Tables 3, 4).

1.5.2.3.7 Additional studies. The Alameda County Study, California, collected income data in 1965, 1974, and 1983. This permitted an "economic hardship" index to be examined in interviewed subjects who were still alive in 1994. The study found that those experiencing economic hardship (not only dire poverty) within the 30-year period were much more likely than others to have had clinical depression and difficulties with activities of daily living. There was a graded relationship with the number of times in 30 years that they had experienced economic hardship as defined. As regards causal direction, the authors considered that all the evidence pointed to hardship antedating depression and difficulties.[171]

The 1978 to 1979 Canada Health Survey found higher rates of symptoms of depression and anxiety in those with lower incomes.[131] In the Australian Health Survey of 1977 to 1978, the strongest correlation found was high mean scores on the GHQ-12, with low incomes.[172]

From a wide-ranging review, Lewis[173] considered that there was good evidence that low income is associated with depressive disorders independent of occupational social class, and that low income might be a cause of high prevalence of disorders in certain groups.

1.5.2.4 *Own occupational social class*

In spite of continuing and increasing doubts about the validity of any social status implications, occupational social class of either the subject or the head of the household remains a prime focus of studies in the UK, but analyses provide equivocal evidence. In other countries, social status implications are bound to be different; comparisons are of doubtful use except in the most general way, and socio-economic status (SES) may be measured in other ways. Dohrenwend,[5] in reviewing the field, found consistent evidence of an inverse relationship of SES with the frequency of psychiatric disorder up to the early 1980s, but less consistency in findings since, although most studies report inverse relationships in men. The nine large-scale population studies under review here give less definite results for this indicator than the other three more precise indicators, somewhat confirming Dohrenwend's conclusion.

1.5.2.4.1 Health Surveys for England. Recently, the 1998 report on the HSE has included analysis of the GHQ-12 scores with markers of social status, and some trend analysis from 1994. In 1998 there was a tendency for GHQ-12 positives (a score of 4 or more) to decrease in frequency with increasing occupational social class of head of household, but this was neither very marked nor consistent[4] (Table 1.27).

TABLE 1.27
HSE 1998: GHQ-12 scores of 4 or more (ORs—95% CIs), by occupational social class of head of household

Occupational social class	*Men*			*Women*		
	%	*OR*	*95% CI*	*%*	*OR*	*95% CI*
I	13	1.24	0.79–1.95	18	0.88	0.61–1.26
II	11	0.98	0.67–1.41	16	0.80	0.60–1.05
IIINM	14	1.01	0.67–1.52	21	0.98	0.74–1.30
IIIM	12	0.83	0.58–1.19	19	0.88	0.67–1.16
IV	13	0.66	0.66–1.41	19	0.84	0.63–1.11
V	16	1		21	1	

Age-standardised %.
Source:[4] (Tables 6.26, 6.31).

1.5.2.4.2 UK National Survey. The first UK National Survey in 1993 also provided somewhat equivocal results. For women, there was a clear social class gradient for neurosis, from 15% in social classes I and II, to 25% in social classes IV and V. This more or less disappeared after adjusting for age, family unit, car access, housing tenure, education, and economic activity, but this is not surprising as these can be viewed to some extent as more specific components of the very general indicator, occupational social class. In men, all classes were similar at 12–14% except for SC I at 6%, which remained after all adjustments[36] (Table 1.28).

Interestingly, functional psychosis showed very high prevalence in SC V in both sexes, but very low prevalence in SC I only for men. This might reflect differences resulting from women being allocated their husband's occupational social class, perhaps protecting them from downward social drift.[26;28]

1.5.2.4.3 Health and Lifestyle Survey. In the HALS baseline survey, there was a general correlation for the whole population aged 18–64 years, of high GHQ-30 scores with low social class (Table 1.29; Table 1.30).

TABLE 1.28
UK National Survey: 1-week prevalence of neurotic disorder (% and unadjusted ORs—95% CIs), by occupational social class

	Men and Women		Men	Women
Social class	*%*	*OR (95%)*	*% (SE)*	*% (SE)*
I	10.2	1	6.0 (1.4)	15.5 (2.1)
II	14.5	1.47 (1.12–1.94)	13.5 (1.0)	15.4 (1.1)
IIINM	18.2	1.89 (1.43–2.52)	13.9 (1.5)	21.3 (1.5)
IIIM	15.8	1.60 (1.21–2.10)	12.4 (0.9)	19.8 (1.2)
IV	18.2	1.98 (1.49–2.63)	12.4 (1.3)	23.5 (1.7)
V	18.5	2.00 (1.43–2.81)	12.9 (2.7)	24.7 (3.1)

Source:[28;3].

TABLE 1.29
HALS: Lifetime occurrence of "depression" (%), by occupational social class

	Males	*Females*
Non-manual	10	18
Manual	14	26

Source:[32] (Table 4).

TABLE 1.30
HALS: Prevalence above threshold on GHQ-30 (%), by socio-economic group, ages 18–64

Occupational group	*Males*	*Females*
Professionals/employers/managers	25	28
Other non-manual	24	32
Skilled manual, etc.	26	34
Semi-skilled/unskilled manual	33	36

n = males 2411; females 3002.
Source:[169] (Tables 6.5, 6.7).

However, for both men and women there was no clear pattern to the distribution of scores according to occupational groups. In the baseline survey, for men aged between 18 and 64, the highest frequency of GHQ-30 scores was in combined occupational social classes I and II (professionals, employers, and managers) in the age-group 18–39; the lowest was in social class III non-manual, in the same age-group. The highest frequency in the age-group 40–64 was also in occupational social classes I and II. Social classes IV and V combined had high frequencies in the 18–39 age-group and low frequencies in the 40–64 age-group.

In the baseline survey, in women the highest GHQ-30 scores were in occupational social classes IV–V (semi-skilled and non-skilled manual workers) in the age-group 18–39; the lowest were in social classes I–II, in the age group 40–64. In the follow-up data, both the highest frequency (in age-group 18–39) and the lowest frequency (in age-group 40–64) were found in the lowest social class (IV–V). The baseline results for women do show a hint of a gradient of negative correlation with social class, but those for men certainly do not, and, given the inherent problems of interpretation of occupational social class in women, it is not surprising that the researchers commented that these results "are difficult to interpret"[30] (Table 1.31).

TABLE 1.31
HALS: Frequency above threshold on GHQ-30 (%), by occupational group

		Men		*Women*	
Occupational group	*Age*	*HALS1*	*HALS2*	*HALS1*	*HALS2*
Professionals/employers/managers	18–39	33	33	26	28
	40–64	24	23	24	28
Other non-manual	18–39	20	27	32	32
	40–64	27	28	28	31
Skilled manual, etc.	18–39	21	21	32	28
	40–64	24	30	33	30
Semi-skilled/unskilled manual	18–39	30	26	39	38
	40–64	23	28	33	27

HALS1 = The Health and Lifestyle Survey 1984–5 (baseline)
HALS2 = The Health and Lifestyle Survey 1991–2 (follow-up)
n = males 1320; females 1786.
Source:[33] (Tables 8.2a, b; 8.5).

1.5.2.4.4 BHPS. The prevalence of GHQ-12 scores of 3 or more in the BHPS varied with occupational social class of either self or head of household, the lowest class having the highest prevalence, but if adjusted for material standard of living this gradient disappeared for men aged below 65.[36] GHQ-12 scores, and changes over time in GHQ-12 scores, were highly correlated with self-assessed health, which showed a clear negative gradient with social class[35] (Table 1.32).

1.5.2.4.5 USA NCS. In the USA NCS of 1990 to 1992, occupational grades showed no clear pattern. It may be that they do not mean the same as in the UK, in terms of social status and its social correlates; perhaps wealth and income are more important as direct indicators of status[46] (Table 1.33).

TABLE 1.32
BHPS: GHQ-12 "cases" above threshold of 3 or more (unadjusted ORs—95% CIs, for social classes IV–V (head of household) compared with I–II), by age and gender

Age	*Men* *OR (95% CI)*	*Women* *OR (95% CI)*
16–35	0.93 (ns)	1.37 (1.01–1.86)
36–55	1.22 (ns)	1.82 (1.31–2.52)
56–75	2.27 (1.36–3.82)	2.48 (1.65–3.72)

Source:[36] (Table 1).

TABLE 1.33
NCS: 12-month prevalence (ORs—95% CIs) of mood disorders and anxiety disorders, by occupation

	Mood disorders			*Anxiety disorders*		
Occupation	*OR (bivariate)*	*OR (multivariate)*	*95% CI*	*OR (bivariate)*	*OR (multivariate)*	*95% CI*
Professional	1	1		1	1	
Sales	1.3	0.8	ns	1.4*	0.7	ns
Services	0.8	0.8	ns	0.9	0.8	ns
Craft	1.1	0.8	ns	1.7***	1.1	ns
Labourers	1.7*	1.0	ns	1.8**	0.8	ns

Source:[46] (Table 1).
* $p < 0.05$, ** $p < 0.001$, *** $p < 0.0001$.

1.5.2.4.6 USA ECA. Although there do not seem to be reports on occupation itself from the main study, the Baltimore follow-up of 1993–96 reported no association between occupational groups and frequency of the common mental disorders.[46]

1.5.2.4.7 Additional studies. The Whitehall II studies were handicapped by excluding all poor and all non-working people, and by their population being a highly selected group of employees. Within their sample, GHQ-30 positives were progressively more frequent with *higher* employment grades. However, higher grades were shown to be more likely to report symptoms, and adjusting for this reversed the gradient, although this was significant only for men. Comparing examinations in 1991 to 1993 and 1995 to 1996, with a mean 36-month gap, deterioration in health, including minor psychiatric disorder indicated by the GHQ-30, was greatest in the lowest employment grades.[174]

"Nervous trouble or persistent depression in the last 12 months" was three times more frequent in lower compared with higher grades. GHQ-30 scores were weakly correlated with sickness absence, which was highest in lower employment grades. Neurosis was a very common reason for sickness absence, increasingly with the length of spells of absence.[138;175;176] Although only a small proportion of the employment grade differential in depression on the GHQ-30 was considered to be accounted for by social selection through upward social mobility, there was some evidence that low levels of depression and high well-being scores at baseline were associated with subsequent upward mobility.[177]

Comparing Whitehall II data with two very different USA studies, the Wisconsin Longitudinal Study and the National Survey of Families and Households, Marmot et al.[168] claim that the consistent results in all three studies, of gradients with the lowest SES category revealing the most symptoms and disorders, suggest robustness for the findings. But the SES indicators varied substantially, and it cannot be assumed that education and occupational status necessarily mean the same in different cultures, especially when many other possible indicators of social status are not considered or controlled for.

A UK 1993 survey of a representative sample of over 3000 residents to test the EuroQoL EQ-5D self-report questionnaire, showed interesting age-group differences in occupational social class distributions of anxiety and depression. Up to age 80, social classes I–II had substantially fewer identified disorders than classes IV–V in every age group, but the middle category, occupational social classes III non-manual and III manual varied, with some rates similar to I–II, some rates similar to IV–V, and some rates in between.[24]

A small study using a score of 2 or more on the GHQ-12 in Northern Ireland in 1986 reminds us that local situations might be quite unrepresentative of modern industrial populations in general. Results showed increasing symptoms with decreasing occupational social class in the Protestant population, and the opposite in the Catholic population.[178]

1.5.2.5 Other SES or composite indices

1.5.2.5.1 USA ECA. The USA ECA studies adopted the Nam-Powers Index, a multiple indicator of socio-economic status (SES) incorporating income, education, and type of occupation. Regier et al.[54] reported a non-significant gradient for affective disorders in total and dysthymia, but a highly significant gradient for anxiety disorders; the OR for the lowest SES group was about 2.5 compared to the highest SES group (Table 1.34). For comparison, it was 8.1 for schizophrenia. For interest, SES was also inversely related to violent behaviour, anti-social personality disorder, and cognitive impairment. However, Horwath and Weissman[55] reported no SES differences for major depression, although there were high rates in the unemployed, and bipolar illness was more common in the least well educated. The New Haven area study found current rates of depression higher in lower SES groups, and life-time rates higher in upper SES groups, a confusing finding possibly reflecting differences in duration of disorder.

TABLE 1.34
ECA: Standardised 1-month prevalence (% and ORs—95% CIs) for DIS categories (all 5 ECA sites), by socio-economic status (Nam-Powers)

Socio-economic status (Nam-Powers)	*Affective disorders* %	*Affective disorders* OR (95% CI)	*Dysthymia* %	*Dysthymia* OR (95% CI)	*Anxiety disorders* %	*Anxiety disorders* OR (95% CI)
1 (high)	4.1	1	2.9	1	4.6	1
2	4.8	1.20 (ns)	3.2	1.19 (ns)	6.4	1.33 (ns)
3	5.9	1.61 (ns)	3.5	1.37 (ns)	8.5	1.84 ($p < 0.0031$)
4 (low)	5.5	1.53 (ns)	3.6	1.37 (ns)	10.5	2.43 ($p < 0.0031$)

Source:[54] (Tables 2,3).

1.5.2.5.2 Additional studies. Studies were conducted in Israel in the 1990s specifically to try to answer the question of social selection or social causation of psychiatric disorders, taking advantage of the diverse Jewish population in terms of immigration history and poverty. The studies used a composite SES classification that could be applied equally to advantaged and disadvantaged ethnic groups. There were SES gradients for the main serious psychiatric disorders, with lower SES groups having the greatest frequencies. The results suggested that social selection ("drift") is most important in explaining the social class differentials in schizophrenia,[129] but that social causation is probably the explanation for social class differentials of depression in women, and anti-social personality disorder or substance abuse in men.[48;179]

A careful, small-scale study in Washington Heights, New York, also concluded that the social causation hypothesis for depression was largely supported, partly through associations with job characteristics, particularly occupational direction, control and planning.[159] This last issue was reviewed by Lennon.[180]

1.5.2.6 Area differences

1.5.2.6.1 The nine studies under review. HSE data from GHQ-12 are also analysed by area type, although these do not necessarily imply clear social class distinctions. Inner London had significantly more, and rural communities had significantly less neurosis than other areas, which were all close to the average for England.[4] In the UK National Survey, both "probable neurosis" and functional psychosis were more common in urban than rural areas.[26] The HALS examined area differences in the UK and found significant north–south differences, excepting Greater London, in the distribution of GHQ-30 scores of 5 or more. The difference varied by occupational social class. SC I–II showed none, SC IV–V showed modest differences, but the greatest differences were in SC III. If the north–south data were adjusted for occupational social class and living conditions, the differences became non-significant.[34] The ECA programme in the USA found symptoms of major depression significantly more common in urban than rural areas, a difference not explained by differences in education.[57]

1.5.2.6.2 Additional studies. An area study in the north-west of England in 1992 sent the GHQ-12 by post to 38,000 people with an overall response rate of 63%. After age and sex standardisation there were very positive correlations of the frequency of GHQ-12 scores of *2 or more* with every measure of area deprivation and disadvantage. These included the UPA (underprivileged area) score, the under age 65 standardised mortality ratio (SMR), lack of amenities, overcrowding, social mobility, and proportions of lone parent families, unemployed, unskilled workers, and ethnic minorities. The three most deprived areas were inner city areas with significantly higher proportions of GHQ-12 positives than the other 19 districts, although they also had substantially lower response rates, which somewhat prejudiced interpretation. Using cut-off scores of 3 or more or 4 or more on the GHQ-12 reduced the numbers but did not change the relativities or correlations.[162]

In the Netherlands, a study of nearly 5000 residents of Amsterdam city used a score of 2 or more on the GHQ-12 to try to disentangle individual and area effects on SES associations with possible psychiatric disorder. The study concluded that individual SES dominated, and that the accumulation of psychiatric disorders in deprived urban areas was largely due to a concentration of individuals with low SES characteristics in these areas.[181] However, it is hard to believe that the two are not inter-related and do not have impact on each other.

1.5.3 Cohort evidence of associations between markers of social position and the common mental disorders

Cohort studies of the links between social position and the common mental disorders have two theoretical advantages over cross-sectional evidence:

- Cohort studies can measure incidence of new cases, rather than prevalence at one point in time, which is influenced by factors that prolong or curtail episodes rather than cause them.
- If social position could be shown to precede the first signs of neurotic disorder, this might indicate the direction of causality; unfortunately, neurotic disorders can often first emerge early in life but be episodic, making it difficult to be sure that social position was really unaffected by early mental states.

The 1946 and 1958 British birth cohorts are the only large population-based long-term samples providing firm evidence of cohort relationships, relevant to the UK, and thus they have been included in the discussion below. In addition, from other studies, there is very limited evidence on early life circumstances, sometimes relying on later recall of early risk factors.

The evidence that emerges is rather mixed and fragmentary. In general it appears that higher rates of disorder in adulthood are associated with:

- multiple disadvantage in childhood, including parental divorce and economic hardship;
- parental psychiatric illness.

Parental occupational social class and childhood chronic physical illness appear not to be associated with adult neurotic illness. It also appears that childhood neurotic symptoms are not associated with adult disorder. However, adolescent behavioural problems in girls may be associated with adult disorders.

1.5.3.1 *Parental occupational social class*

Parental occupational social class was not generally related to psychiatric symptoms or disorder, with few exceptions.

1.5.3.1.1 UK birth cohorts. In the 1946 birth cohort study, PSE scores for neurosis showed no relationship to father's social class for men at age 36. For women at age 36 there was a strong relationship but only in that there was a *higher* prevalence in the lowest category ("in or previously in unskilled manual work") compared with all others.[72] In the 1958 birth cohort study, there were minimal differences in scores on the Malaise Inventory (MI).[77]

1.5.3.1.2 Stockholm cohort. However, in the 1963 Stockholm cohort of people born in 1953, parental occupational social status was significantly associated with psychiatric disorder in men, as determined by the military conscription board at age 19; sons of unskilled workers had rates twice as high as those of sons of upper middle class families. However, the validity of the diagnosis is very doubtful. Most interestingly, those whose occupational status was higher at age 27 than their father's had high ratings for coping ability and low rates for psychiatric disorder. Those whose status at age 27 was lower than their father's had low ratings for coping ability and high rates for psychiatric disorder.[182]

1.5.3.1.3 The Whitehall studies. In the Whitehall II studies of London civil servants, adjusting for father's social class made little difference to the distribution of GHQ-30 scores by employment grade. However, the *lowest* frequencies were for men in the lowest employment grade who had fathers in manual occupations.[138] In comparing this study with two USA studies, Marmot et al.[168] claim that they all suggest that the social status of the family of origin has no clear associations with adult symptoms or disorder. The PHPS, using GHQ-12, found no gradient with occupational social class of parents.

1.5.3.2 Multiple disadvantage in childhood

Although parental social class appears not to be very important in direct relationship with adult psychiatric symptoms from these studies, it is itself closely associated with many important features of childhood and early adult life that may relate to later mental symptoms. These include poorer economic conditions in childhood and adulthood, lower educational qualifications, less secure employment, more psycho-social job stress, less social support, and lower incomes.

1.5.3.2.1 1946 birth cohort. In the 1946 birth cohort at age 36, although early benefits seemed to convey no advantage, multiple disadvantages appeared to have a cumulative effect on the frequency of PSE-diagnosed disorder,[74;183] and a high "childhood adversity score" was associated with higher PSE symptom scores at age 36. The social class distribution of multiple adversity was not clarified.

Parental divorce or separation was associated with more in-patient psychiatric treatment by age 26, neurosis in women and delinquency in men up to age 36, and higher PSF scores at age 43, but the latter only in single, divorced, or remarried women.[73;74;184]

It should be recalled that there was very little differentiation of frequency of disorder by social class of family of origin. These findings are interesting in the light of evidence that disadvantages tend to accumulate in low-status groups measured by wealth, income, education, housing, or unemployment. This might again argue for disadvantage associated with psychiatric disorder being focused upon certain groups in society not identified as a specific stratum of occupational social class.[183]

1.5.3.2.2 1958 cohort. In the 1958 birth cohort at age 23 and 33, high MI scores were associated, among other things, with childhood parental divorce and pre-marital pregnancy. High scores were also associated with parental divorce when the subject was a young adult, especially when combined with own divorce, but there was no increase of scores for parental death at any time. Although parental occupational social class was not very significant in itself, it was closely associated with important features of childhood associated with subsequent high MI scores, including poorer economic conditions in childhood. Researchers concluded that early factors may not determine inequalities in psychological health, but may increase the risks of experiencing later causal factors and, perhaps, increasing their deleterious effects.[78;79]

1.5.3.2.3 Other studies. Americans' Changing Lives (ACL) survey data related most childhood adversities (but not parental divorce) to first onset of depression, but few to recurrence.[185]

1.5.3.3 *Parental psychiatric disorder*

In the American NCS, adult depression, anxiety disorder, alcohol or other drug abuse, and anti-social personality disorder were associated strongly with parental psychiatric disorder, but only weakly with childhood adversity except for anti-social personality disorder.[45]

1.5.3.4 *Adolescent behaviour*

In the UK1946 birth cohort,[183] the strongest predictor of adult anxiety and depression in women was their anti-social behaviour as adolescent girls, which must imply some common factor before adulthood, either inherited or experienced.

1.5.3.5 *Chronic physical illness*

People who experienced at least 3 months of chronic illness after the age of 21 showed more psychiatric disorder, but those who experienced chronic illness in childhood showed little difference from others in respect of later psychiatric disorder, although boys showed more "nervous habits".[186] These were not associated with adult psychiatric disorder for which there was "remarkably little evidence for strong associations with features of childhood".[74] From much earlier studies, Rutter[187] had suggested that so-called neurotic symptoms in children were not much related to neurosis in adulthood.

1.5.3.6 Early influences on educational attainment

In the USA it was noted from ECA data that early-onset alcohol abuse tended to reduce educational achievement, status of occupation, and personal income in adult life, all associated with psychiatric disorder.[59;60] Similarly, NCS data showed that early-onset anxiety disorders, mostly in girls, and conduct disorders, mostly in boys, were strongly associated with later psychiatric disorder, but also with not finishing school or college, non-marriage, not working, and low SES[44] (Table 1.35; Table 1.36).

TABLE 1.35
NCS: Effects of prior psychiatric disorder on failure to make educational transitions; (ORs and 95% CIs)

	Anxiety disorder		*Mood disorder*	
	OR	*95% CI*	*OR*	*95% CI*
Failure to complete high school among 8th grade graduates	1.4	1.1–1.8	1.5	1.1–1.9
Failure to enter college among high-school graduates	1.4	1.2–1.8	1.6	(ns)
Failure to complete college among college entrants	1.4	1.2–1.6	2.9	1.4–5.8

Source:[188] (Table 2).

TABLE 1.36
NCS: Effect of early-onset disorders and educational achievement

	Probability of NOT finishing high school		*Probability of finishing college*	
	SE	*OR*	*SE*	*OR*
No early onset disorder		1		1
Major affective disorder	0.672	1.26	0.344	1.08
Major anxiety disorder	0.207	2.16	0.029	0.27
Substance dependence	1.515	0.88	2.031	0.59
Conduct disorder	1.141	3.07	0.694	0.45
Other disorder	0.129	1.56	0.195	0.56

Source:[44] (Table 2).

1.5.3.7 Personality and coping strategies

McLeod and Kessler[189] found little research on personality features such as feelings of powerlessness and low self-esteem in relation to psychiatric symptoms or disorder and socio-economic status. It is possible that childhood socialisation, including education, affects reactions to life events and capacity to cope.

Earlier research reporting that people with low levels of education used the least effective coping strategies has been little followed-up.[190] In a twin study, coping strategies of "turning to others" and "problem solving" were associated with lower rates of depression and anxiety, but the strategy of denial was associated with higher rates.[191] The authors suggested that there might be genetic influences on the development of coping behaviour.

A broad life-history approach might be needed to elucidate the genetic, pre-natal, childhood and adult factors that contribute to the development and maintenance of psychiatric disorder, especially anxiety and depression, assuming that health is a life-long development for individuals, and inequalities in health are likely to be a product of gradually accumulating negative factors at all times of life.[192] Something similar was concluded by Bebbington[193] after reviewing the evidence on gender differences in depression.

1.5.4 Risk factors for the common mental disorders that are also related to social position

A number of risk factors for the common mental disorders are also related to social position. These factors all have substantial literatures of their own. They arise in the major studies discussed in previous chapters in a minor way, but should be noted as possibly important factors likely to have associations with socio-economic status. The following sections cannot provide full reviews but record what arises from the major studies detailed above, with some additional literature.

Physical illness emerges strongly in association with the common mental disorders and this clearly raises the possibility of causal relationships either way, or common causes for both. Life events have long been accepted as being important precursors of common mental disorders but it also seems likely that disadvantaged people generally experience more stressful life events than others. Social support and social networks have been subject to substantial investigation in this context, but the results are less clear. Conditions of work may produce stressful events and permanently stressful social environments, but also may supply supportive relationships and networks. Working conditions tend to be distributed very differently according to social class, income levels, or educational background.

1.5.4.1 Physical illness and disability

Physical illness and disability are often included in surveys focusing primarily on psychiatric symptoms and disorder, but published analyses relating both to socio-economic status are not common, although it is well established that most measures of morbidity and mortality show negative gradients with social class.[1;144]

1.5.4.1.1 HSE. Frequencies of GHQ-12 scores of 4 or more on the annual HSE were highly correlated with both recent acute sickness and long-standing illness, the latter increasing steadily with age, although GHQ scores did not.[25]

1.5.4.1.2 UK National Survey. In the UK National Survey, a very close relationship was shown between neurosis and physical complaints whether general or specific. Significantly more of those with a neurosis had a long-standing physical complaint, a musculo-skeletal complaint, or a genito-urinary complaint, than those with no neurosis. Although complaints increased with age, the association with neurosis was positive at all ages, and varied little with the psychiatric diagnosis.[3]

1.5.4.1.3 The Health and Lifestyle Survey. In the HALS, there was a strong association between GHQ-30 scores and both current symptoms of physical illness and limiting long-term illness. Of special interest, HALS subjects were followed-up after 7 years and GHQ-30 scores of 5 or more were associated with a significant increase in *mortality*, even after adjusting for age, sex, smoking behaviour, sleeping difficulties, limiting disease, and unnatural deaths. Smoking retained a significant relationship with excess mortality, but was also associated with GHQ-30 scores of 5 or more. There was approximately a linear relationship between the risk of dying in the 7-year period and the number of symptoms recorded on the GHQ-30, especially in men. This excess mortality related to probable psychiatric disorder varied by occupational social class, with an OR of 1.55 for manual compared to non-manual occupations.[31]

1.5.4.1.4 British Household Panel Survey. In the BHPS, physical illness was negatively associated with occupational social class and positively associated with GHQ-12 scores of 3 or more.[36]

1.5.4.1.5 UK birth cohorts. At age 36, the 1946 birth cohort showed higher treatment rates for "emotional disorders" if they had had a chronic physical illness (3 months or more) after the age of 21.[74] The high PSE scores at age 36 in those unemployed and not seeking work were largely related to chronic sickness and disability.[72;194] In the 1958 birth cohort at age 23 there was no social class variation for limiting long-standing illness, and little at age 33, but there was substantial variation in self-rated health which was associated with high malaise (MI) scores.[76]

1.5.4.1.6 The US ECA. In the USA ECA area of New Haven, after various adjustments, home-bound status related to physical illness remained a strong association of depression of first onset. Social isolation appeared to modify the effects of poverty and home-bound status, but researchers concluded that increased risks of depression in the elderly are strongly related to increases in physical illness, which were related also to low income.[57]

1.5.4.1.7 Australian National Mental Health Survey of 1997. In the Australian National Mental Health Survey of 1997, physical conditions were reported more frequently in those with probable mental disorders. In particular, about 50% of people with affective or anxiety disorders (they were treated as separate categories in these data) reported physical conditions. The more separate psychiatric diagnoses people were allocated, the more likely they were also to report physical conditions.[68]

1.5.4.1.8 Additional studies. In the Whitehall II studies, there was a close linear relationship between psychiatric morbidity recorded as a score of 5 or more on the GHQ-30, and number of physical symptoms, but virtually none with long-term physical illness. Sickness absence tended to be recorded for either physical or psychiatric reasons, but sickness absence for physical reasons may be exacerbated by psychiatric symptoms.[195]

1.5.4.2 Life events

1.5.4.2.1 UK National Survey. All people interviewed in the UK National Survey were asked about stressful life events in the past 6 months, based on the List of Threatening Life Events.[196;197] There was a strong linear relationship between having higher CIS-R scores and the experience of more than one stressful life event. This also applied to each separate life event, with the strongest relationship shown for "having a serious problem with a close friend, relative or neighbour", "marital separation or break-up of a steady relationship", and a "financial crisis". Analysis by frequency of "probable neurotic disorder" (CIS-R score of 12 or more) produced very similar results, except that experiencing physical illness was also among the strongest associated individual life events. Taking into account many socio-demographic and economic factors, the presence of a probable neurotic disorder was positively and significantly associated with having experienced two or more stressful life events in the 6 months prior to interview, with an OR of 2.5.[166]

1.5.4.2.2 HALS. In the HALS, there was a close correlation between high scores on the GHQ-30 in 1984–85 and high scores in 1991–92; people divorcing between these dates had had the highest scores in 1984–85.[30] High frequencies of GHQ-30 scores of 5 or more were associated with more frequent life events, especially if recalled as "stressful". One stressful life event doubled the frequency of high GHQ-30 scores, but the possibility of recall bias was considered to make this unreliable.[30]

1.5.4.2.3 BHPS. In the BHPS, GHQ-12 scores decreased for those getting married during the year of follow-up, and increased for those divorcing or separating.[35] In a review, Bruce[135] found evidence from several sources that low SES was associated not only with more stressful life events, but also with more impact from those experienced.

1.5.4.2.4 1958 cohort. In the 1958 birth cohort at ages 23 and 33, high MI scores, especially indicative of depression, were associated, among other things, with high rates of adverse life events.

1.5.4.2.5 Additional studies. McLeod and Kessler[189] disaggregated both SES and life events from five USA community surveys assessing psychological health and depressive symptoms.

The predominant pattern was of more negative life events the lower the income, education, or occupational status, especially income. But psychological distress reactions to events were also influenced by the same three factors, with some variation by type of event. The increased vulnerability of low-status people to life events was not only due to shortage of financial resources.

Although employment status is examined above, the various stages of the unemployment process can be seen as life events. Hamilton et al.[198] reported that the effects of anticipating and experiencing job loss were worst on lower-status workers and the less well educated. Kessler et al.[199] reported psychological distress with all phases of the unemployment process. Re-employment reduced levels, but, surprisingly, the most distressed were more likely to be re-employed.

Kessler[42] reviewed the literature on life events and depression and summarised the results as follows: there is consistently an association between exposure to stressful life events and subsequent onset of major depression. The degree of association depends on the measures used, being stronger with "contextual" measures than check lists. Severe events are more likely to produce depression than less severe events. Although most depressed people report a recent stressful life event, most people experiencing such events do not become depressed. There is a wider issue than "events", as psycho-social factors may represent long-term experiences and it is not yet clear the degree to which they might have causal effects on mental health.[200]

In the Whitehall II analyses, material difficulties considered as "stressors", and life events, were reckoned to account for about one-third of the employment grade differential in depression on the GHQ-30, rather more for life events.[177] Life events generally increased in frequency with lower occupation grade for men, but the opposite was true for women. Interestingly in this context, with regard to alcohol consumption, the frequency of GHQ-30 scores of 5 or more was lowest in women non-drinkers and near lowest in men non-drinkers.[201]

1.5.4.3 *Social support*

Support at a time of stress, from a person in a close relationship, has been shown to be protective for depression,[202] but social support can mean many different things in the literature.

1.5.4.3.1 HSE. In the HSE annual surveys, lack of perceived social support, as measured in the HALS and National Survey, was closely correlated with occupational social class and equivalised household income, increasing from social class I to social class V, but only weakly correlated directly with GHQ-12 scores.[7;25] The relationship, therefore, of GHQ-12 scores and lack of social support was not clear.

1.5.4.3.2 UK National Survey. The UK National Household Survey used the same measure of perceived social support as the HSE and HALS, together with a measure of the extent of the social network, and involvement in social activities. The proportion of people perceiving a severe lack of social support increased progressively with CIS-R scores, and a severe lack of social support was strongly associated with probable neurosis. Stressful life events and lack of social support were independently associated with probable neurosis, so that 46% of those with severe lack of social support and experiencing two or more stressful life events in the previous 6 months had a probable neurosis, compared to only 9% of those with none of either factor. Both CIS-R scores and probable neurosis were also associated with smaller social networks, and CIS-R scores were closely related to the number of social and leisure activities participated in.[166]

1.5.4.3.3 HALS. In the HALS, "contact with family and friends" was not much different in all occupational groups and showed only very limited associations with malaise, but malaise was related to "perceived social support" (from seven questions on close relationships) and an "index of roles and available attachments" (created by combining several social variables), particularly for men in manual occupations. This relationship with malaise was stronger even than for physical illness. At the 7-year follow-up, reduced social support was associated with increased malaise, especially in older age-groups and men in manual occupations of all ages. Perceived "ongoing" lack of social support in women was strongly associated with high malaise scores. Living alone and seeing relatives less than once a week was associated with more malaise in men than in women. Individual men and women in all age-groups who improved their "index of roles and available attachments" consistently reported lower malaise scores at follow-up. Neither the initial nor the follow-up report includes any analysis of GHQ-30 scores related to social support measures.

1.5.4.3.4 ECA. In the New Haven area of the USA ECA, after various adjustments, low levels of social contact remained strong associations of depression of first onset. Social isolation apparently modified the effects of poverty and home-bound status. Researchers proposed that much of the effect of poverty might be mediated through social isolation, but not necessarily living alone, which was not itself correlated.[57]

1.5.4.3.5 Additional studies. In the Whitehall II analyses, social support at work was reckoned to account for about one-third of the employment-grade differential in depression on the GHQ-30.[177] Negative aspects of social support were associated with higher sickness absence rates. However, higher rates of "close confiding relationships" and good social support networks were associated with higher rates of sickness absence (all causes), possibly due to encouragement to take sick leave.[203]

In the review of five USA community studies,[189] analysis could not discriminate between social support and resilience of personality, the two major components of vulnerability proposed by others. From the literature, it was not clear that social support does vary consistently with SES, nor that poor social networks are necessarily associated with mental distress. The position is complex and not yet elucidated.

1.5.4.4 Work characteristics

1.5.4.4.1 HSE. In the very limited analyses available from the annual HSE since 1993, men in social classes I and II, and women in social class II reported the highest stress levels, controlled for age, and people with a "high work pace" reported more stress affecting their health. Social classes I and II were more likely to have a high pace at work, but very much less likely to have little variety and low control than manual social classes.[7]

1.5.4.4.2 Additional studies. Work characteristics were of particular interest in the Whitehall II studies which found, after adjusting for age and employment grade, that four factors were all associated with decreasing frequencies of probable psychiatric disorder as measured by a GHQ-30 score of 5 or more. These were, in order of importance:

- Increasing levels of social support in the job.
- Degree of control over their own work.
- Variety in work.
- Opportunities to use their skills.

These factors also contributed to a greater sense of well-being, and greater global satisfaction. Subjective work assessments were more closely associated than official, objective job assessments, for which only degree of control remained significant.

For depression and anxiety, the pace of work and degree of control were the most important factors. However, the ABS instrument used showed an association between reporting negative job conditions and reporting GHQ symptoms, and adjusting for this reduced the association with job support and control to very little. Men and women reporting "high strain" work situations had more than twice the rate of probable psychiatric disorder than those reporting "low strain".[133]

Most of the employment-grade differential in depression (GHQ-30) and psychological well-being (as recorded on the ABS) could be explained by different work characteristics, including skill discretion and decision authority.[204] Sickness absence was strongly associated with jobs rated low in variety, use of skills, and control, especially in men.[175] In the USA, increased job demands, decreased decision latitudes, and increased job insecurity were all associated with high rates of depression.[159]

1.6 CONCLUSIONS

1.6.1 General conclusions

In reviewing the results of the included studies, we have divided the evidence on the links between social position and the common mental disorders into three main groups:

- Evidence of statistical associations between disorders and the main markers of social position in adults, from cross-sectional studies.
- Evidence from cohorts, especially the prospective birth cohorts, linking early factors to later occurrence of disorder.
- Evidence on linked risks, such as adverse life events, physical illness, social networks, and work circumstances (with evidence for cross-sectional or relatively short-term longitudinal associations).

In terms of the main body of evidence on the cross-sectional links between social position and neurotic illness, a fairly clear set of conclusions can be drawn. In eight of the nine included studies, there is evidence of an association between less privileged social position and higher prevalence of the common mental disorders on at least one of the available indicators. No study shows a contrary trend with any indicator, although for some individual indicators in particular studies, no clear trend was evident. This is summarised in Table 1.37.

TABLE 1.37
Number of included studies reporting associations with higher rates of the common mental disorders, by dimensions of less privileged social position

		Less education	*Unemployment*	*Lower income or material circumstances*	*Low social status*
Positive association	Men and women separately	2	3*	2	2
	Men and women combined (separate data not given)	2	3	4	1
	Total positive	**4**	**6**	**6**	**3**
No clear association		1	1	0	3
Inverse association		0	0	0	0
Number of studies	**Total reporting**	**5**	**7**	**6**	**6**
reporting associations	No data	4	2	3	3

* In one study, positive only for men; women equivocal.

If a higher prevalence of disorder in the less privileged groups (unadjusted for other aspects of social position) is taken as a "positive association" then, in relation to those studies reporting these associations:

- Less education was positive in four out of five studies.
- Unemployment showed positive associations in six out of seven studies, although in one study the association was positive only for men.
- Low income, wealth, assets, or markers of material standard of living were positive in all six studies.
- Less privileged occupational social class was positive in three studies out of six.
- No studies showed an inverse relationship.

This crude overview suggests some robustness of findings despite the many methodological concerns relating to the literature reviewed. It also suggests that, of the four indicators of social position for which evidence is available, the least useful is occupational social class. (Note: A recent large-scale national survey in Germany[223] provisionally gives similar positive associations with education, unemployment, and a social class index, with no negative ones.)

While counting numbers of positive studies gives some sense of the consistency of findings, it does not convey the degree to which prevalence is increased in less privileged groups. In general, deprived groups seldom had as much as a doubling in prevalence of neurotic disorder or a subset of, e.g., mood disorders, compared to the most privileged groups. For example, measures of education reported in different studies have more consistency than most of the other markers of social position. The odds ratios from reporting studies included:

- In Britain, those with no qualifications had an odds ratio of less than 1.3 (1.29 for men, 1.26 for women) compared to those with A levels, for recent neurotic disorder in the first national Psychiatric Morbidity Survey.
- In the US, those with 0 to 11 years of education had an odds ratio of 1.3 for mood disorder in the past 12 months, compared to those with 17 or more years of education.
- In the Netherlands, those with 0–11 years of education had an odds ratio of 1.55 (1.22–1.98) for mood disorders compared to those with 16 plus years of education.
- In Australia, those who did not complete secondary school had an odds ratio of 1.53 compared to those with post-school qualifications, for affective disorders.

On the other hand, reports of differences for income or material standard of living were much more diverse in the markers used. For income, for example:

- In the Health Survey for England the odds ratio for the lowest quintile was 1.53 for men (1.11 for women) for GHQ case-ness, compared to the highest quintile.
- In the Netherlands, odds ratios of 1.56 (1.20–2.03) were reported for the lowest quartile compared to the top quartile for mood disorders.
- In the US, odds ratios of 2 were reported for those earning $0–$19,000 compared to those earning $70,000 plus, for mood disorders, from the National Comorbidity survey.

The lack of comparability in the measures of illness and relative education or income in these examples illustrates the fact that mathematical pooling of results would be invalid. Instead, this project undertook analyses of the most detailed British study, exploring effect sizes and establishing whether markers were independent of each other. Results of this work are presented in Report 2.

The apparent cross-sectional associations may justify some targeting of efforts to deal with the common mental disorders in less privileged groups, but cannot establish whether, on the whole, poor social position causes common mental illnesses, or vice versa. Cohort evidence has the potential to help here, but the little available evidence is fragmentary and supports only tentative conclusions. In general it appears that higher rates of disorder in adulthood are associated with multiple disadvantage in childhood, including parental divorce and economic hardship, and parental psychiatric illness. Despite this, parental occupational social class, in itself, is not generally an important factor.

For early psychological problems as a cause of educational failure and lowered adult social position, the evidence is very limited. Childhood neurotic symptoms (or childhood chronic physical illness) appear not to be associated with adult neurotic illness. However, adolescent behavioural problems in girls may be associated with adult disorders, and adolescent alcohol abuse in boys is associated with lowered educational attainment. Overall, it is likely that directions of causation are not simple; the relative contributions of each factor in the general population are unclear.

In overview, this systematic review has identified nine population-based studies meeting the inclusion criteria. These studies had large samples and adequate measures of mental health and indicators of social disadvantage. In eight of these, there is evidence of an association between less privileged social position and higher prevalence of the common mental disorders, on at least one of the available indicators. No study shows a contrary trend with any indicator, although for some individual indicators in particular studies no clear trend was evident. Incidentally, the study providing no evidence of an association with indicators of disadvantage (the Health and Lifestyle Survey) had a response rate for the postal questionnaire mental health measure of only 54%.

In assessing this result, we should remember that there are important limitations in the available evidence. Chief among these are the following:

- Response rates in the selected studies varied from as low as 54% up to above 80%: as response may well be influenced by both the presence of psychiatric symptoms and by deprivation, this lack of response may have the effect of minimising observed differences.
- Only limited analyses focused on social disadvantage and the common mental disorders have thus far been published from the available studies.

- Bias in reporting of results is possible, although the controversy over whether a link exists between social position and the common mental disorders would have encouraged publication of both negative and positive results.
- Measures of mental illness vary greatly across the studies, and the absence of a "gold standard" for the identification of cases of the common mental disorders greatly hampers evaluation of the validity of these measures.
- Social inequality is usually associated with multiple disadvantage, and disentangling the risks associated with individual markers is inherently difficult.
- Given the different concepts, instruments, and measures used in the different studies, formal pooling of results and quantitative meta-analysis would not produce meaningful results. Similarly, quantitative testing for biased reporting of results was not possible.
- Most of the evidence available is based on cross-sectional studies, which cannot clarify the nature of possible causal mechanisms.

Despite the limitations:

- The accumulated evidence derives from nine large-scale community-based studies carried out during the last 20 years.
- There were consistent links between the common mental disorders and one or more markers of social disadvantage in eight of the nine studies.
- This consistency, in spite of the studies having been carried out with different instruments and measures, and in different settings, suggests that the findings are robust.

Set out below are some specific conclusions relating to each of the markers of social inequality. Most of the following refers to what we have called common mental disorders, but are often referred to in the literature as minor mental illnesses, minor or non-psychotic psychiatric disorders, neuroses or neurotic disorders, or emotional disorders. Frequently the focus is largely or specifically anxiety and depression. Psychiatric symptoms per se cannot be excluded as their accumulation and severity are usually the means of identifying "disorders" (with all the problems of thresholds and validity discussed above), and data are often presented analysed as numbers of symptoms as well as threshold-defined disorders.

1.6.2 The higher prevalence of the common mental disorders in less privileged groups: Issues of cause in general

One of the issues necessarily arising out of the finding of consistent excesses of common mental disorders among those who experience social disadvantage in various ways is to what extent causal factors might lie in inheritance, in childhood experience, or in more proximal adult circumstances and experiences. Almost certainly all these are important in some individuals and some disorders, but it is also possible that for many individuals there is an accumulation of risk factors throughout life and an aggregation of factors as contributory causes. Thus, genetic predispositions may be fulfilled or not according to circumstances and experience during childhood or adulthood. Risk factors arising in childhood from, say, parental divorce, neglect, abuse, gross impoverishment, or incomplete education may give rise to mental disorder or not according to adult conditions. Some risk factors arising in childhood, such as poor education, will almost inevitably increase the likelihood of additional risk factors in adult life—low occupational status, income and material resources, and unemployment. On the other hand, circumstances arising entirely in adult life may be overwhelming in producing depression and anxiety in individuals generally resilient. Apart from genetic inheritance, possible causal factors in both childhood and adulthood may arise within the close family or the wider community.

This complex theoretical position can only partly be addressed by the studies here reviewed, and many more focused aetiological studies are needed to disentangle genetic predisposition, resilience, coping capacity, and responses to noxious environments and stressful events. However, what evidence arises to add to the debate is detailed below. It must be remembered that statistical associations in populations do not imply causality and, if there is causality, the direction of effect might be either way or both. For example, the close inter-relationship between depression and anxiety and physical illness may reveal simple causal, one-way relationships in particular individuals, but in others there may be a circular "feed-back" mechanism involving both—and, in yet others, both may in truth be part of a more complex single syndrome if we could properly understand it.

1.6.3 Specific associations indicating possible causal factors

(1) Childhood factors, likely to be distributed unequally by social class, also show a mixed picture in these studies, although multiple disadvantage is probably associated with later depression and anxiety. Parental divorce emerges several times as a negative factor, but not always. Factors that limit educational achievement, and thus (in general) later occupational status, income, and social resources, have been identified in some studies, including parental psychiatric disorder and teenage anxiety, conduct, or alcohol disorders. There is some concern with the development of coping capacity, but little that is clear in this particular literature.

(2) From these studies there is little evidence that parental occupational social class is important, although many factors representing disadvantage in childhood might be.
(3) Although there is some inconsistency, perhaps related to differences in measures and context, most of these studies show a close relationship between common mental disorders in general, or anxiety and depression in particular, and physical illness. This may have been identified as physical symptoms, system complaints, diagnosed physical disorders, or long-term limiting illness and disability, but, in most cases, they are all associated with higher frequencies of psychiatric symptoms and common mental disorders. One study convincingly demonstrates a higher mortality related to common mental disorders as identified on the GHQ-30. This is important in the light of well-established social class or socio-economic status differentials in the UK in mortality, both in general and for most specific causes, as well as evidence of differentials in physical morbidity.
(4) A few studies show work characteristics of lack of control, variety, and skill use to be associated with neurosis, recognising that jobs with these features tend to be low-status, low social class, requiring limited education, and poorly paid.
(5) The relationship of stressful life events to depression and anxiety barely needs confirmation from the few of these studies addressing the issue, but the likely social class distribution of both the frequency of and negative response to stressful life events might be emphasised, as they tend to reinforce the disadvantages of people in lower occupational social classes, on low incomes, or having experienced low levels of education to help them develop adequate coping strategies.
(6) There is substantial evidence from recent large-scale UK studies of the important association of perceived lack of social support with increased levels of common mental disorders.

1.6.4 Implications of the main associations

(1) People of lower socio-economic status, however measured, are disadvantaged, including higher frequencies of the common mental disorders. But they also tend to live in communities and cultures that are disadvantaged. This has already known policy implications.

Certain areas, communities, groups, cultures, and environments are associated, almost certainly causally, with higher frequencies of psychiatric symptoms and common mental disorders. Many deleterious factors are distributed very unequally according to social class, such as noxious environments, poor human services, smoking, drinking, drug taking, and violence.

Differential social and geographical mobility ("drift") of people with severe psychosis may be reflected in relatively high prevalence in "lower" class areas and communities, but the evidence suggests that the far more common depression and anxiety are causally related to adult conditions and experiences. People brought up in disadvantaged families and/or communities probably carry increased mental health risks, mediated in part by poor education, low incomes, and low-status work. All these things may affect duration as well as onset and thus increase prevalence in populations.

(2) Occupation (and therefore, occupational social class) is a broad indicator of disadvantage in relation to mental health status, but its significance and social meaning must vary in different communities and cultures. It interacts with most other indicators, particularly education, income, and area of residence. However, of the four indicators for which evidence was available, occupational social class was the least consistent and the least effective at discriminating social differentials. Occupational social class differentials in the common mental disorders are not the strongest and most consistent, and it must be seen as a general indicator that needs to be "unpacked" before it can properly be interpreted.

(3) Education emerges strongly as an indicator of differentials in psychiatric symptoms and common mental disorders in many different social contexts. In some cases "qualifications achieved" seems to be the most useful, in others, "years of completed education" or "age at completion" appears a better indicator. There probably needs to be more work to detail and standardise these, and work out exactly what they are indicating. They could provide clear policy information in order, for example, to target an especially vulnerable group of young people who leave school early or without any qualifications.

(4) Income and material resources are key indicators of disadvantage in mental health, but also interact with many other variables, not least education, occupation, and unemployment, which tend to accumulate in the same individuals and groups.

The excess of psychiatric symptoms and common mental disorders found in most social inequalities research is not only a product of a sub-class of severely disadvantaged people. There is clear evidence that prevalence of symptoms and disorders increases progressively with socio-economic status even in the absence of overt poverty or obvious deprivation. Inequality itself, not only deprivation, appears to be important, and this has given rise to explanations in terms of relatively reduced social capital, sense of belonging, and control over one's life. The extent of inequality in society may be as important in this context as the existence of a distinctly impoverished sub-group, although the latter should be the first priority for action.

(5) There is already much evidence of mental health disadvantages related to unemployment, confirmed by the studies considered here. Unemployment interacts with education, income, housing, and occupational social class. The event of becoming unemployed appears to be a particular risk factor and implies the potential for preventive intervention. Other stressful life events also appear to have an impact and are probably more common among people of low income and material resources, poor education, and low job status.

These indicators are all measured in adult life but represent a lifetime of experience. Education takes us back to school years, but what are the causes of poor education? Apart from demonstrable low intelligence, they might include, for example, illness in childhood, personality factors, family characteristics, poor schools, and local subcultures. If those leaving school early or without qualifications represent a vulnerable group to target for preventive intervention as regards future mental ill-health, they equally represent a group already suffering damage, the causes of which deserve full investigation. The limited evidence from these studies suggests that certain mental and emotional disorders in adolescence are strong predictors of psychiatric disorder in adulthood, as well as the socio-economic indicators of disadvantage.

1.6.5 Implications for research and policy

(1) At the worst levels of social inequality shown to be associated with anxiety and depression among many other disadvantageous consequences, it does not need doctor-diagnosed illness in individuals or major surveys in populations to show that serious poverty, deprivation, environmental degradation, and social stress should be high on the political agenda. That is simply a matter of equity, justice, and human rights.

(2) The excess of common mental disorders in disadvantaged people, whether measured by occupational social class, education, unemployment, income, or material possessions, is now well enough established to warrant further policy initiatives to ensure that access to effective diagnosis and treatment is improved, especially at the primary health-care level, and especially in communities with high levels of social disadvantage.

(3) The excess of common mental disorders is probably not best described by the broad hierarchical model of occupational social class. That is, rather than a bottom "layer" across society, it is probably specific groups who are most disadvantaged in this context, defined by combinations of factors including education, income, housing, social support,

and physical illness amongst others. For policy, this offers the possibility of identifying the most affected groups and targeting them with additional resources over a prolonged period.

(4) The research relating mental ill-health to socio-economic status and related factors has already produced a wealth of useful evidence, but general conclusions useful to policy makers are to some extent prejudiced by the use of different instruments and measures which produce data and analyses that are incompatible and non-comparable in detail. It is not easy to get agreement on indicators and instruments because underlying concepts vary and each group of researchers has already invested a great deal of time and effort into developing and validating the one they favour. However, for the future of this field of research and the most effective and efficient use of research funds, there should be a combined effort to agree on, standardise, and validate a small range of instruments and indicators, out of those currently in use and in process of development, which would represent the principal options for future studies.

This applies to measuring mental health (for example resilience of personality; coping capacity) and mental ill-health as both symptoms and common mental disorders, including issues of instrument thresholds, separation of defined syndromes, and the meaning of "comorbidity". It applies to measures of personal function, disability, and social disadvantage. It applies to measures of socio-economic status, income, education, and other indicators of social inequality. It applies to measures of childhood adversity, life events, and social support.

(5) More research will, no doubt, be needed, but there are, it appears, many databases already existing which should be fully exploited to answer the key questions on mental health inequalities as much as they can before new populations are recruited. This includes the birth cohorts, the annual HSE, and others in the UK, where it seems that, in spite of much already published, much more could be extracted.

(6) Future research needs very clear formulation of questions relating to income, education, early experiences, and so on. For example, many studies include data on psycho-social factors in adulthood or childhood adversity, but it is doubtful if the epidemiology of these phenomena is well understood in human populations. Similarly, it is not at all clear that occupational status, income levels, or educational achievement, for example, have the same social meaning in different countries or even in different cultures within one country. What are the processes by which such things influence mental health? What possible interventions might arise in family policy or educational practice, for example? Some authors raise these issues but research journals are not likely to permit much space to them in publications.

It may be that more theoretical, conceptual work needs to be done to underpin these questions, or that there needs only to be better communication and closer working between sociologists and social anthropologists on the one hand, and epidemiologists, psychiatrists, and psychologists on the other. There is little in this literature that addresses issues of culture and of sub-cultures, and their impact on the mental health and mental health risks of individuals. There are some important questions raised about communal, societal influences on experience and behaviour, and therefore on health, as opposed to individual actions and attitudes that tend to inform current research as well as political cultures.

This gap needs to be filled if we are to extend our understanding of the vulnerabilities and resiliences of disadvantaged individuals in particular contexts, the societal factors that place people most at risk of the common mental disorders, and help or hinder their recovery, and the services that might reduce their risks of illness and the duration of their dysfunction, and improve the overall quality of their lives.

1.7 APPENDIX A: PSYCHIATRIC SURVEYS PROVIDING ADDITIONAL EVIDENCE

The studies summarised below do not meet the strict inclusion criteria for the systematic review, but do give some relevant valid and detailed data on specific issues of importance to understanding the nature of the association between the common mental disorders and markers of less privileged social position. Data from these studies have been discussed in various sections of the main report under the heading "additional studies". Here their main features and findings are presented, so that readers may readily follow up any particular aspects of interest to them.

1.7.1 The Whitehall Studies; 1967–70 and 1995; 1985–88

The first Whitehall study (Whitehall I) was a cross-sectional survey of 19,019 London civil servants in 1967 to 1970, with a follow-up after approximately 25 years, in 1995.[205] There were several indicators of socio-economic status, but the only mental health related measures were self-assessed current general health, alcohol consumption, and current medications.

Whitehall II collected data from 10,314 London civil servants aged 35–55 in 1985–1988, using a self-administered questionnaire and clinical screening tests. Follow-up was in 1991 to 1993 and 1995 to 1996. The

GHQ-30 was used, treating a score of 5 or more as positive, after examining receiver operating characteristics (ROCs) and this was subject to some validation against the CIS in a sub-sample.[206] The Affect Balance Scale (ABS), Framingham Type-A Personality Scale, and questions reporting subjectively stressful life events, personal difficulties, hostility, and "locus of control" were also used. In the 1991 follow-up, the SF-36 was administered, recording "general mental health".

Civil Service grade of employment was available as an indicator of socio-economic status, together with parents' occupation and educational level, and measures of income[138] The most important limitation of this study is that it includes only employed people, and those within only one socio-economic sector of employment, and only in London.

GHQ-30 positives were progressively more frequent in higher grades of employment, but validation studies showed that higher grades tended to report more for the same morbidity, and when adjusted for this, the socio-economic gradient was reversed, significantly in men but not significantly in women. The picture given by ABS results was very confusing. What associations there were could mostly be "explained" by different work characteristics, especially skill discretion and decision authority.

The very limited and mixed associations of GHQ-30 results with employment grade must be interpreted in the context of there being no unemployed and no poor people in the study, but the Civil Service may also select out people likely to develop, or in the early stages of development of, neurotic symptoms. In general, father's occupational social class appeared not much to affect the distribution of GHQ-30 scores of 5 or more according to employment grade, but the lowest frequencies were for men in the lowest employment grade with fathers from manual occupations!.[138]

Psychiatric symptoms recorded by the GHQ-30 were very weakly correlated with sickness absence, but grade of employment was strongly correlated with sickness absence, the most short or long spells being in the lowest grades. The results relating sickness absence to social networks and close confiding relationships were confusing.[175]

Reasons officially recorded for sickness absence were not considered reliable in respect of any psychiatric symptoms, but after validation against the GP's diagnosis, psychiatric disorder, largely neurosis, was the third most common cause of sickness absence in women, and the fourth in men. In both men and women it was second most common for very long spells of absence. Neurosis clearly defined and neurosis ill-defined were recorded separately by GPs but showed similar patterns. Sickness absence related to neurosis was highly related to length of spell, being a very small proportion of short spells, a moderate proportion of long spells, and a high proportion of very long spells.[176]

In relation to alcohol consumption, the frequency of positive GHQ-30 scores was lowest in women and near lowest in men non-drinkers, and showed a gradient with increased consumption, especially in women.[201] High GHQ-30 scores were highly correlated with the number of physical symptoms, showing a close, linear relationship. However, there was virtually no relationship with long-term illness once psychiatric diagnoses had been removed.[207]

In regard to the work situation, increasing levels of skill-use and variety in work, degree of control over own work, and social support in the job, were all associated with decreasing frequencies of probable psychiatric disorder as measured by a GHQ-30 score of 5 or more, as well as a greater sense of well-being, and greater global satisfaction. Subjective work assessment was more closely associated than official, objective job assessments, for which only degree of control remained significant. For depression and anxiety, the pace of work and degree of control were the most important factors.[133]

In a study comparing data from Whitehall II, the Wisconsin Longitudinal Study (WLS) of relatively privileged white Americans, and the more representative US National Survey of Families and Households (NSFH), the authors claim that the data suggest that social status of family of origin is of little importance in this context, having no clear associations with adult symptoms or disorder.

Although these three studies generally show clear SES gradients for depression and psychological well-being, the lowest SES category showing most symptoms or disorders, the SES indicators showing this gradient varied between education levels and employment grade.[168] There is difficulty in interpreting these data, because the studies are very different. There is no reason to believe that education and occupational status mean precisely the same in different cultures, with different social conventions, and there are many other possible indicators of social status not considered, including, for example, income, wealth, and housing tenure.

1.7.2 Israeli studies in the 1990s

These examined psychiatric disorder and SES in nearly 5000 adults born in Israel, to try to elucidate the social selection (drift) or social causation issue. They compared the relatively advantaged Ashkenazim, generally of European migrant origin, and the relatively disadvantaged Sephardim, generally of African migrant origin. There was a full range of SES groups in each. Results suggested that social selection is probably the most important process creating SES differentials in schizophrenia, and social causation is probably the most important for depression in women and anti-social personality disorder or substance abuse in men.[48;179]

1.7.3 USA Americans' Changing Lives (ACL), 1986 and 1989

A multi-stage, stratified, area probability sample of non-institutionalised adults aged 25 or more in mainland USA was interviewed in 1986 and followed-up in 1989. A 70% initial response rate (3617 interviews at time 1) and a follow-up rate of 83% gave 2867 interviews at time 2. At time 2 only, one modified DIS "stem" question was asked—"ever felt sad for a whole week etc". 41.7% said "yes", and "life-time" rates are based on this. If the most recent episode was within the last 12 months, more questions were asked and better data obtained. 10.2% had had an episode within that period (14.5% first time; 62.5% recurrences; 23% chronic).

Kessler and Magee[185] examined the relationships of childhood adversities and adult depression, but with no social class or SES analysis. Seven of eight childhood adversities (the exception is parental divorce) were significantly related to first onset of depression, but only three adversities—family history of mental illness, family history of violence, and parental divorce (less strongly)—were related to recurrence. Recent depression was strongly related to previous depression.

House et al.[208] presented data for SES distributions but only for physical illness; also for the USA 1985 National Health Interview Survey (55,690 subjects). Their conclusion, however, is interesting: ". . . morbidity and functional limitations, prior to age 75 at least, are concentrated (both absolutely and relatively) in the lowest socio-economic strata of our society". SES was defined in four classes as a composite of years of education (three divisions: 16+; 12–15; 11–) and annual income (two divisions at $20,000). They claim that very similar results are obtained by education alone, but income enhances the differences.

1.7.4 Christchurch Psychiatric Epidemiology Study, New Zealand, 1986

The Christchurch Psychiatric Epidemiology Study interviewed a sample of 1498 adults aged 18 to 64 years. They used the DIS to make DSM-III diagnoses, and to compare their results with USA ECA data.[109;209] They found very high prevalence rates for depression, which appeared to be higher in younger cohorts and appearing at earlier ages.[210] Published work so far appears not to have addressed the issues of socio-economic diversity.

1.8 APPENDIX B: PSYCHIATRIC SURVEYS NOT INCLUDED IN THE REVIEW

In this appendix we summarise the details and results of some well-conducted surveys that identified the common psychiatric conditions, but did not meet the inclusion criteria for the systematic review. The evidence from the studies included in the main report above can be regarded as superseding that from the studies summarised below, at least for the core issues of the systematic review.

1.8.1 The West London Survey of Psychiatric Morbidity, 1977

A large-scale survey of people living in the environs of Heathrow Airport arose out of concerns about the effect of aircraft noise and focused on relating noise levels to psychiatric disturbance; 5885 people were interviewed.[211] The survey used a list of physical and psycho-somatic symptoms, the GHQ-30 using 5 or more as an indication of "case-ness", and questions on long-standing illness and reduced activities from the General Household Survey (GHS). Validation of the GHQ by psychiatrist interview on a sub-sample was not very encouraging; only two-thirds of GHQ positives (5+) were confirmed as cases, and of those considered cases by the psychiatrist, two-thirds had scored 5 or more on the GHQ but one-third had scored under 5. So, in this study, specificity was low and sensitivity very low. For socio-economic status the survey recorded the occupation of the head of household and age of termination of education.

The results were very mixed and confusing related to socio-economic status, with different findings from the GHQ and from questions related to consulting a GP for psychological problems. The men in the lowest SES group with high GHQ scores consulted GPs the least! It was suggested that cultural attitudes prevail in which minor mental illness, or psychological symptoms, are not considered appropriate for consulting the GP.[212]

Lewis and Wilkinson[213] compared results from the GHQ-30 in this study with those from the HALS. The latter had substantially higher rates of presumed "case-ness", even after adjustment for various factors including occupational social class, but no analysis of the latter was included.

GHQ-30 scores were relatively independent of chronic illness or disability.[212]

1.8.2 Canada Health Survey, 1978–79

A national sample of 31,688 people was surveyed from 12,000 households excluding the northern territories, Indian reservations, remote areas, and people in institutions. The survey involved an interview, physical measurement, and self-administered questionnaire. For mental health, the survey adapted the Affect Balance Scale (ABS)[119] to indicate global unhappiness and "distress", and the Health Opinion Survey[214] to record symptoms of anxiety and depression. Neither gives standardised diagnostic categories.

Income and education data were collected as well as occupational social class.[215]

Both "depression and anxiety", and "distress" showed a mixed picture, with high frequencies in the middle categories of "disorder" more common in those with lower incomes and with poor educational qualifications, although much of this was within the unemployed. Occupational social class gave a mixed picture, though again unemployment generally increased the rates. Unemployment in all groups was associated with higher frequencies of symptoms and distress.[131]

1.8.3 Ontario Health Survey; Mental Health Supplement (1990)

The Ontario survey was designed to complement the USA NCS by using very similar methods[216] applied to the resident population of Ontario aged 15 or over. It was limited to private dwellings, excluding institutions, the homeless, native people's reserves, very remote areas, and foreign service personnel. Its stratified (urban/rural), multi-stage sampling method selected first enumeration areas, then households in each selected area, then adults in each selected household. Out of 14,758 households, the authors contacted 88.1%, and selected 13,002 individuals, of whom 9953 were eventually interviewed. There were fewer males and non-Canadian born people, and more rural dwellers and people aged over 65 than expected from the 1990 census figures.

Like the NCS, the survey used the UM-CIDI to make DSM-III and ICD-10 diagnoses. It also used the Mini Mental State Examination for those aged 65 and over. The survey recorded individual and household income, education level achieved, and aspects of housing, occupation, and employment. Overall, the survey obtained a frequency of 18.6% of people aged 15–64 with a "psychiatric disorder" in the previous year.[217] Unfortunately, no social or economic status analyses seem to have been published so far for prevalence of disorder.

Service use, especially in comparison with the USA, has been a major focus of publication. In service use, proportionately more care was received by women, urban dwellers, and those on "public assistance", especially in urban areas.[218] 6.9% of Canadian adults reported a visit in the previous year to the health sector for psychiatric disorder, compared to 8.8% of Americans. Americans of high income and low morbidity were much more likely to receive psychiatric care than similar Canadians; Americans of low income and high morbidity were much less likely to receive care than similar Canadians. In general, Americans with higher incomes were most likely to receive care at all levels of morbidity; Canadians of low income were most likely to receive care at all levels of morbidity.

For Ontario, there were no significant variations in either general medical or specialist service use according to income, but there was for specialist services according to education. Surprisingly, compared to those who failed to finish high school, all other groups showed significantly higher frequencies of receiving specialist mental health care—high-school graduates (OR 1.4); those with some college experience (OR 2.0); college graduates (OR 3.3).[19]

1.8.4 Western Australia Survey, 1971

Two surveys were performed simultaneously, one community sample and one sample of people attending GPs in the same community, using the GHQ-60. The community survey sampled all residents of the city of Perth and surrounding rural areas, aged between 15 and 69 years, excluding those in hospital or expecting hospital admission that week. (This strange exclusion was to sample only "healthy" people!) A 1% sample, using probability according to size of sample areas, produced 2324 GHQ-60 records, a response rate of about 60%.

Higher-class men and women were over-represented according to census returns, and lower-class men were under-represented. In general, men, non-married, foreign born, recent migrants, and lower social classes were all under-represented in the sample. Social class was defined using the UK RG classification (but failing to divide SC-III into non-manual and manual), and the Australian National University six-fold classification of occupations. As is frequently the case, only one-third of women could be given their own occupational class, others being allotted the class of their husbands. A score of 12 or more on the GHQ-60 was counted a "case" of "minor psychiatric morbidity". No further diagnosis was made.

The two (Australian) lower classes together had significantly higher prevalence rates of minor psychiatric morbidity (GHQ-60) than the higher four classes, for all men and for Australian born men (19.6% vs 11.1%); (also for foreign-born men but this was not statistically significant). The sample of men was only 920. Prevalence of minor psychiatric morbidity in women did not vary either by own social class where working, husband's social class when not working, or between the two employment groups.[153]

In the GP survey, there was no clear pattern in the social class distribution of high GHQ-60 scores for men; employed women showed higher rates with higher social class. The general findings thus suggested more minor morbidity in lower-class men not reflected in GP consultations, and more GP consultations by upper social class women not reflecting any higher prevalence of morbidity.[219]

It might be noted that the Australian Health Survey of 1977–78 found clear gradients for educational achievement; the least educated having the highest GHQ-12 mean scores.[172]

1.8.5 Project Metropolitan—Stockholm Cohort Study 1953–63 (follow-up 1980, age 27)

Every child living in Stockholm metropolitan area in 1963, and born in 1953, was registered, and early information gleaned from delivery records. They were followed-up in 1980, at age 27, with about 90% contact rate. However, all men were examined by the military conscription board at age 19, and about 11% were rejected as being too disabled for military service on the grounds of psychiatric disorder. Further study of the diagnoses found that only 2% of those rejected had serious disorders; about 66% had "neurotic symptoms" and 13% personality disorder or drug/alcohol dependence. The validity of this measure for epidemiological analysis must be in grave doubt.

More interesting, perhaps, the study applied a measure of "coping ability" expressed as ability to function under stress, based on "a global assessment by the team of psychiatrists and psychologists involved in the draft board examination". This measure is said to be highly correlated with concurrent psychiatric disorder. Socio-economic status was based on father's (or single mother's) occupation at the time of birth, and own occupation at follow-up, in three classes.[182]

The Stockholm cohort study found a clear association in men between low occupational status at age 27 and high rates of psychiatric disorder as determined by the military conscription board at age 19. Those whose status was higher than their father's had high ratings for coping ability and low rates for psychiatric disorder. Those whose status was lower than their father's had low ratings for coping ability and high rates for psychiatric disorder.[182] A 1970–71 survey of adults in "former Stockholm County" had found psychiatric disorder of moderate or severe degree significantly more prevalent in occupational social class III than II or I in both men and women.[220]

1.8.6 Upper Bavaria Field Study, some time before 1982

The study used the CIS in hour-long interviews by trained psychiatrists with 1536 subjects sampled from small-town rural areas in Upper Bavaria. Prevalence of "disorders in need of treatment" on CIS was 23.6% of lower social class subjects and 15.4% of upper and middle social class subjects.[221] Social class was a rather similar occupation-based system to the RG system in the UK.[222] Surprisingly, psychotropic drug use was less in lower social classes although not significantly so (also apparent—and significantly—in Hannover from another survey). This applied to all "health-status" groups—"no health problem"; "physical only"; "psychiatric only"; "physical and psychiatric".

1.8.7 The USA National Survey of Families and Households (NSFH) (1987–88)

This cross-sectional survey also collected retrospective data on one interviewed member of a multi-stage sample of households; out of 33,869 households selected there were 74% successful initial interviews. They included a global self-assessment of current "general health" but no measures of mental health, mental symptoms, or disorder.

1.9 NOTES

1. Acheson D. *Independent Inquiry into Inequalities in Health.* London: The Stationery Office, 1998.
2. Marmot M, Wilkinson R. *Social Determinants of Health.* Oxford: Oxford University Press, 1999.
3. Meltzer H, Gill B, Petticrew M, Hinds K. *The Prevalence of Psychiatric Morbidity among Adults Living in Private Households.* 1. London: ONS, 1995.
4. Erens B, Primatesta P. *Health Survey for England: Cardiovascular Disease 1998.* London: The Stationery Office, 1999.
5. Dohrenwend BP. Socio-economic status (SES) and psychiatric disorders: are the issues still compelling? *Social Psychiatry and Psychiatric Epidemiology* 1990;**25**:41–7.
6. Health Education Authority. *Health in England 1998: Investigating the Links Between Social Inequalities and Health.* London: Health Education Authority, 2000.
7. DoH. *Health Survey for England, Cardiovascular Disease, 98; Self-Assessed Health, 1994–1998.* DoH web page (January 2000). London: DoH, 2000.
8. Murray C, Lopez AD. *The Global Burden of Disease.* Harvard: Harvard School of Public Health, 1996.
9. Meltzer H, Gill B, Petticrew M, Hinds K. *The Office of Population Censuses and Surveys Survey of Psychiatric Morbidity in Great Britain—Report 8 Adults With a Psychotic Disorder Living in the Community.* London: ONS, 1996.
10. Piccinelli M, Gomez Homen F. *Nations for Mental Health: Gender Differences in the Epidemiology of Affective Disorders and Schizophrenia.* Geneva: World Health Organization, 1997.
11. Nazroo J. *Ethnicity and Mental Health: Findings from a National Community Survey.* London: Policy Studies Institute, 1997.
12. Nazroo J. *The Health of Britain's Ethnic Minorities: Findings from a National Survey.* London: Policy Studies Institute, 1997.
13. Nazroo J. Rethinking the relationship between ethnicity and mental health: The British Fourth National Survey of Ethnic Minorities. *Social Psychiatry and Psychiatric Epidemiology* 1998;**33**:145–8.
14. Dohrenwend BP. "The problem of validity in field studies of psychological disorders" revisited. *Psychological Medicine* 1990;**20**:195–208.

15. Piccinelli M, Homen FG. *Gender Differences in the Epidemiology of Affective Disorders and Schizophrenia*. Geneva: WHO, 1997.
16. Harrison G, Glazebrook C, Brewin J, Cantwell R, Dalkin T, Fox R et al. Increased incidence of psychotic disorders in African Caribbean migrants to the UK. *Psychological Medicine* 1997;**27**:799–806.
17. Shah A. Ethnicity and common mental disorders. In D Melzer, T Fryers, R Jenkins (Eds.), *Social Inequalities and the Distribution of the Common Mental Disorders*, pp. 171–223. Hove: Psychology Press, 2004.
18. Gill B, Meltzer H, Hinds K , Petticrew M. *Psychiatric Morbidity Among Homeless People*, 7. London: ONS, 1996.
19. Katz SJ, Kessler RC, Frank RG, Leaf P, Lin E. Mental health care use, morbidity, and socioeconomic status in the United States and Ontario. *Inquiry* 1997;**34**:38–49.
20. Katz SJ, Kessler RC, Lin E, Wells KB. Medication management of depression in the United States and Ontario. *Journal of General Internal Medicine* 1998;**13**:77–85.
21. Olfson M, Kessler RC, Berglund PA, Lin E. Psychiatric disorder onset and first treatment contact in the United States and Ontario. *American Journal of Psychiatry* 1998;**155**:1415–22.
22. Goldberg DP, Gater R, Sartorius N, Ustun TB, Piccinelli M, Gureje O et al. The validity of two versions of the GHQ in the WHO study of mental illness in general health care. *Psychological Medicine* 1997;**27**:191–7.
23. Bennett N, Dodd T, Flatley J, Freeth S, Bolling K. *Health Survey for England 1993*. London: HMSO, 1995.
24. Kind P, Dolan P, Gudex C, Williams A. Variations in population health status: Results from a UK national questionnaire survey. *British Medical Journal* 1998;**316**:741.
25. Prescott-Clarke P, Primatesta P. *Health Survey for England 1995. Vol I Findings*. London: The Stationery Office, 1997.
26. Jenkins R, Bebbington PE, Brugha T, Farrell M, Gill B, Lewis G et al. The National Psychiatric Morbidity Surveys of Great Britain—strategy and methods. *Psychological Medicine* 1997;**27**:765–74.
27. Lewis G, Bebbington PE, Brugha T, Farrell M, Gill B, Jenkins R et al. Socio-economic status, standard of living, and neurotic disorder. *Lancet* 1998;**352**:605–9.
28. Jenkins R, Lewis G, Bebbington P, Brugha T, Farrell M, Gill B. The National Psychiatric Morbidity Surveys of Great Britain: Initial findings from the Household Survey. *Psychological Medicine* 1997;**27**:775–89.
29. Singleton N, Bumpstead R, O'Brien M, Lee A, Meltzer H. *Psychiatric Morbidity Among Adults Living in Private Households, 2000*. London: The Stationery Office, 2001.
30. Huppert FA, Whittington JE. Longitudinal changes in mental state and personality measures. In BD Cox, FA Huppert, MJ Whichelow (Eds), *The Health and Lifestyle Survey: Seven Years On*, pp. 133–54. Aldershot: Dartmouth, 1993.
31. Huppert FA, Whittington JE. Symptoms of psychological distress predict 7-year mortality. *Psychological Medicine* 1995;**25**:1073–86.
32. Blaxter M. Evidence of inequality in health from a national survey. *Lancet* 1987;**2**.
33. Cox BD, Huppert FA, Whichelow MJ. *The Health and Lifestyle Survey: Seven Years On*. Aldershot: Dartmouth, 1993.

34. Lewis G, Booth M. Regional differences in mental health in Great Britain. *Journal of Epidemiology and Community Health* 1992;**46**:608–11.
35. Buck N, Gershuny J, Rose D, Scott J. *Changing Households: The British Household Panel Survey, 1990–1992*. Colchester: ESRC Research Centre on Micro-Social Change, 1994.
36. Weich S, Lewis G. Material standard of living, social class, and the prevalence of the common mental disorders in Great Britain. *Journal of Epidemiology and Community Health* 1998;**52**:8–14.
37. Weich S, Lewis G. Poverty, unemployment and common mental disorders: Population based cohort study. *British Medical Journal* 1998;**317**:115–19.
38. Kendler KS, Gallagher TJ, Abelson JM, Kessler RC. Lifetime prevalence, demographic risk factors, and diagnostic validity of non-affective psychosis as assessed in a US community sample: The National Comorbidity Survey. *Archives of General Psychiatry* 1996;**53**:1022–31.
39. Wittchen H-U, Kessler RC, Zhao S, Abelson J. Reliability and clinical validity of UM-CIDI DSM-III-R generalized anxiety disorder. *Journal of Psychiatric Research* 1995;**29**:95–110.
40. Regier DA, Kaelber CT, Rae DS, Farmer ME, Knauper B, Kessler RC et al. Limitations of diagnostic criteria and assessment instruments for mental disorders: Implications for research and policy. *Archives of General Psychiatry* 1998;**55**:109–15.
41. Kessler RC, Zhao S. Overview of descriptive epidemiology of mental disorders. In CA Aneshensel, JC Phelan (Eds), *Handbook of the Sociology of Mental Health*, pp. 127–50. New York: Plenum, 1999.
42. Kessler RC. The effects of stressful life events on depression. *Annual Review of Psychology* 1997:191–214.
43. Kessler RC, Zhao S, Blazer DG, Swartz M. Prevalence, correlates, and course of minor depression and major depression in the national comorbidity survey. *Journal of Affective Disorders* 1997;**45**:19–30.
44. Jayakody R, Danziger S, Kessler RC. Early onset psychiatric disorders and male socio-economic status. *Social Science Research* 1998;**27**:371–87.
45. Kendler KS, Davis CG, Kessler RC. The familial aggregation of common psychiatric and substance use disorders in the National Comorbidity survey: A family history study. *British Journal of Psychiatry* 1997;**170**:541–8.
46. Muntaner C, Eaton WW, Diala C, Kessler RC, Sorlie PD. Social class, assets, organizational control and the prevalence of common groups of psychiatric disorders. *Social Science and Medicine* 1998;**47**:2043–53.
47. Kessler RC, Frank RG. The impact of psychiatric disorders on work loss days. *Psychological Medicine* 1997;**27**:861–73.
48. Dohrenwend BP, Schwartz S. Socio-economic status and psychiatric disorders. *Current Opinion in Psychiatry* 1995;**8**:138–41.
49. Eaton WW, Regier DA, Locke BZ, Taube CA. The epidemiologic catchment area program of the national institute of mental health. *Public Health Reports* 1981;**96**:319–25.
50. Kessler RC. Building on the ECA: The National Comorbidity Survey and the children's ECA. *International Journal of Methods in Psychiatric Research* 1994;**4**:81–94.
51. Srole L, Fischer AK. The Midtown Manhattan Longitudinal Study vs "the Mental Paradise Lost" doctrine: A controversy joined. *Archives of General Psychiatry* 1980;**37**:209–21.
52. Myers JK, Weissman MM, Tischler GL, Holzer CE, Leaf P, Orvaschel H et al.

Six-month prevalence of psychiatric disorder in three communities. *Archives of General Psychiatry* 1984;**41**:959–67.
53. Regier DA, Narrow WE, Rae DS. The epidemiology of anxiety disorders: The Epidemiologic Catchment Area (ECA) experience. *Journal of Psychiatric Research* 1990;**24**:3–14.
54. Regier DA, Farmer ME, Rae DS, Myers JK, Kramer M, Robins LN et al. One-month prevalence of mental disorders in the United States and socio-demographic characteristics: The Epidemiologic Catchment Area study. *Acta Psychiatrica Scandinavica* 1993;**88**:35–47.
55. Horwath E, Weissman MM. Epidemiology of depression and anxiety disorders. In MT Tsuang, M Tohen, GEP Zahner (Eds), *Textbook in Psychiatric Epidemiology*, pp. 317–44. New York: Wiley, 1995.
56. Blazer D, George LK, Landerman R, Pennybacker M, Melville ML, Woodbury M et al. Psychiatric disorders: A rural/urban comparison. *Archives of General Psychiatry* 1985;**42**:651–6.
57. Bruce ML, Hoff RA. Social and physical health risk factors for first-onset major depressive disorder in a community sample. *Social Psychiatry and Psychiatric Epidemiology* 1994; **29**:165–71.
58. Bruce ML, Takeuchi DT, Leaf PJ. Poverty and psychiatric status: Longitudinal evidence from the New Haven Epidemiologic Catchment Area study. *Archives of General Psychiatry* 1991;**48**:470–4.
59. Swanson JW, Holzer CE III, Ganju VK, Jono RT. Violence and psychiatric disorder in the community: Evidence from the Epidemiologic Catchment Area surveys. *Hospital and Community Psychiatry* 1990;**41**:761–70.
60. Mullahy J, Sindelar J. Life-cycle effects of alcoholism on education, earnings and occupation. *Inquiry* 1989;**26**:272–82.
61. Orn H, Newman S, Bland R. Design and field methods of the Edmonton survey of psychiatric disorders. *Acta Psychiatrica Scandinavica Suppl* 1988;**338**:17–23.
62. Bland RC, Newman SC, Orn H. Period prevalence of psychiatric disorders in Edmonton. *Acta Psychiatrica Scandinavica Suppl* 1988;**338**:33–42.
63. Bland RC, Stebelsky G, Orn H, Newman SC. Psychiatric disorders and unemployment in Edmonton. *Acta Psychiatrica Scandinavica Suppl* 1988;**338**:72–80.
64. Newman SC, Bland RC. Life events and the 1-year prevalence of major depressive episode, generalized anxiety disorder, and panic disorder in a community sample. *Comprehensive Psychiatry* 1994;**35**:76–82.
65. Bijl RV, Ravelli A, van Zessen G. Prevalence of psychiatric disorder in the general population: Results of The Netherlands Mental Health Survey and Incidence Study (NEMESIS). *Social Psychiatry and Psychiatric Epidemiology* 1998;**33**:587–95.
66. de Graaf R, Bijl RV, Smit F, Ravelli A, Vollebergh WA. Psychiatric and sociodemographic predictors of attrition in a longitudinal study: The Netherlands Mental Health Survey and Incidence Study (NEMESIS). *American Journal of Epidemiology* 2000;**152**:1039–47.
67. Spijker J, Bijl RV, de Graaf R, Nolen WA. Determinants of poor 1-year outcome of DSM-III-R major depression in the general population: Results of The Netherlands Mental Health Survey and Incidence Study (NEMESIS). *Acta Psychiatrica Scandinavica* 2001;**103**:122–30.
68. McLennan, W. *Mental Health and Well-Being: Profile of Adults, Australia*. 1. Canberra: Australian Bureau of Statistics, 1998.
69. Andrews G, Henderson S, Hall W. Prevalence, comorbidity, disability and

service utilisation: Overview of the Australian National Mental Health Survey. *British Journal of Psychiatry* 2001;**178**:145–53.
70. Atkins E, Cherry N, Douglas JWB, Kiernan KE, Wadsworth MEJ. The 1946 British birth cohort: An account of the origins, progress and results of the National Survey of Health and Development. In SA Mednick, AE Baert (Eds), *Prospective, Longitudinal Research:An Empirical Basis for the Primary Prevention of Psycho-social Disorders*, pp. 25–30. Oxford: OUP, 1981.
71. Wadsworth MEJ, Mann SL, Rodgers B, Kuh DJL, Hilder WS, Yusuf EJ. Loss and representativeness in a 43 year follow up of a national birth cohort. *Journal of Epidemiology and Community Health* 1992;**46**:300–4.
72. Rodgers B. Socio-economic status, employment and neurosis. *Social Psychiatry and Psychiatric Epidemiology* 1991;**26**:104–14.
73. Wadsworth MEJ, Kuh DL. Childhood influences on adult health: A review of recent work from the British 1946 national birth cohort study, the MRC National Survey of Health and Development. *Paediatric and Perinatal Epidemiology* 1997;**11**:2–20.
74. Rodgers B. Adult affective disorder and early environment. *British Journal of Psychiatry* 1990;**157**:539–50.
75. Jones P, Rodgers B, Murray R, Marmot M. Child developmental risk factors for adult schizophrenia in the British 1946 birth cohort. *Lancet* 1994;**344**:1398–402.
76. Manor O, Matthews S, Power C. Comparing measures of health inequality. *Social Science and Medicine* 1997;**45**:761–71.
77. Power C, Manor O. Explaining social class differences in psychological health among young adults: A longitudinal perspective. *Social Psychiatry and Psychiatric Epidemiology* 1992;**27**:284–91.
78. Power C, Matthews S, Manor O. Inequalities in self rated health in the 1958 birth cohort: Lifetime social circumstances or social mobility? *British Medical Journal* 1996;**313**:449–53.
79. Rodgers B, Power C, Hope S. Parental divorce and adult psychological distress: Evidence from a national birth cohort: A research note. *Journal of Child Psychology and Psychiatry and Allied Disciplines* 1997;**38**:867–72.
80. Hope S, Rodgers B, Power C. Marital status transitions and psychological distress: Longitudinal evidence from a national population sample. *Psychological Medicine* 1999;**29**:381–9.
81. Montgomery SM, Cook DG, Bartley MJ, Wadsworth MEJ. Unemployment pre-dates symptoms of depression and anxiety resulting in medical consultation in young men. *International Journal of Epidemiology* 1999;**28**:95–100.
82. CLS. Publications arising from the 1970 British Cohort Study. London: Centre for Longitudinal Studies, Institute of Education, 1999.
83. Schinnar AP, Rothbard AB, Kanter R, Yoon SJ. An empirical literature review of definitions of severe and persistent mental illness. *American Journal of Psychiatry* 1990;**147**:1602–8.
84. Goldberg DP, Huxley P. *Common Mental Disorders: A Bio-Social Model.* London: Routledge, 1992.
85. Jenkins R, Newton J, Young R. *The Prevention of Depression and Anxiety: The Role of the Primary Care Team.* London: HMSO, 1992.
86. Dohrenwend BS, Dohrenwend BP, Link B, Levav I. Social functioning of psychiatric patients in contrast with community cases in the general population. *Archives of General Psychiatry* 1983;**40**:1174–82.
87. Rose G. *The Strategy of Preventive Medicine.* Oxford: OUP, 1992.

88. Marmot MG. Improvement of social environment to improve health. *Lancet* 1998;**351**:57–60.
89. Lewis G. Observer bias in the assessment of anxiety and depression. *Social Psychiatry and Psychiatric Epidemiology* 1991;**26**:265–72.
90. Huppert FA, Walters DE, Day NE, Elliott BJ. The factor structure of the General Health Questionnaire (GHQ-30). A reliability study on 6317 community residents. *British Journal of Psychiatry* 1989;**155**:178–85.
91. Rose G. The mental health of populations. In P Williams, G Wilkinson, K Rawnsley (Eds), *The Scope of Psychiatric Epidemiology*. London: Routledge, 1989.
92. Kessler RC, McGonagle KA, Zhao S, Nelson CB, Hughes M, Eshleman S et al. Lifetime and 12-month prevalence of DSM-III-R psychiatric disorders in the United States: Results from the National Comorbidity Survey. *Archives of General Psychiatry* 1994;**51**:8–19.
93. Kessler RC, Nelson CB, McGonagle KA, Liu J, Swartz M, Blazer DG. Comorbidity of DSM-III-R major depressive disorder in the general population: Results from the US National Comorbidity Survey. *British Journal of Psychiatry* 1996;**168**:17–30.
94. Kessler RC, Wittchen HU, Abelson JM, McGonagle KA, Schwartz N, Kendler KS et al. Methodological studies of the CIDI in the US National Comorbidity Survey. *International Journal of Methods in Psychiatric Research* 1998;**7**:33–55.
95. Lewis G, Pelosi AJ, Araya R, Dunn G. Measuring psychiatric disorder in the community: A standardized assessment for use by lay interviewers. *Psychological Medicine* 1992;**22**:465–86.
96. Goldberg DP. *The Detection of Psychiatric Illness by Questionnaire*. London: OUP, 1972.
97. Lindelow M, Hardy R, Rodgers B. Development of a scale to measure symptoms of anxiety and depression in the general UK population: The psychiatric symptom frequency scale. *Journal of Epidemiology and Community Health* 1997;**51**:549–57.
98. Bartlett CJ, Coles EC. Psychological health and well-being: Why and how should public health specialists measure it? Part 2: Stress, subjective well-being and overall conclusions. *Journal of Public Health Medicine* 1998;**20**:288–94.
99. Anderson J, Huppert F, Rose G. Normality, deviance and minor psychiatric morbidity in the community: A population-based approach to general health questionnaire data in the health and lifestyle survey. *Psychological Medicine* 1993;**23**:475–85.
100. Goldberg DP, Cooper B, Eastwood MR, Kedward HB, Shepherd M. A standardised psychiatric interview for use in community surveys. *British Journal of Preventive and Social Medicine* 1970;**24**:18–23.
101. Brugha TS, Bebbington PE, Jenkins R, Meltzer H, Taub NA, Janas M et al. Cross validation of a household population survey diagnostic interview: A comparison of CIS-R with SCAN ICD-10 diagnostic categories. *Psychological Medicine* 1999;**29**:1029–42.
102. Brugha TS, Bebbington PE, Jenkins R. A difference that matters: Comparisons of structured and semi-structured diagnostic interviews of adults in the general population. *Psychological Medicine* 1999;**29**:1013–20.
103. Rutter ML, Tizard J, Whitmore K. *Education, Health and Behaviour*. London: Longman, 1970.
104. Rodgers B, Pickles A, Power C, Collishaw S, Maughan B. Validity of the

Malaise Inventory in general population samples. *Social Psychiatry and Psychiatric Epidemiology* 1999;**34**:333–41.
105. Grant G, Nolan M, Ellis NA. A re-appraisal of the Malaise Inventory. *Social Psychiatry and Psychiatric Epidemiology* 1990;**25**:170–8.
106. Rodgers B, Mann SA. The reliability and validity of PSE assessments by lay interviewers: A national population survey. *Psychological Medicine* 1986;**16**:689–700.
107. Robins LN, Helzer JE, Croughan J, Ratcliff KF. National Institute of Mental Health Diagnostic Interview Schedule: Its history, characteristics and validity. *Archives of General Psychiatry* 1981;**38**:381–9.
108. Robins LN. Epidemiology; reflections on testing the validity of psychiatric interviews. *Archives of General Psychiatry* 1985;**42**:918–24.
109. Wells JE, Bushnell JA, Hornblow AR, Joyce PR, Oakley-Browne MA. Christchurch Psychiatric Epidemiology Study, Part I: Methodology and lifetime prevalence for specific psychiatric disorders. *Australian and New Zealand Journal of Psychiatry* 1989;**23**:315–26.
110. Kessler RC, Andrews G, Mroczek D, Ustun TB, Wittchen HU. The WHO Composite International Diagnostic Interview Short Form (CIDI-SF). *International Journal of Methods in Psychiatric Research* 1998;**7**:171–85.
111. Zigmond A, Snaith R. The hospital anxiety and depression scale. *Acta Psychiatrica Scandinavica* 1983;**67**:361–70.
112. Payne JN, Coy J, Milner PC, Patterson S. Are deprivation indicators a proxy for morbidity? A comparison of the prevalence of arthritis, depression, dyspepsia, obesity and respiratory systems with unemployment rates and Jarman scores. *Journal of Public Health Medicine* 1993;**15**:161–70.
113. Beck AT. *Cognitive Therapy and the Emotional Disorders*. New York: International Universities Press, 1976.
114. McHorney CA, Ware JE, Raczek A. The MOS 36-item Short Form Health Survey (SF-36); II: Psychometric and clinical tests of validity in measuring physical and mental health constructs. *Medical Care* 1993;**31**:247–63.
115. Garratt A, Ruta D, Abdalla M et al. The SF-36 health survey questionnaire: An outcome measure suitable for routine use in the NHS? *British Medical Journal* 1993;**306**:1440–4.
116. Brazier JE, Harper R, Jones NMB et al. Validating the SF-36 health survey questionnaire: A new outcome measure for primary care. *British Medical Journal* 1992;**305**:160–4.
117. Lyons R, Lo S, Littlepage B. Comparative health status of patients with 11 common illnesses in Wales. *Journal of Epidemiology and Community Health* 1994;**48**:388–90.
118. Bowling A, Bond M, Jenkinson C, Lamping DL. Short Form 36 (SF-36) health survey questionnaire: Which normative data should be used? Comparisons between the norms provided by the Omnibus Survey in Britain, the Health Survey for England, and the Oxford Healthy Life Survey. *Journal of Public Health Medicine* 1999;**21**:255–70.
119. Bradburn NM. *The Structure of Psychological Well-being*. Chicago: Aldine, 1969.
120. Bartlett CJ, Coles EC. Psychological health and well-being: Why and how should public health specialists measure it? Part I: rationale and methods of the investigation, and review of psychiatric epidemiology. *Journal of Public Health Medicine* 1998;**20**:281–7.

121. Susser MW, Watson W, Hopper K. *Sociology in Medicine*. London: OUP, 1985.
122. Worsley P. Class. In P Worsley (Ed.), *The New Introducing Sociology*, pp. 365–406. London: Penguin, 1987.
123. Townsend P, Davidson N, Whitehead M. *Inequalities in Health: The Black Report and The Health Divide*. London: Penguin, 1988.
124. Carstairs V, Morris R. *Deprivation and Health in Scotland*. Aberdeen: Aberdeen University Press, 1991.
125. Jefferys M. Health, illness and medicine. In P Worsley (Ed.), *The New Introducing Sociology*, pp. 197–237. London: Penguin, 1987.
126. Joshi H. The cost of caring. In C Glendenning, J Millar (Eds.), *Women and Poverty in Britain*, Brighton, UK: Wheatsheaf Books, Harvester Press, 1987.
127. Jarman B. Underprivileged area: Validation and distribution. *British Medical Journal* 1984;**289**:1587–92.
128. Townsend P. Deprivation. *Journal of Social Policy* 1987;**16**:125–46.
129. Freeman H. Schizophrenia and city residence. *British Journal of Psychiatry* 1994;**164**:39–50.
130. Hilfiker D. Are we comfortable with homelessness? *Journal of the American Medical Association* 1989;**262**:1375–6.
131. D'Arcy C, Siddique CM. Unemployment and health: An analysis of Canada Health Survey data. *International Journal of Health Services* 1985;**15**:609–35.
132. Moser KA, Fox AJ, Jones DR. Unemployment and mortality in the OPCS longitudinal study. In RG Wilkinson (Ed.), *Class and Health*, pp. 75–87. London: Tavistock, 1986.
133. Stansfeld SA, North FM, White I. Work characteristics and psychiatric disorder in civil servants in London. *Journal of Epidemiology and Community Health* 1995;**49**:48–53.
134. Wadsworth MEJ. Serious illness in childhood and its association with later-life achievement. In RG Wilkinson (Ed.), *Class and Health*, pp. 50–74. London: Tavistock, 1986.
135. Bruce ML. Socio-economic status and psychiatric disorders. *Current Opinion in Psychiatry* 1990;**3**:696–9.
136. Winkleby MA, Jatulis DE, Frank E, Fortman SP. Socio-economic status and health: How education, income and occupation contribute to risk factors for cardio-vascular disease. *American Journal of Public Health* 1992;**82**:816–20.
137. Sorlie PD, Backlund E, Keller J. US mortality by economic, demographic and social characteristics; the National Longitudinal Mortality Study. *American Journal of Public Health* 1995;**85**:949–56.
138. Pilgrim JA, Stansfeld S, Marmot M. Low blood pressure, low mood? *British Medical Journal* 1992;**304**:75–8.
139. Kawachi I, Kennedy BP, Lochner K, Prothrow-Smith D. Social capital, income inequality, and mortality. *American Journal of Public Health* 1997;**87**:1491–8.
140. Wilkinson RG. Socio-economic differences in mortality: Interpreting the data on their size and trends. In RG Wilkinson (Ed.), *Class and Health; Research and Longitudinal Data*, pp. 1–20. London: Tavistock, 1986.
141. Wilkinson RG. *Unhealthy Societies*. London: Routledge, 1996.
142. Ellison GTH. Income inequality, social trust, and self-reported health status in high-income countries. In NE Adler, MG Marmot, BS McEwen, J Stewart (Eds), *Socio-economic Status and Health in Industrial Nations*, pp. 325–8. New York: New York Academy of Sciences, 1999.

143. Kohler L, Martin J. *Inequalities in Health and Health Care*. Goteborg: Nordic School of Public Health, 1985.
144. Drever F, Whitehead M. *Health Inequalities: Decennial Supplement*. London: The Stationery Office, 1997.
145. Adler NE, Marmot MG, McEwen BS, Stewart J. *Socio-economic Status and Health in Industrial Nations*. New York: New York Academy of Sciences, 1999.
146. Liberatos P, Link BG, Kelsey JL. The measurement of social class in epidemiology. *Epidemiologic Reviews* 1988;**10**:87–121.
147. Worsley P. Introduction. In P Worsley (Ed.), *The New Introducing Sociology*, pp. 11–47. London: Penguin, 1987.
148. Hart N. The social and economic environment and human health. In R Detels, WW Holland, J McEwen, GS Omenn (Eds), *Oxford Texbook of Public Health*, pp. 95–123. Oxford: OUP, 1997.
149. Pater JE. *The Making of the National Health Service*. London: King's Fund, 1981.
150. Elliott BJ, Huppert FA. In sickness and in health: Associations between physical and mental well-being, employment and parental status in a British nationwide sample of married women. *Psychological Medicine* 1991;**21**:515–24.
151. Baum A, Garofalo JP, Yali AM. Socio-economic status and chronic stress. In NE Adler, MG Marmot, BS McEwen, J Stewart (Eds), *Socio-economic Status and Health in Industrial Nations*, pp. 1131–44. New York: New York Academy of Sciences, 1999.
152. Weyerer S, Dilling H. Psychiatric and physical illness, socio-demographic characteristics, and the use of psychotropic drugs in the community: Results from the Upper Bavarian Field Study. *Journal of Clinical Epidemiology* 1991;**44**:303–11.
153. Finlay-Jones RA, Burvill PW. The prevalence of minor psychiatric morbidity in the community. *Psychological Medicine* 1977;**7**:475–89.
154. Karasek RA, Theorell T. *Healthy Work: Stress, Productivity, and the Reconstruction of Working Life*. New York: Basic Books, 1990.
155. Eaton WW, Anthony JC, Mandel W, Garrison R. Occupations and the prevalence of major depressive disorder. *Journal of Occupational Medicine* 1990;**32**:1079–87.
156. Karasek RA. Job demands, job decision latitude, and mental strain: Implications for job re-design. *Administrative Science Quarterly* 1979;**24**:285–306.
157. Diener E, Emmons RA, Larson RJ, Griffin S. The Satisfaction with Life Scale. *Journal of Personality Assessment* 1985;**49**:71–5.
158. Stansfeld SA, Fuhrer R, Head J, Ferrie J, Shipley M. Work and psychiatric disorder in the Whitehall II study. *Journal of Psychosomatic Research* 1997;**43**:73–81.
159. Link BG, Lennon MC, Dohrenwend BP. Socio-economic status and depression: The role of occupations involving direction, control and planning. *American Journal of Sociology* 1993;**98**:1351–87.
160. Hoisington E, Stevens G. Occupational prestige and the 1980 US labor force. *Social Science Research* 1987;**16**:74–105.
161. Roos PA, Treiman DJ. Dot scales for the 1970 census classification. In AR Miller, DJ Treiman, PS Cain, PA Roos (Eds), *Work, Jobs and Occupations: A Critical Review of the Dictionary of Occupational Titles*, pp. 336–89. Washington, DC: National Academy Press, 1980.

162. Harrison J, Barrow S, Creed F. Mental health in the North West Region of England: Associations with deprivation. *Social Psychiatry and Psychiatric Epidemiology* 1998;**33**:124–8.
163. Pamuk E, Makuc D, Heck K, Reuben C, Lochner K. *Health United States, 1998; Socio-Economic Status and Health Chartbook*. Hyattsville, Maryland, USA: National Centre for Health Statistics, 1998.
164. Kessler RC. A dis-aggregation of the relationship between socio-economic status and psychological distress. *American Sociological Review* 1982;**47**:752–64.
165. Taylor SE, Seeman TE. Psycho-social resources and the SES–health relationship. In NE Adler, MG Marmot, BS McEwen, J Stewart (Eds), *Socio-economic Status and Health in Industrial Nations*, pp. 210–25. New York: New York Academy of Sciences, 1999.
166. Meltzer H, Gill B, Petticrew M, Hinds K. *Economic Activity and Social Functioning of Adults with Psychiatric Disorders. OPCS Surveys of Psychiatric Morbidity in Great Britain, 3*. London: HMSO, 1995.
167. Kessler RC, Zhao S. The prevalence of mental illness. In AV Horwitz, TL Scheid (Eds), *Sociology of Mental Health and Illness*, pp. 58–78. Cambridge: Cambridge University Press, 1999.
168. Marmot MG, Ryff CD, Bumpass LL, Shipley M, Marks NF. Social inequalities in health: Next questions and converging evidence. *Social Science and Medicine* 1997;**44**:901–10.
169. Cox BD, Blaxter M, Buckle ALJ, Fenner NP, Golding JF, Gore M et al. *The Health and Lifestyle Survey*. Cambridge: Health Promotion Research Trust, 1987.
170. Kessler RC, Davis CG, Kendler KS. Childhood adversity and adult psychiatric disorder in the US National Comorbidity Survey. *Psychological Medicine* 1997;**27**:1101–19.
171. Lynch JW, Kaplan GA, Shema SJ. Cumulative impact of sustained economic hardship on physical, cognitive, psychological and social functioning. *New England Journal of Medicine* 1997;**337**:1889–95.
172. Broadhead P. Social status and morbidity in Australia. *Community Health Studies* 1985;**9**:87–98.
173. Lewis G. Depression and public health. *International Review of Psychiatry* 1996;**8**:289–94.
174. Hemingway H, Shipley MJ, Stansfeld S, Marmot M. Sickness absence from back pain, psychosocial work characteristics and employment grade among office workers. *Scandinavian Journal of Work, Environment and Health* 1997;**23**:121–9.
175. North FM, Syme SL, Feeney A, Head J, Shipley M. Explaining socio-economic differences in sickness absence: The Whitehall II study. *British Medical Journal* 1993;**306**:361–6.
176. Stansfeld S, Feeney A, Head J, Canner R, North F, Marmot M. Sickness absence for psychiatric illness: The Whitehall II study. *Social Science and Medicine* 1995;**40**:189–97.
177. Stansfeld SA, Head J. Explaining social class differences in depression and well-being. *Social Psychiatry and Psychiatric Epidemiology* 1998;**33**:1–9.
178. Cairns E. Social class, psychological well-being and minority status in Northern Ireland. *International Journal of Social Psychiatry* 1988;**35**:231–6.
179. Dohrenwend BP, Levav I, Schwartz S, Naveh G, Link BG, Skodol AE et al.

Socio-economic status and psychiatric disorders: The causation—selection issue. *Science* 1992;**255**:946–51.
180. Lennon MC. Work conditions as explanations for the relation between socio-economic status, gender and psychological disorders. *Epidemiologic Reviews* 1995;**17**:120–7.
181. Reijneveld SA, Schene AH. Higher prevalence of mental disorders in socio-economically deprived urban areas in the Netherlands: Community or personal disadvantage? *Journal of Epidemiology and Community Health* 1998;**52**:2–7.
182. Timms DWG. Social mobility and mental health in a Swedish cohort. *Social Psychiatry and Psychiatric Epidemiology* 1996;**31**:38–48.
183. Rodgers B. Behaviour and personality in childhood as predictors of adult psychiatric disorder. *Journal of Child Psychology and Psychiatry and Allied Disciplines* 1990;**31**:393–414.
184. Wadsworth MEJ. Follow-up of the first national birth cohort: Findings from the Medical Research Council National Survey of Health and Development. *Paediatric and Perinatal Epidemiology* 1987;**1**:95–117.
185. Kessler RC, Magee WJ. Childhood adversities and adult depression: Basic patterns of association in a US national survey. *Psychological Medicine* 1993;**23**:679–90.
186. Pless IB, Cripps HA, Wadsworth MEJ. Chronic physical illness in childhood: Psychological and social effects in adolescence and adult life. *Developmental Medicine and Child Neurology* 1989;**31**:746–55.
187. Rutter ML. Relationships between child and adult psychiatric disorders. *Acta Psychiatrica Scandinavica* 1972;**48**:3–21.
188. Kessler RC, Foster CL, Saunders WB, Stang PE. Social consequences of psychiatric disorders, I: Educational attainment. *American Journal of Psychiatry* 1995;**152**:1026–32.
189. McLeod JD, Kessler RC. Socio-economic differences in vulnerability to undesirable life events. *Journal of Health and Social Behavior* 1990;**31**:162–72.
190. Pearlin LJ, Schooler C. The structure of coping. *Journal of Health and Social Behavior* 1978;**19**:2–21.
191. Kendler KS, Kessler RC, Heath AC, Neale MC et al. Coping: A genetic epidemiological investigation. *Psychological Medicine* 1991;**21**:337–46.
192. Wadsworth MEJ. Health inequalities in the life course perspective. *Social Science and Medicine* 1997;**44**:859–69.
193. Bebbington P. The origins of sex differences in depressive disorder: Bridging the gap. *International Review of Psychiatry* 1996;**8**:295–332.
194. Rodgers B. Models of stress, vulnerability and affective disorder. *Journal of Affective Disorders* 1991;**21**:1–13.
195. Jenkins R. Minor psychiatric morbidity in employed young men and women and its contribution to sickness absence. *British Journal of Industrial Medicine* 1984;**42**:147.
196. Brugha TS, Bebbington P, Tennant C, Hurry J. The list of threatening experiences: A subset of 12 life event categories with considerable long-term contextual threat. *Psychological Medicine* 1985;**15**:189–94.
197. Brugha TS, Cragg D. The list of threatening experiences: The reliability and validity of a brief life events questionnaire. *Acta Psychiatrica Scandinavica* 1990;**82**:77–81.
198. Hamilton VL, Broman CL, Hoffman WS, Renner DS. Hard times and

vulnerable people: Initial effects of plant closing on autoworkers' mental health. *Journal of Health and Social Behavior* 1990;**31**:123–40.

199. Kessler RC, Turner JB, House JS. Intervening processes in the relationship between unemployment and health. *Psychological Medicine* 1987;**17**:949–61.
200. Stansfeld SA, Fuhrer R, Cattell V, Wardle J, Head J. Psycho-social factors and the explanation of socio-economic gradients in common mental disorder. *Health Variations* 1999;**4**:4–5.
201. Marmot M, Holland WW. Preventive medicine and the health of a nation. *Journal of Epidemiology and Community Health* 1993;**47**:1–5.
202. Brown GW, Harris T, Adler Z, Bridge L. Social support, self-esteem and depression. *Psychological Medicine* 1986;**16**:813–31.
203. Stansfeld SA, Rael EGS, Head J, Shipley M, Marmot M. Social support and psychiatric sickness absence: A prospective study of British civil servants. *Psychological Medicine* 1997;**27**:35–48.
204. Stansfeld SA, Bosma H, Hemingway H. Psychosocial work characteristics and social support as predictors of SF-36 health functioning: The Whitehall II study. *Psychosomatic Medicine* 1998;**60**:247–57.
205. Clarke R, Breeze E, Sherliker P, Shipley M, Youngman L, Fletcher A et al. Design, objectives, and lessons from a pilot 25 year follow up re-survey of survivors in the Whitehall study of London Civil Servants. *Journal of Epidemiology and Community Health* 1998;**52**:364–9.
206. Stansfeld SA, Smith GD, Marmot M. Association between physical and psychological morbidity in the Whitehall II study. *Journal of Psychosomatic Research* 1993;**37**:227–38.
207. Ferrie JE, Shipley MJ, Stansfeld S, Smith GD. Health effects of anticipation of job change and non-employment: longitudinal data from the Whitehall II study. *British Medical Journal* 1995;**311**:1264–9.
208. House JS, Kessler RC, Herzog R, Mero RP, Kinney AM, Breslow MJ. Age, socio-economic status and health. *Milbank Quarterly* 1990;**68**:383–411.
209. Oakley-Browne MA, Joyce PR, Wells JE, Bushnell JA, Hornblow AR. Christchurch Psychiatric Epidemiology Study, Part II: Six month and other period prevalences of specific psychiatric disorders. *Australian and New Zealand Journal of Psychiatry* 1989;**23**:327–40.
210. Joyce PR, Oakley-Browne MA, Wells JE, Bushnell JA, Hornblow AR. Birth cohort trends in major depression: Increasing rates and earlier onset in New Zealand. *Journal of Affective Disorders* 1990;**18**:83–9.
211. Tarnopolsky A, Morton-Williams J. *Aircraft Noise and Psychiatric Disorders.* London: Social and Community Planning Research, 1980.
212. Williams P, Tarnopolsky A, Hand D, Shepherd M. Minor psychiatric morbidity and general practice consultations: The West London Survey. *Psychological Medicine* 1986;**16**.
213. Lewis G, Wilkinson G. Another British disease? A recent increase in the prevalence of psychiatric morbidity. *Journal of Epidemiology and Community Health* 1993;**47**:358–61.
214. Leighton DC, Harding JS, Macklin DB, Macmillan AM, Leighton AH. *The Character of Danger*. New York: Basic Books, 1963.
215. Health and Welfare Canada. *The Health of Canadians: Report of the Canada Health Survey*. Ottawa: Statistics Canada, 1981.
216. Boyle MH, Offord DR, Campbell D, Catlin G, Goering P, Lin E et al. Mental health supplement to the Ontario Health Survey: Methodology. *Canadian Journal of Psychiatry* 1996;**41**:549–58.

217. Offord DR, Boyle MH, Campbell D, Goering P, Lin E, Wong M et al. One-year prevalence of psychiatric disorder in Ontarians 15 to 64 years of age. *Canadian Journal of Psychiatry* 1996;**41**:559–63.
218. Lin E, Goering P, Offord DR, Campbell D, Boyle MH. The use of mental health services in Ontario: Epidemiologic findings. *Canadian Journal of Psychiatry* 1996;**41**:572–7.
219. Finlay-Jones RA, Burvill PW. Contrasting demographic patterns of minor psychiatric morbidity in general practice and the community. *Psychological Medicine* 1978;**8**:455–66.
220. Halldin J. Prevalence of mental disorder in an urban population in central Sweden in relation to social class, marital status and immigration. *Acta Psychiatrica Scandinavica* 1985;**71**:117–27.
221. Weyerer S, Dilling H, Kohl R, Martens H. Social class and mental disorders: A study of the use of medical services. *Social Psychiatry* 1982;**17**:133–41.
222. Pflantz M, Basler HD, Schwoon D. Use of tranquillising drugs by a middle-aged population in a West German city. *Journal of Health and Social Behavior* 1977;**18**:194–205.
223. Wittchen HU, Carter RM, Pfister H, Montgomery SA, Kessler RC. Disabilities and quality of life in pure and comorbid generalized anxiety disorder and major depression in a national survey. *International Clinical Psychopharmacology* 2000;**15**(6):319–28.

REPORT TWO

Quantifying associations between social position and the common mental disorders in Britain

David Melzer, Tom Fryers, Brenda McWilliams and Rachel Jenkins

---

Address for correspondence: Dr David Melzer, Institute of Public Health, Forvie Site, Robinson Way, Cambridge CB2 2SR, UK. Email: dm214@medschl.cam.ac.uk

We thank Professor Terry Brugha for his invaluable input on the survey instruments and diagnostic issues. We acknowledge the help of The Data Archive, University of Essex, for supplying material relating to the National Survey of Psychiatric Morbidity.

This work was undertaken by the University of Cambridge who received funding from the Department of Health; the views expressed in this publication are those of the authors and not necessarily those of the Department of Health.

Contents: Report two

List of tables and figure: Report two

TABLES

FIGURE

2.1 INTRODUCTION

Mental disorders are major causes of disability and premature death, especially in working adults. The "Global Burden of Disease" study[1] for the World Bank and World Health Organization estimated that mental disorder is responsible for 38% of all years lived with a disability in females and 25% in males, in the established market economies. While the severe "psychotic" mental illnesses are often highly disabling to sufferers, they are also relatively rare in the general population. The majority of the burden of mental illness derives, in fact, from the less severe but far more numerous "neurotic disorders" or "common mental disorders", and it is this latter category that provides the focus for this report.

In 1998 the UK Department of Health commissioned a systematic review of recent epidemiological studies on mental health and social inequalities in developed countries. In Report 1, the results of the re-examination of large recent studies from developed countries were presented, clarifying the nature of links between the common mental (or "neurotic") disorders and social position, measured by occupational social class, education, material circumstances, or employment. Nine large well-conducted studies from the UK, North America, Holland, and Australia met inclusion criteria, with good markers of mental disorders and social position. Of these, eight showed an association between one or more markers of less privileged social position and higher prevalence of the common mental disorders. For some individual indicators in particular studies, no clear trend was evident, but no study showed a contrary trend with any indicator. Markers showing this relationship most consistently include unemployment, less education, and low income or material standard of living. Occupational social class was the least consistent marker. Overall risks in relatively deprived groups were seldom raised by more than a risk ratio of 2, for prevalence of the common mental conditions.

Because of the lack of consistency in measures and approaches, and the patchy nature of the published accounts from these studies, the review in Report 1 was unable to explore the reported markers of social position further. It was not possible, for example, to explore inter-relationships of markers, or identify the best markers for the more disabling common conditions, occurring with significant disability. Therefore, further exploration of these markers was undertaken in the most detailed available "local" data, namely the 1993 national Survey of Psychiatric Morbidity in Great Britain[2;3] and the results are reported below. (The second National Psychiatric Survey has recently reported its basic results, but detailed analyses are not as yet available for this later study. However, initial reports indicate few differences from the first survey.)

In addition to the household survey, ONS national psychiatric surveys were also carried out on sub-populations covering psychotic conditions, homeless people, and people in prison. In these specialised surveys there was ample evidence of social deprivation among psychotic patients, as well as high prevalence rates of illness in homeless and imprisoned populations. The focus of this further analysis, however, is on neurotic disorder in the general population.

2.1.1 Previously published results from the national Survey of Psychiatric Morbidity (household sample)

OPCS (now the Office for National Statistics) published a series of reports on the national Household Psychiatric Survey.[4–6] Analyses were based on symptom scores and specific neurotic disorders identified through "lay" interview, using the Clinical Interview Schedule (CIS-R).[7] The resulting data indicated that overall one in seven adults aged 16 to 64 had some sort of neurotic health problem (based on a score of 12 or more on the interview instrument) in the week prior to interview. Table 2.1 summarises the prevalence results for specific disorders from the published data. The table shows that the most frequent category of neurotic disorder identified in the survey was "mixed anxiety and depressive disorder", accounting for nearly half of all cases. Patients were placed in this category if more precise diagnoses did not apply, according to the instrument's algorithms for classifying symptoms into diagnoses.

TABLE 2.1
Prevalence of specific neurotic disorders

	Rate per 1000	*% of group with neurotic disorders*
Mixed anxiety and depressive disorder	77	48
Generalised anxiety disorder	31	19
Depressive episode	21	13
All phobias	11	7
Obsessive compulsive disorder	12	8
Panic disorder	8	5
All neurotic disorders	160	100

Source:[2] p. 76.

In multivariate analyses of factors associated with neurotic disorder, the likelihood of having neurotic disorder in those who were unemployed was reported as twice that of working people. Women, people living alone, those living in rented rather than owned accommodation, and in urban rather than rural settings also had raised rates. In addition, multivariate analyses were carried out to identify factors associated with each of the specific neurotic conditions.

Significantly, those with neurotic disorders were estimated by the OPCS study to have far lower incomes than those without these disorders: the median weekly gross income among those with a neurotic disorder was about £90 compared with £150 for the general population.

Lewis et al.[8] have published a more detailed analysis of the associations between measures of socio-economic status and neurotic disorder from the OPCS household survey, and concluded that there was an independent association between low standards of living and the prevalence of neurotic disorder. Housing tenure and access to cars were used as measures of standard of living, and both were associated with higher prevalence of neurotic disorder, even after adjustment for other socio-economic and demographic variables. They estimated that about 10% of the neurotic disorder in the UK could be attributed to the increased prevalence in those without cars who rented their homes.

Two major problems arise from this published work. First, the analysis of factors associated with neurotic disorders was limited to a restricted set of explanatory factors, and did not always incorporate factors known from the previous literature to be important underlying risks, such as the presence of physical illness, the occurrence of adverse life events, and the lack of social support. Second and more fundamentally, the analyses were restricted to the diagnostic dimension and did not incorporate measures of the functional impact or disability associated with neurotic disorder.

2.1.2 Diagnosis and disability in the general population

Two main issues shape the analysis of mental health inequalities: the identification of mental conditions in surveys and the definition of social position. The general approach adopted in dealing with these issues in our analysis is summarised below.

One reason for the lack of clarity in the previous literature on neurotic disorder and social inequalities in the general population may be due to the difficulties in diagnosing illness in epidemiological surveys. Approaches to defining the presence of neurotic disorder in surveys are controversial,[9] with a range of concerns, including establishing the thresholds for identifying clinical "cases". There are at least three dimensions that are relevant to the definition of case-ness, namely severity of symptoms, chronicity (the time the symptoms have lasted), and disability.

The OPCS Survey employed the Clinical Interview Schedule (CIS-R)[7] and identified neurotic symptoms and diagnostic "case-ness" during the week before interview. The CIS-R involves eliciting psychological symptoms and does not take their functional impact on everyday life (the associated disability) into account in arriving at a diagnosis. This approach can be justified as some patients can suffer substantial psychological distress but continue to function, while others with relatively mild symptoms can sometimes show marked disruption in activities of daily living. On the other hand, mental symptoms are widespread, showing a continuous distribution in the general population, and as a result, the definition of "case-ness" is to some extent arbitrary. The cut-off of 12 or more symptoms on CIS-R in the previous week, chosen for the analysis of the OPCS survey, represents a substantial burden of psychological distress, and was chosen as equating to clinical cases who would be considered in need of at least clinical monitoring, if not early treatment.

While increasing symptom number and severity is generally associated with increasing disability, a number of other factors determine difficulties in functioning in everyday life. These factors include:

- coping behaviours, styles, and abilities;
- environmental factors including family, workplace, and peer support;
- personality trait;
- illness behaviour.

Neurotic disorder combined with disability is of additional policy concern and therefore we have developed a range of definitions of neurosis, defining sub-groups with increasing levels of functional impairment or disability, for use in exploring links with social inequality.

Further methodological difficulties are present in defining social inequalities. In general, social inequalities are taken here to cover population sub-groups identified by markers of less privileged socio-economic status or material circumstances, or less education. In addition, differences between gender and ethnic groups provide important dimensions, as do differences between disabled and non-disabled groups, single parents and others, and unemployed or economically inactive groups and others. Inevitably, these various attributes overlap, and the majority of measures have some degree of statistical association with each other. In our analyses, we have tried to incorporate as wide a set of definitions of social inequality as are available from the study data. We have then tried to identify those measures that provide the closest statistical association with our range of measures of neurotic disorder in the general population. We should also note, however, that the available measures of inequality are probably each markers of a number of more specific factors that might be involved in neurotic disorder.

In analysing the cross-sectional OPCS study, it should also be noted that causal pathways cannot be identified. Thus, if neurotic disorder is shown to be associated with unemployment, it is not possible in this data to identify which came first. Unfortunately, longitudinal data relevant to the question of whether social inequality causes neurotic disorder, or vice versa, are scarce.

2.1.3 Overview of the report

In the brief overview of the relevant existing published output from the OPCS national household psychiatric survey set out above, it is apparent that further work is needed for three main purposes, aiming to:

- incorporate the functional impact or disability dimension of neurotic disorder as a supplement to diagnostic information derived from the CIS-R;
- quantify the strength of associations between the social position markers and the disorders with or without disability;
- explore the inter-relationship or independence of markers associated with neurotic disorder, using a series of statistical models.

In the sections that follow, we describe the detailed methods used in this analysis, and then present the results, covering the distribution of characteristics in the study sample, the associations between markers of social inequality and neurotic disorder adjusted only for age and gender differences, and finally, the associations between markers in comprehensive multivariate logistic regression models.

2.2 METHODS

2.2.1 Outline of the national Psychiatric Morbidity Survey study methods

The Department of Health, the Scottish Home and Health Department, and the Welsh Office commissioned the OPCS household survey, and fieldwork was carried out between April and September 1993. The population surveyed consisted of adults aged 16 to 64 years living in private households in England, Wales, and Scotland (excluding the Highlands and Islands).

2.2.1.1 Sample

The Postcode Address File (PAF) provided the sampling frame for the survey, as this gives a good representation of private households. Within each of the initially selected 200 postal sectors, 90 delivery points were chosen. These 18,000 addresses were visited by trained interviewers to identify private households with at least one person aged 16 to 64 years. The Kish grid method was used to select one person from each household.[10]

After excluding those addresses that were ineligible because either they contained no private households or if a private household, contained no one within the eligible age range, 12,730 adults were selected for interview. Of these, 10,108 people agreed to be interviewed (approximately four out of five people selected).

2.2.1.2 Weighting

The final sample interviewed was weighted in three stages. First, weights for non-response (refusals and non-contacts) associated with household size were applied. Second, weights were applied to take account of different probabilities of selecting informants in different-sized households. Third, weights were applied to represent the age–sex structure of the total national population living in private households. The product of these three weights was applied, followed by a correcting factor to return the weighted sample size to its original size.

2.2.1.3 Identification of mental disorder

The Clinical Interview Schedule—Revised (CIS-R)[11] was used to measure neurotic psychopathology. Survey respondents were questioned about the presence of 14 symptoms in the past month and their frequency, severity, and duration in the past week. Diagnoses were obtained by looking at the answers to various questions and applying algorithms based on ICD-10 diagnostic criteria.[12]

Estimates of the prevalence of psychosis were obtained by first screening respondents for presently occurring symptoms. A questionnaire was developed specifically for this purpose—the Psychosis Screening Questionnaire (PSQ).[13] Potential cases were followed up with a clinician interview using Schedules for Clinical Assessment in Neuropsychiatry (SCAN).[14;15]

Alcohol and drug dependence details were obtained from each interviewed adult by means of a self-completion questionnaire. The components of alcohol dependence measured were: loss of control, symptomatic behaviour, and binge drinking. Drug dependence was measured by questions on: frequency of drug use, stated dependence, inability to cut down, need for larger amounts, and withdrawal symptoms.

2.2.1.4 Instruments used for deprivation, social class, and disability

Everyone interviewed was asked questions on Schedule A, which covered:

- socio-demographics;
- general health questions;

- the Clinical Interview Schedule (Revised) (CIS-R);
- the Psychosis Screening Questionnaire.

Those scoring above the threshold (scoring 12 or more) on the CIS-R and those with potential psychotic illnesses were asked Schedule B questions covering:

- longstanding illness;
- medication and treatment;
- health;
- social and voluntary care services;
- activities of daily living and informal care;
- recent stressful life events;
- social activities;
- social networks and social support;
- education and employment;
- finances
- smoking and alcohol consumption.

Those scoring less than 12 on the CIS-R were asked questions on Schedule C, which was an abridged version of Schedule B (omitting longstanding illness, medication, and service use, as they were assumed to have no mental health problems).

2.2.2 Measures of social position used in the new analysis

The answers to questions on Schedule A of the OPCS survey questionnaire provided information on potential measures of deprivation that are summarised in Table 2.2. These are divided into four main areas, covering education, occupation, status, and material circumstances.

TABLE 2.2
Markers of socio-economic position

Dimension	*Measure*
Education	Age left school Qualifications
Occupation	Work status—full-time, part-time, unemployed, or economically inactive
Social status, based on occupation	Registrar General's Social Class
Income and wealth (material circumstances)	Housing type Housing tenure Car ownership

Initial exploratory work indicated that some grouping of responses was appropriate. For example, ages at which people had left school were split into a dichotomous variable, because models indicated that groups either side of this split had similar risks for neurotic disorder in regression models.

2.2.2.1 *Statistical analysis*

As described above, the sampling procedure of the OPCS survey involved identifying households within 16 regions of England, Wales, and Scotland (excluding the Highlands and Islands), and then randomly choosing one adult within each household to interview. As a result, adults living together in a household were less likely to be selected: for example, adults in households with two adults were half as likely to be included as those where they were living alone; in households of three, one-third as likely, and so on. In addition, there was some non-response and refusal to participate in the study, and an overall need to weight the data back to the age–sex structure of the studied adult population.

The necessary weights for exploring the data are provided by the OPCS. Initial analysis was carried out in SPSS,[16] employing these weights. While this method provides accurate estimates of percentages and odds ratios, errors can occur in the estimation of confidence intervals due to the complex nature of the sampling. To take account of the complex sampling, a replicate weighting program (WesVar 3.0)[17] was used for final estimates. The Jacknife method was used to calculate estimates, which is the standard approach to the analysis of complex sample surveys.[18]

In line with the general approach, logistic regression models were developed on the weighted data in SPSS. The resulting models were then tested in WesVar, using the replicate weight approach, producing more accurate confidence intervals.

2.3 DIAGNOSTIC GROUPS AND DISABILITY

In this section we will report the rationale for selecting a range of measures of mental illness, incorporating information on functional limitation or disability.

2.3.1 Neurotic disorder: Grouped or individual conditions?

The first major analytical choice is whether to explore the relationship with markers of social inequalities for neurotic disorders as a whole or to identify discrete diagnostic entities within this category. In the OPCS survey, 48% of neurotic cases were assigned to a residual category of "mixed anxiety and depressive disorder".

Brugha et al.[19] have published the results of a comparison study of the diagnostic instrument and classifications used by "lay" interviewers in the OPCS study compared to diagnoses resulting from the symptoms recorded by psychiatric clinicians, using the SCAN interview (Schedules for Clinical Assessment in Neuropsychiatry).[15] In detailed analyses, Brugha et al.[19] showed that there were significant discrepancies between the two interviews. For example, marked discrepancies were found in the identification of phobic disorders and sensitivity for identifying depression was also poor in the "lay" interview. Generalised anxiety disorders accounted for most CIS-R anxiety disorders but were rare on SCAN interview. Obsessive-compulsive disorder was similarly common on CIS-R but rare in the clinical interview. Given these findings, the meaningfulness of identifying discrete groups within the neurotic "case" category appears doubtful, and as a result we have chosen not to subdivide the "cases" into specific diagnostic entities.

2.3.1.1 *Drug and alcohol dependence*

Some analyses of mental health problems include alcohol and drug dependence as diagnostic categories. In this analysis we have not included these conditions, on the basis that their cause and distribution are different from those of the common psychiatric disorders. It is clear from Table 2.3 that only a minority of those suffering from alcohol or drug dependence in the OPCS survey had neurotic disorders as well.

TABLE 2.3
Numbers of people by neurotic disorder status and the presence of alcohol or drug dependence

	Number without neurotic disorder	*Number with neurotic disorder*	*Total*
Total in the survey sample	8545	1563	10108
Alcohol dependence	341	143	484
Drug dependence	117	97	214

Data on alcohol dependence was not available for 324 people.

2.3.2 The disability dimension

As discussed in the introduction, increasing attention is being focused on the presence not only of a diagnosis of neurotic disorder, but also on functional limitation or disability.[20] At the end of the CIS-R interview, respondents were asked whether their mental symptoms had limited the things they do. First, they were asked whether in the past week mental symptoms had "stopped you from getting on with things you used to do or would like to do", and if the respondent answered "no" to this question, whether mental symptoms had made "things more difficult, even though you had got everything done". Table 2.4 shows that of the 1562 cases of neurotic disorder in the weighted sample, 84% felt that their mental symptoms had made things harder or had stopped them, and 54% felt that symptoms stopped them from doing things. Clearly the very broad questions used to determine whether things were harder identifies the great majority of the whole neurotic group, and even the narrower question identifies over half of the sample.

Having been stopped from "getting on with things that you used to or would like to do" could include people with relatively small functional limitations, given the broad nature of the question. Nevertheless, the question does identify a group half the size of all those with neurotic disorder and therefore this criterion was used to define a group of people with "limiting neurotic disorder".

TABLE 2.4
Number (%) of cases of any neurotic disorder on CIS-R results, by whether mental symptoms stopped respondents from doing things they used to or would like to do

	Number	*%*
Neurotic disorder (total)	1562	100
"Things" stopped or harder because of mental symptoms	1312	84
"Things" stopped because of mental symptoms	837	54

Table 2.5 shows data on the relationship between limiting neurotic disorder and limitations in activities of daily living (ADLs). In the category of limiting disorder (based on mental symptoms having stopped the person

TABLE 2.5
Numbers of people with limiting neurotic disorder who have difficulty in activities of daily living (ADLs)

	Yes	*No*	*% with difficulties*
Difficulty with ablutions	78	753	9
Difficulty using transport	131	699	16
Difficulty with medical care	19	805	2
Difficulty with household activities	142	680	17
Difficulty with practical activity	201	609	25
Difficulty with paperwork	135	694	16
Difficulty managing money	100	719	12
One or more ADLs	341	493	41
Two or more ADLs	207	627	25
Three or more ADLs	139	695	17

$n = 819$.

from doing "things") 59% of the group still had no difficulties in any of the measured activities of daily living. The final category of disabling neurotic disorder was therefore developed, by excluding those with no ADLs from the group with limiting disorder.

Limitations in activities of daily living occur in many people who have physical illness, and therefore this criterion was only applied to those who attributed limitations to mental symptoms.

2.3.3 The final diagnostic categories used in the analysis

In view of the need to use both diagnostic and symptom count based definitions of neurosis, and to incorporate functional limitations and disabilities (difficulties in at least one activity of daily living), six different categories were used in the analysis. The main set were based on CIS-R-diagnosed neurotic disorder and the following categories were used:

- *Disorder*: was present in those people with any "neurotic" diagnosis on CIS-R.
- *Limiting disorder*: neurosis was present on CIS-R and the person reported that the mental symptoms had stopped them from getting on with things they used to do or would like to do.
- *Disabling disorder*: was present if a person had limiting disorder and also had at least one ADL difficulty.

In addition, a sensitivity analysis was carried out based on symptom scores of 12 or more on the CIS-R, avoiding possible problems arising from the diagnostic algorithms in the instrument. The three definitions used were otherwise equivalent to those for "case-ness".

Table 2.6 summarises the prevalences for each category. The table shows that while neurotic disorder is relatively common (affecting over 15% of the

TABLE 2.6
Numbers and prevalence (%) of each category of neurotic disorder or symptom groups

	N	%
Neurotic disorder	1563	15.5
Limiting disorder	837	8.3
Disabling disorder	340	3.4
Symptomatic	1430	14.1
Limiting symptoms	792	7.8
Disabling symptoms	325	3.2

n = 10,108.

population), disabling neurotic disorder is far less frequent, and affects only 3.4%. The symptom-based definitions show similar patterns.

2.3.4 Duration of symptoms

Table 2.7 presents data on the percentage of people in each neurotic disorder group who said that their symptoms had been present for 6 months or more, or 1 year or more. Of those with neurotic disorder, 63% had had an average length of symptom presence of 6 months or more, and 49% for a year or more. The data for disabling neurotic disorder were 72% for 6 months or more and 57% for 12 months or more. People with long-standing symptoms, therefore, dominate these diagnostic categories, even though the case identification was based on the presence of disorder in the week before interview.

As certain types of symptoms and syndromes tend to fluctuate in severity, it should be remembered that during any one year there will be a higher prevalence of disorder in the general population than in any one week. In addition, approximately one in five of those sampled for the OPCS

TABLE 2.7
Duration of symptoms

	6 months or more			*1 year or more*		
	Disorder %	*Limiting disorder* %	*Disabling disorder* %	*Disorder* %	*Limiting disorder* %	*Disabling disorder* %
How long with pain	61	60	68	53	50	58
How long feeling tired	56	57	65	40	40	49
How long with problems of concentration	62	63	70	44	43	51
How long with problems with sleep	65	66	76	50	48	60
How long feeling irritable	58	60	71	43	44	54
How long spent worrying about health	60	62	70	47	48	59
How long feeling sad, miserable or depressed	57	59	71	40	41	53
How long worrying about things	61	63	74	46	46	56
How long with feelings of anxiousness	63	62	72	48	48	59
How long have you been phobic	76	77	79	68	69	71
How long with feelings of panic	72	70	78	62	59	66
How long repeating actions	68	64	66	56	54	55
How long with obsessional thoughts	56	60	71	39	44	52
Mean of above	63	63	72	49	49	57

survey refused to take part, and it is thought that there may be a higher prevalence of neurotic disorder in survey non-responders.[20]

Andrews[21] has suggested that the 1-year prevalence of neurotic disorder in this study may be around a third higher, at 24% (rather the 15.5% one week prevalence).

2.4 FACTORS POTENTIALLY ASSOCIATED WITH NEUROTIC DISORDER: DESCRIPTIVE STATISTICS

In reporting the results of our analyses, we first present simple tabulations of the factors to be explored in identifying the associates of neurotic disorder. We then present the results of univariate analyses of the measures of inequality adjusted only for age and gender. This is followed by the results of the full multivariate analysis, in which we seek to identify the principal factors that are associated with neurotic disorder, adjusting for a comprehensive set of known risk factors.

Tables 2.8 to 2.10 summarise data on the prevalence of our three definitions of neurotic disorder, by all the potentially associated factors on which data are available in the OPCS study. Table 2.8 gives numbers of people with each category of disorder by age and sex. Household size was a key factor in the sampling for the survey, and Table 2.9 summarises the data on the prevalence of the three definitions of disorder by this factor.

Many of the variables examined were either those from the original questionnaires or those that had been derived by OPCS. Some were collapsed into fewer categories, such as qualifications, age left school, and social class (Table 2.10). The summary variable for number of stressful life events was recoded to exclude the item relating to the respondent's own serious illness over the last 6 months (this variable then ranged from 0 to 10 and was grouped into none, one, two, or more). This recoding was done because data on illness status were available separately, and also to remove the possibility of mental illnesses being included in reported life events.

The recent occurrence of stressful life events is an important risk factor for neurotic disorder, according to the published literature. Table 2.11 summarises the data relating to each of these identified in the OPCS survey, together with a summary measure, based on the numbers of events that occurred.

The presence of physical illness is also a well-validated risk factor for neurotic disorder, and Table 2.12 summarises data relating to these. Again, a summary variable is presented, based on the numbers of physical illness ICD-10 categories present.

TABLE 2.8
Numbers (%) of people with each category of common mental disorder, by age and sex

	Total	*Disorder* Number	%	*Limiting disorder* Number	%	*Disbling disorder* Number	%
Total	10,108	1563	15	837	8	340	3
Subject's age in 10-year groups							
55–64	1589	212	13	111	7	73	5
45–54	1910	313	16	173	9	82	4
35–44	2148	358	17	182	8	70	3
25–34	2520	400	16	212	8	63	3
16–24	1941	280	14	159	8	51	3
Subject's sex							
Female	5032	963	19	489	10	183	4
Male	5076	600	12	348	7	157	3

TABLE 2.9
Numbers (%) by household size (numbers living in the household) and neurotic disorder

	Total	*Disorder* Number	%	*Limiting disorder* Number	%	*Disabling disorder* Number	%
Household size							
5–10	1349	217	16	128	9	45	3
4	2537	351	14	180	7	61	2
3	2308	359	16	178	8	68	3
2	3044	445	15	247	8	113	4
1	870	191	22	104	12	53	6

TABLE 2.10
Numbers (%) with disorder by markers of socio-economic inequality

		Disorder		*Limiting disorder*		*Disabling disorder*	
	Total	*Number*	*%*	*Number*	*%*	*Number*	*%*
Accommodation type							
Flat bedsit other	1484	319	21	178	12	77	5
House terrace	3078	533	17	288	9	119	4
House semi	3358	446	13	228	7	107	3
House detached	2170	261	12	141	6	38	2
Accommodation tenure							
Rent (other)	916	164	18	86	9	26	3
Rent (LA/HA)	1860	440	24	239	13	134	7
Mortgage	5657	757	13	405	7	135	2
Owned	1660	199	12	106	6	45	3
Number of cars							
None	1783	422	24	235	13	125	7
1	4606	706	15	375	8	145	3
2+	3710	434	12	227	6	70	2
Country							
Wales	511	85	17	49	10	23	5
Scotland	709	104	15	60	8	28	4
England	8888	1375	15	728	8	289	3
Locality							
Urban	6673	1129	17	605	9	254	4
Rural/semi-urban	3434	433	13	231	7	86	3
Family unit type							
Child of lone parent	344	53	15	30	9	9	3
Child of couple	1116	120	11	73	7	21	2
One person only	1349	276	20	150	11	71	5
Lone parent	572	158	28	90	16	42	7
Couple 1+ child	4079	609	15	310	8	118	3
Couple no child	2648	346	13	183	7	80	3
Number of children							
3+	657	120	18	64	10	26	4
2	1614	238	15	132	8	37	2
1	1792	308	17	169	9	63	4
None	6044	896	15	472	8	213	4
Number of adults aged 16–64							
4–7	1330	190	14	106	8	42	3
3	1881	284	15	137	7	52	3
2	5426	766	14	414	8	159	3
1	1471	323	22	180	12	86	6

TABLE 2.10
Continued

	Total	Disorder		Limiting disorder		Disabling disorder	
		Number	*%*	*Number*	*%*	*Number*	*%*
Number of adults aged 65+							
One or more	544	72	13	39	7	17	3
None	9564	1490	16	798	8	323	3
Ethnicity							
Other	85	16	19	11	13	6	7
Asian or oriental	365	54	15	40	11	15	4
West Indian or African	158	26	16	11	7	4	3
White or European	9414	1459	15	771	8	315	3
Age left school							
15– or no school	3048	567	19	311	10	176	6
16+ or still in education	7031	990	14	521	7	164	2
Qualifications							
None	2875	525	18	295	10	154	5
A/O/CSE/other	4832	729	15	376	8	134	3
Degree/technical/higher national diploma/ nursing	2298	293	13	156	7	47	2
Social class							
Never worked	254	33	13	28	11	12	5
Armed forces	107	13	12	6	6	1	1
IV+V	2058	365	18	198	10	100	5
IIIM	2866	438	15	229	8	100	3
IIINM	1512	270	18	141	9	51	3
I+II	3284	437	13	230	7	75	2
Work status							
Economically inactive	2333	475	20	298	13	177	8
Unemployed	865	219	25	120	14	54	6
Working part time	1680	266	16	125	7	27	2
Working full time	5209	596	11	289	6	81	2

TABLE 2.11
Prevalence of neurotic disorder by presence of stressful life events and perceived social support score

		Disorder		*Limiting disorder*		*Disabling disorder*	
	Total	*Number*	*%*	*Number*	*%*	*Number*	*%*
	10108	1563	15	837	8	340	3
Relative seriously ill							
Missing	328	7	2	5	2	0	0
Yes	1315	299	23	175	13	82	6
Immediate relative died							
Missing	331	6	2	5	2	0	0
Yes	319	74	23	46	14	23	7
Close relative died							
Missing	330	6	2	5	2	0	0
Yes	1537	301	20	165	11	80	5
Had a separation							
Missing	333	7	2	6	2	0	0
Yes	524	159	30	93	18	31	6
Problems with relatives							
Missing	336	8	2	6	2	0	0
Yes	899	331	37	197	22	94	10
Made redundant							
Missing	329	6	2	5	2	0	0
Yes	425	88	21	47	11	17	4
Seeking work for 1 month or more							
Missing	327	6	2	5	2	0	0
Yes	1156	259	22	133	12	51	4
Financial crisis							
Missing	328	6	2	5	2	0	0
Yes	496	177	36	103	21	39	8
Problems with police							
Missing	329	6	2	5	2	0	0
Yes	165	64	39	33	20	14	8
Something lost or stolen							
Missing	328	6	2	5	2	0	0
Yes	684	173	25	104	15	43	6
Number of stressful life events (excluding self illness)							
Missing	326	6	2	5	2	0	0
2+	1833	538	29	303	17	136	7
1	3063	520	17	290	9	109	4
0	4886	499	10	239	5	94	2
Perceived social support score (grouped)							
Missing	433	26	6	17	4	7	2
Severe lack	916	263	29	157	17	78	9
Moderate lack	2565	424	17	235	9	94	4
No lack	6193	849	14	429	7	161	3

TABLE 2.12
Prevalence of physical illness by defined neurotic disorder

	Total	*Disorder* Number	%	*Limiting disorder* Number	%	*Disabling disorder* Number	%
Cancers	80	30	38	18	23	12	15
Endocrine/metabolic	266	54	20	37	14	23	9
Central nervous system	317	87	27	56	18	34	11
Eye complaints	106	13	12	10	9	5	5
Ear complaints	150	25	17	12	8	9	6
Heart, vessels, circulation	568	120	21	77	14	52	9
Respiratory	712	161	23	96	13	42	6
Digestive	345	108	31	64	19	32	9
Genito-urinary	193	90	47	43	22	18	9
Musculo-skeletal	1277	356	28	210	16	141	11
Infections, parasites	24	6	25	4	17	2	8
Blood disorders	45	11	24	8	18	3	7
Skin complaints	179	45	25	26	15	12	7
Other	50	26	52	13	26	4	8
Number of non-mental ICD-10 system complaints							
Two or more	764	255	33	159	21	103	13
One only	2561	535	21	297	12	137	5
None	6783	773	11	381	6	100	1

2.5 THE UNIVARIATE ASSOCIATION BETWEEN MARKERS OF SOCIO-ECONOMIC STATUS AND NEUROTIC DISORDER

The social position of individuals is generally measured using markers of social status, income or wealth, occupation, and education. In this section we explore the available variables relevant to these dimensions, while ignoring for the moment other potential risk factors for neurotic disorder.

Table 2.13 sets out the odds ratios for the univariate associations between each marker of social position and neurotic disorder. In this table the associations are adjusted for age and sex only, and the replicate model has adjusted the data and confidence intervals for the complex nature of the sample. The table shows clearly that all measures of less privileged socio-economic position show strong associations with each of the categories of neurotic disorder. There is a general tendency for the size of these risks to increase with increasing disability.

The largest odds ratios for limiting disorder (with risks of 2 or more) were for living in a flat, bedsit, or other accommodation compared to living

TABLE 2.13
Age–sex-standardised odds ratios (95% CI) for each potential measure of inequality separately, for each definition of mental disorder, based on replicate model estimates

	Age–sex-standardised odds ratios					
Variable and	*Disorder*		*Limiting disorder*		*Disabling disorder*	
comparison category	*OR*	*95% CI*	*OR*	*95% CI*	*OR*	*95% CI*
Nature of accommodation						
House detached						
Flat, bedsit, or other	2.1	1.7–2.5*	2.0	1.7–2.5**	3.3	2.2–4.9**
House terraced	1.6	1.3–1.9*	1.5	1.3–1.9*	2.4	1.6–3.6**
House semi-detached	1.2	0.9–1.4	1.1	0.9–1.4	1.9	1.3–2.8*
Housing tenure						
Owned						
Rent other	1.6	1.3–1.9*	1.6	1.3–1.9*	1.5	0.8–2.6*
Rent LA/HA	2.1	1.7–2.6**	2.0	1.6–2.4**	2.9	2.4–3.5**
Mortgaged	1.1	0.9–1.3	1.0	0.8–1.2	0.9	0.6–1.3
Car ownership						
2 or more cars						
None	2.4	2.0–2.9**	2.5	2.1–3.1**	4.4	3.0–6.5**
One	1.4	1.2–1.7*	1.4	1.2–1.7*	1.8	1.5–2.2*
Work status						
Working full-time						
Economically inactive	1.9	1.6–2.3*	2.6	2.2–3.2**	5.6	3.8–8.3**
Unemployed	2.7	2.2–3.3**	2.8	2.3–3.4**	4.3	2.9–6.4**
Working part-time	1.2	1.0–1.4*	1.2	1.0–1.5*	1.2	0.8–1.7*
Social class						
I+II						
IV+V	1.5	1.2–1.8*	1.5	1.2–1.8*	2.3	1.6–3.5**
IIIM	1.2	1.0–1.5*	1.2	1.0–1.5*	1.5	1.3–1.9*
IIINM	1.4	1.2–1.8*	1.3	1.1–1.6*	1.7	1.4–2.0*
Never worked	1.0	0.6–1.8	1.6	0.9–2.8	2.6	1.2–5.8**
Armed forces	0.8	0.4–1.8	0.8	0.3–2.1	0.4	0–>1000*
Qualifications						
Degree/technical/hnd/nursing						
No qualifications	1.6	1.3–1.9*	1.6	1.4–2.0*	2.7	1.9–4.1**
A level, O level, CSE, or other	1.2	1.0–1.5*	1.2	1.0–1.5*	1.6	1.1–2.4*
Age left school						
16+ or still						
15– or never	1.6	1.3–1.9*	1.7	1.4–2.0*	2.5	2.0–3.0**

* significant at $p < 0.05$: ** odds ratio 2 or more.

in a detached house, being unemployed or economically inactive compared to being in full-time work, and having no car or van compared to two or more.

Many of these markers of social position measure overlapping attributes, and show significant statistical correlations with each other. In addition, certain measures may be less valid in populations aged 16 to 64 years. For example, occupationally based social class classifies people on factors including job skill and the degree to which the respondent manages other people. However, many 16- to 25-year-olds will not have entered or only recently entered the job market, from full-time education. Seniority in the workplace depends partly on experience and younger adults will not have had enough time to rise to supervisory roles in the workplace.

To deal with this problem, we have entered all these measures into a multivariate model. In Table 2.14 we present the result of the multivariate model of markers of social position (plus age and gender) only. Factors entered were selected from conventional weighted forward regression models, and significant coefficients were then estimated in the replicate model programme, to ensure accurate estimation of confidence intervals.

It is clear from this analysis that markers of poorer material circumstances (covering housing tenure and lack of car ownership), less education, and being economically inactive or unemployed are the significant associated factors. Occupationally based social class (a marker of status) does not emerge as a significant factor in the multivariate model. Markers of education identifying education qualifications did not enter the multivariate model, and instead only the marker of having left schooling by the age of 15 remained in the model.

2.6 THE MULTIVARIATE IDENTIFICATION OF THE PRINCIPAL RISK FACTORS FOR NEUROTIC DISORDER

The same extended set of demographic, socio-economic status, physical disease, and other variables set out descriptively in Section 2.4 were regressed in multivariate models against each definition of neurotic disorder. This was carried out in SPSS, initially, using forward logistic regression techniques and employing the OPCS weights for the data. All the variables that were significantly and independently associated with each of these types of illness were then explored further, using a replicate weighting programme, to produce accurate confidence intervals for the odds ratios, adjusted for the complex nature of the sample. The results are set out in Table 2.15.

Models with both an expanded set of individual life events and physical illnesses as well as summary variables (numbers of each) were explored. The

TABLE 2.14

Multivariate models results (odds ratios and 95% confidence intervals) of markers of wealth, education, and occupation, adjusted for age-group and gender

		Disorder		*Limiting disorder*		*Disabling disorder*	
Variable and comparison category		*OR*	*95% CI*	*OR*	*95% CI*	*OR*	*95% CI*
Age group							
16–24	55–64	0.71	0.59–0.87**	0.62	0.51–0.75**	1.03	0.70–1.53
	45–54	1.20	0.98–1.46	1.17	0.96–1.43	1.72	1.16–2.54**
	35–44	1.21	0.99–1.47	1.11	0.91–1.34	1.42	0.96–2.10
	25–34	1.14	0.94–1.39	1.06	0.87–1.29	1.03	0.70–1.53
Gender							
Male	Female	1.57	1.29–1.91**	1.23	1.01–1.50**	0.90	0.74–1.09
Type of accommodation							
Detached house	Flat, bedsit or other	1.31	1.08–1.59**	1.30	1.07–1.58**	1.42	0.96–2.10
	Terraced	1.19	0.97–1.44	1.15	0.95–1.40	1.40	0.95–2.08
	Semi-detached	0.95	0.78–1.16	0.93	0.77–1.13	1.25	0.84–1.84
Housing tenure							
Owned	Rent other	1.31	1.08–1.59**	1.27	1.04–1.55**	1.22	0.68–2.20
	Rent from LA or HA	1.46	1.20–1.78**	1.31	1.08–1.59**	1.60	1.08–2.37**
	Mortgage	1.17	0.96–1.43	1.19	0.97–1.44	1.23	0.83–1.83

Car or van ownership							
2+	None	1.46	1.20–1.78**	1.51	1.24–1.83**	1.80	1.22–2.67**
	One	1.20	0.98–1.46	1.22	1.00–1.49**	1.27	0.86–1.88
Age left school							
16 years plus	Up to 15 (including no education)	1.32	1.09–1.61**	1.38	1.13–1.68**	1.72	1.41–2.09**
Work status							
Working full time	Economically inactive	1.68	1.38–2.05**	2.34	1.92–2.85**	4.26	2.88–6.31**
	Unemployed	2.16	1.78–2.63**	2.27	1.87–2.76**	2.97	2.01–4.40**
	Working part time	1.20	0.98–1.46	1.22	1.00–1.49**	1.13	0.76–1.67
Social class							
I+II	Never worked	0.57	0.31–1.02	0.76	0.42–1.36	0.76	0.35–1.67
	Armed forces	0.73	0.33–1.59	0.69	0.26–1.84	0.36	0–>1000
	IV+V	0.93	0.77–1.13	0.90	0.74–1.10	1.07	0.72–1.59
	III M	0.97	0.80–1.18	0.94	0.77–1.15	0.91	0.75–1.11
	III NM	1.17	0.96–1.43	1.08	0.89–1.32	1.13	0.76–1.67

** identifies odds ratios that are significant at the 5% level.

TABLE 2.15

Odds ratios (95% confidence intervals) for a comprehensive set of factors associated with neurotic disorder

Variable and reference category	Category	Disorder OR	Disorder 95% CI	Limiting disorder OR	Limiting disorder 95% CI	Disabling disorder OR	Disabling disorder 95% CI
Age group							
vs 16–24	55–64	0.62	0.42–0.92*	0.54	0.45–0.66*	0.71	0.48–1.05
	45–54	1.02	0.84–1.24	1.00	0.68–1.48	1.15	0.64–2.07
	35–44	1.06	0.87–1.29	0.99	0.81–1.20	1.05	0.58–1.89
	25–34	1.07	0.88–1.30	1.04	0.86–1.27	0.92	0.62–1.37
Gender							
vs Male	Female	1.68	1.38–2.05*	1.26	1.03–1.53*	0.92	0.76–1.12
Tenure							
vs Owned	Rent other	1.31	1.08–1.59*	1.26	0.85–1.86	1.04	0.58–1.87
	Rent from LA or HA	1.34	1.10–1.63*	1.17	0.96–1.43	1.40	0.95–2.08
	Mortgage	1.17	0.96–1.43	1.20	0.98–1.46	1.21	0.82–1.79
Number of cars or vans							
vs 2 or more cars	No cars	1.23	1.01–1.50*	1.21	0.99–1.47	1.39	0.94–2.06
	1 car	1.09	0.90–1.33	1.08	0.89–1.32	1.11	0.75–1.64
Age left education							
vs 16 years or more	Up to 15 (including no education)	1.26	1.03–1.53*	1.28	1.06–1.56*	1.60	1.32–1.95*
Work status							
vs Working full-time	Economically inactive	1.42	1.17–1.73*	1.95	1.61–2.38*	3.32	2.24–4.91**
	Unemployed	1.30	1.07–1.58*	1.34	1.10–1.63*	1.63	1.10–2.42*
	Working part time	1.13	0.93–1.37	1.15	0.95–1.40	1.03	0.70–1.53

Ethnicity							
vs White/European	Other	1.17	0.65–2.11	1.70	0.94–3.06	2.97	1.12–7.92**
	Asian/oriental	1.15	0.78–1.70	1.49	1.01–2.21*	1.46	0.67–3.20
	West Indian/African	0.79	0.54–1.18	0.73	0.40–1.31	0.66	0.30–1.45
Urban residence							
vs urban	Semi-urban or rural	1.14	0.94–1.39	1.08	0.89–1.32	1.19	0.97–1.44
Family type							
vs couple no children	Child of lone parent	0.97	0.66–1.44	1.04	0.58–1.87	0.74	0.34–1.62
	Child of couple	0.89	0.60–1.31	1.15	0.64–2.07	1.45	0.54–3.86
	One person	1.17	0.79–1.74	1.23	0.83–1.83	1.55	0.86–2.8
	Lone parent	1.43	1.18–1.74*	1.63	1.10–2.42*	1.97	1.10–3.55*
	Couple 1+ children	1.14	0.77–1.69	1.23	0.83–1.83	1.79	0.99–3.22
Household size							
vs One	5 to 10	0.73	0.50–1.09	0.78	0.53–1.15	0.61	0.28–1.33
	Four	0.69	0.47–1.02	0.66	0.44–0.97*	0.55	0.25–1.20
	Three	0.81	0.55–1.20	0.76	0.51–1.12	0.68	0.31–1.50
	Two	0.79	0.53–1.16	0.88	0.59–1.30	1.04	0.48–2.28
Number of life events							
vs None	2+	3.16	2.60–3.84**	3.16	2.60–3.84**	3.25	2.20–4.82**
	One	1.75	1.44–2.13*	1.90	1.56–2.31*	1.80	1.48–2.19*
Social support							
vs No lack	Unknown	1.46	0.99–2.16	1.62	0.90–2.91	2.03	0.93–4.45
	Severe lack	2.14	1.76–2.60**	2.14	1.76–2.60**	2.23	1.50–3.29**
	Moderate lack	1.25	1.02–1.52*	1.21	0.99–1.47	1.12	0.75–1.65
Number of physical illnesses							
vs None	Two or more	3.46	2.84–4.20**	0.82	3.14–4.65**	6.42	4.34–9.51**
	One	1.86	1.53–2.26*	1.95	1.61–2.38*	2.69	2.21–3.27**

* significant at $p < 0.05$: ** odds ratio 2 or more.

latter performed well, with results being very similar for models with individual illness or life events compared to summary models (see Sensitivity analysis below). The latter are therefore presented here.

Table 2.15 shows that the well-established pattern of older age, the absence of stressful life events, and the presence of a supportive social network are all protective against neurotic disorder. The table also shows that being physically ill, being economically inactive or unemployed, having finished full-time education by the age of 15 years, or being a single parent are all associated with significantly raised risks of illness.

Interestingly, the odds ratios for the main inequality risk factors tend to increase in size for the more severe "disabling neurotic disorder". In this category, an odds ratio of above 6 was present for those having two or more physical illnesses, and above 2 for those who had had two or more adverse life events, or a severe lack of social support.

It should be noted that factors such as living in rented accommodation and not having a car did not emerge as significant factors for limiting or disabling disease. Note also that in disabling illness, the association with female gender disappears.

In terms of ethnic group differences, greater risks of limiting disorder were present for people of Asian or oriental ethnicity, but this did not reach statistical significance for disabling disorder. The "other" ethnic grouping was based on 85 respondents and represents a residual category.

2.6.1 Sensitivity analysis

Redoing the above analysis with symptom-count-based categories produced essentially the same pattern of results. In analyses of factors associated with limiting neurotic symptoms, housing tenure emerged as an additional significant factor, with higher risks in all those who do not own their own homes. For ethnicity, Asians had raised risks of limiting symptoms, but not the other categories.

For disabling neurotic symptoms, again all the significant risks for disabling disorder were similar, but two additional factors reached statistical significance: being aged 55–64 (vs 16–24), and living in accommodation rented from local authorities or housing associations.

Models were also explored that included individual disease groups and individual life events. In these, disease counts remained in the model, with small additional risks associated with a small number of specific conditions, including cancer. For life events, counts also remained in the model, with recent financial crises and problems with relatives also remaining in, but adding little explanatory power to the model.

2.6.2 Overview of results

Table 2.16 summarises the statistically significant factors associated with limiting neurotic disorder, the middle category of the three used in these analyses. The table shows that all the markers of social position were significantly associated with limiting neurotic disorder separately, but the social status or class measure did not stay in the multivariate socio-economics risk model. In the comprehensive model incorporating family type, physical illness, life events, and support groups, markers of income and wealth (accommodation type and tenure, car ownership) were no longer statistically significant, suggesting that their "effect" may be due to these more specific factors that replaced them in the comprehensive model.

For all neurotic disorders, the results were very similar, except that housing tenure and car ownership remained significant factors, in the comprehensive risk model.

TABLE 2.16
Factors associated with limiting neurotic disorder in the range of models

Variables	*Univariate socio-economic status risks*	*Multivariate socio-economic status risks*	*Multivariate comprehensive risk model*
Age group	×	×	×
Gender	×	×	×
Socio-economic markers			
Housing type	×	×	
Housing tenure	×	×	
Car ownership	×	×	
Age left education	×	×	×
Highest educational qualification	×		
Work status	×	×	×
Social class	×		
Additional factors			
Family type (lone parents)			×
Ethnicity (Asian)			×
Life events			×
Lack of social support			×
Physical illness			×
Rural or semi-urban residence			
Household size			

× indicates significant association present. The shaded panels indicate that the additional factors were not included in the models.

The analysis of disabling neurotic disorder produced similar results (Table 2.17), except that age and gender ceased to be significant factors. Interestingly, Asian ethnicity was a significant factor in the comprehensive

TABLE 2.17
Factors associated with disabling neurotic disorder in the range of models

Variables	*Univariate socio-economic status risks*	*Multivariate socio-economic status risks*	*Multivariate comprehensive risk model*
Age group	×	×	
Gender	×		
Socio-economic markers			
Housing type	×	×	
Housing tenure	×	×	
Car ownership	×	×	
Age left education	×	×	×
Highest educational qualification	×		
Work status	×	×	×
Social class	×		
Additional factors			
Family type (lone parents)			×
Ethnicity (Asian)			
Life events			×
Lack of social support			×
Physical illness			×
Rural or semi-urban residence			
Household size			

× indicates significant association present. The shaded panels indicate that the additional factors were not included in the models.

model for limiting neurotic disorder, but not for all neurotic or disabling neurotic disorders.

2.7 ACCESS TO TREATMENT

Identifying neurotic disorder and its associated disability would be of limited value if care were already being delivered to those involved. Table 2.18 shows that while the great majority of those with each type of disorder have seen GPs to discuss a physical health problem in the previous 12 months, less than half had done so to discuss a mental health problem. Levels of treatment with, for example, anti-depressants were low in 1993, with only 13% of those with disabling disorder taking these medications.

Data on receipt of counselling are available only for those with neurotic disorder: 9% of the disorder group, 11% of the limiting disorder group, and 15% of those with disabling disorder were receiving counselling at the time of the interview. These patterns of low access to treatment have been reported from studies in other countries.[21]

TABLE 2.18
Access to treatment: Percentage of diagnostic groups receiving each category of care or treatment

	No neurotic disorder %	*Neurosis* %	*Limiting disorder* %	*Disabling disorder* %
Past 12 months, spoken to GP about a physical condition	62	78	79	88
Past 12 months, spoken to GP about a mental condition	7	35	39	47
Taking the following at the time of interview:				
Hypnotics	0	2	3	5
Anxiolytics	0	2	4	7
Anti-depressant drugs	0	6	8	13
Taking drugs used in psychoses and related conditions	1	1	1	2
Been out-patient for a physical problem during past year?	2	41	44	55
Been out-patient for a mental problem during the past year?	0	4	5	7
Been out-patient for a physical and mental problem during the past year?	0	1	1	1

Multivariate models were developed to identify factors associated with talking to a GP about a mental health problem during the last 12 months. These showed that there was no evidence that markers of relative deprivation or inequality were associated with less seeking of care (see Section 2.8).

Reasons suggested in the literature for the low rates of treatment include issues of access to clinicians, but also negative attitudes to the conditions and available treatments among those who have the disorders.[22] Clearly, therefore, there is a need to extend access and uptake to effective diagnosis and treatment, in order to reduce the suffering and disability associated with these conditions. In the next section, we will explore the nature of high prevalence subgroups of neurotic disorder that may deserve special attention in the context of social inequalities.

2.8 HIGH-RISK SUBGROUPS FOR NEUROTIC DISORDER: THE PROSPECTS FOR TARGETING OF INTERVENTIONS

As discussed above, older age, the absence of stressful life events, and the presence of a supportive social network are all protective against limiting neurotic disorder. However, being a lone parent, being physically ill, unemployed, or economically inactive, or having left school at or before age 15 were all associated with significantly raised risks of neurotic disorder. Disability (measured as difficulty with one or more activity of daily living) was used in the analysis as part of the definition of neurotic disorder categories, and people with disabilities form an additional group with high prevalence of neurotic disorder.

From this analysis, these (overlapping) sub-groups of people with a high risk of neurotic disorder were studied as potentially constituting specific target groups for improving care, within a comprehensive approach to reducing the morbidity associated with mental health inequalities.

Lone parents are the smallest group in the general population in the national survey (6% of those aged 16–64) but 28% of this group had neurotic disorder (Table 2.19). It should be noted, however, that there has been a strong upward trend in the numbers of lone-parent households, and the estimate presented here may be artificially low.

TABLE 2.19
High-risk groups as a percentage of the population aged 16–64, and the percentage of each high-risk group who suffer from neurotic disorder

	Group as a % of the population aged 16–64	*Prevalence of neurotic disorder in each group (%)*
1. Lone parents	6*	28
2. Two or more physical illness groups	8	33
3. Unemployed	9	25
4. People with disabilities: Difficulty with one or more activities of daily living (ADLs)	16	31
5. Economically inactive	23	20
6. Left school at age 15 or earlier	30	19

* may be an underestimate: see text.

People with two or more physical illnesses (involving different ICD-10 disease systems) made up only 8% of the general population, but 33% of this group had neurotic disorder.

These high-risk groups overlap: the top three together make up 20% of the population, and 27% of this combined group had neurotic disorder. Perhaps more importantly from a disease control perspective, these three groups (people who were unemployed, had two or more physical illnesses, or were lone parents) contributed 36% of all those with neurotic disorder, 39% of those with limiting disorder, and 51% of those with disabling neurotic disorder. The contribution of each group to the total with each category of neurotic disorder is summarised in Table 2.20.

TABLE 2.20
Percentage contribution of each high-risk group to the total of those suffering from each category of neurotic disorder

Total number in sample	*Neurotic disorder N = 1562, 100%*	*Limiting disorder N = 836, 100%*	*Disabling disorder N = 341, 100%*
1. Lone parents	10	11	12
2. Two or more physical illnesses	16	19	30
3. Unemployed	14	14	16
4. People with disabilities	32	41	(100)
5. Economically inactive	31	36	52
6. Left school at age 15 or earlier	36	37	52

High-risk groups overlap.

In order to explore more fully the nature of these high-risk groups (to inform any potential targeting of interventions) we summarise key features of each group in Table 2.21. In overview, the lone parent and unemployed groups with neurotic disorder were younger, with the lowest percentage of cases aged 45–64. The great majority of the cases in the group who had left school before age 16 were in the older age groups.

Not surprisingly, there were high percentages of females among cases who were lone parents or economically inactive. Only a minority in all groups of cases had no educational qualifications, the exception being in the group who had left full-time schooling before the age of 16. In terms of paid occupation, it is clear that a sizeable minority of those who were unemployed or economically inactive in each group had been unemployed for less than 5 years, suggesting that there may be considerable scope for achieving a return to work, if care and treatment are improved. Interestingly, 72% of those who were unemployed and 41% who were economically inactive with neurotic disorder had worked during the previous 0 to 4 years before interview.

Between 44% and 56% of people in the high-risk groups had spoken to a GP about a mental problem during the previous 12 months, suggesting that there is considerable scope for improving access or use of professional care.

2.8.1 Lone parents

Lone parents are people of particular concern, as their neurotic disorder may affect their children. In the study, 12.3% of households were headed by lone parents. However, Social Trends 30[23] reported that 19% of families were headed by a lone parent in 1991–92, and this percentage has since

TABLE 2.21

Distribution (% of each group) of key characteristics within the whole population, all those with neurotic disorder and those with neurotic disorder in high-risk groups

			With neurotic disorder					
Number in sample and base for %	*Whole population 10108 %*	*All neurotic disorder 1564 %*	*1. Lone parents 158 %*	*2. Two or more physical illnesses 255 %*	*3. Unemployed 219 %*	*4. One or more ADL 507 %*	*5. Economically inactive 477 %*	*6. Left school by age 15 566 %*
Age group								
16–24	19	18	19	6	29	15	17	6
25–44	46	48	55	37	49	37	34	34
45–64	35	34	26	57	22	48	49	60
Gender								
Female	50	62	91	61	47	55	72	61
Qualifications								
Degree/technical/HND/nursing	23	19	13	17	13	13	9	5
A level/O level/CSE/other	48	47	45	37	51	41	39	26
No qualifications	29	34	42	46	35	45	52	69
Work								
Working part or full time	68	55	38	38	N/A	35	N/A	43
Unemployed for 0 to 4 years	4	23	32	25	72	30	41	25
Economically inactive or unemployed for 5 or more years	28	22	30	36	28	35	59	32
Seeking care								
Spoken to a GP about a mental problem, last year	12	35	44	51	33	44	45	56

risen to 24% (in 1998–99). Some of this difference may be due to differences in definitions; the Social Trends (General Household Survey) definition includes children aged 16 to 18 in full-time education.

Table 2.22 summarises the distribution of children in the weighted sample population. In the household survey, 10% of children were living in lone parent households. Only 3% of all children were living in lone parent households where the parent had a neurotic disorder, thus making targeting of this high-risk group a relatively limited and focused issue.

TABLE 2.22
Numbers (%) of children in lone-parent households

	Number of children	*%*
Children in all households	7206	100
Children in lone-parent households	704	10
Lone parent with neurotic disorder	200	3

2.9 DISCUSSION

2.9.1 Reasons for work

In Report 1 we presented the results of the systematic review of the larger studies relevant to this association. The review showed that eight of the nine studies meeting the selection criteria reported two or more indicators of less privileged social position associated with increased rates of "neurotic" mental disorder. No studies have shown an inverse association. However, differences in detailed definitions of social position markers and mental health status made quantitative estimation across studies invalid. We therefore analysed the OPCS national Psychiatric Morbidity Survey data-set, to provide the best available quantitative estimates of the studied associations for use in British policy making.

In exploring the available data, the general approach taken was to:

- include a range of measures of disorder, including evidence of limitations that the interviewed respondents attribute to their mental symptoms, and of disabilities;
- explore the primary associations first, with age- and gender-adjusted models of the association between each definition of neurotic disorder and each marker of social position;
- explore the markers of social position together, to identify the best markers;

- explore the markers plus more specific risk factors in comprehensive multivariate models

The results confirm that there are strong primary associations between all available markers of less privileged social position and higher prevalence of neurotic disorder. More specific analysis indicates that this overarching pattern may partly be due to the higher prevalence in specific groups, especially lone parents, physically ill people, and the unemployed.

The analysis of the distribution of neurotic disorder within the population reporting disabilities also confirms the estimates produced by the WHO Global Burden of Disease study.[1] As predicted by the WHO Global Burden of Disease estimates, neurotic disorder made a large contribution to all reported disability in the survey: for example, 38% of those with more severe disabilities (difficulties with three or more activities of daily living) had a limiting neurotic disorder.

2.9.2 Methodological issues

In evaluating these results it is important to remember some limitations of the study. One major limitation of this work, based on cross-sectional data, is that it is impossible to determine whether less privileged material circumstances cause disabling neurotic disorder, or vice versa. As discussed in the review of other studies, the available evidence does provide some support for a causal link, with deprived circumstances causing the common mental disorders. It is important, however, that the direction of causality in the link between neurotic disorder and inequality is fully clarified, with a longitudinal study.

A second major limitation of this analysis is that important issues were absent from the available data—including, for example, caring status (carers have high rates of depression), and histories of abuse. In addition to the household survey, OPCS psychiatric surveys were also carried out on sub-populations covering psychotic conditions, homeless people, and people in prison. In these specialised surveys there was ample evidence of social deprivation among psychotic patients, as well as high prevalence rates of illness in homeless and imprisoned populations.

A third limitation is that the survey may have somewhat under-counted some groups of people with neurotic disorder. The response rate for the survey (around 80%) is relatively good, but it is likely that those not responding will have had higher rates of illness than those who did respond. As set out above (Section 2.8.1), there is some evidence that lone parents may have been somewhat under-represented in the survey.

In Section 2.3 we discussed the diagnostic problems of the survey data. In this analysis, we have used a range of broad categories, aiming to maximise the validity of the definitions chosen. No attempt has been made to analyse the individual syndromes separately. The addition of a limitations and disability dimension also adds to the validity of the identification of "cases" of illness in the data.

Further difficulties exist in defining and measuring "social inequality" (see Section 2.2.2). In this analysis, we have concentrated on "social class" or social position, based on the well-established theories of the existence of hierarchies within contemporary society, evident in the distribution of material resources, education, and social status. As these notions are broad and overlapping (although somewhat weighted to specific elements within social position), it is inevitable that more specific measures will tend to displace broader measures in statistical analyses. The more specific markers, however, are of use in identifying specific sub-groups who may have special characteristics of policy importance.

Having acknowledged the limitations of the study, we should also note some of its strengths. These include its national population representativeness, and the availability of a comprehensive set of markers of neurotic disorder, disability, and social position. Its large size, with over 10,000 respondents, also provides a great deal of statistical power to explore the studied relationships. The analysis itself has provided a hierarchy of models, which can be used to identify both broad markers as well as more specific identifiers of groups with high rates of neurotic disorder.

2.9.3 The results

In terms of results, the analysis has extended previous analyses. As reported earlier, 15.5% of the general population aged 16–64 have neurotic disorder, but this analysis has shown that 8.3% have limiting neurotic disorder (reporting that their mental symptoms stopped them doing things) and 3.4% have disabling neurotic disorder (reporting limiting disorder with difficulty doing at least one activity of daily living). These categories of neurotic disorder (or "common mental disorders") are each composed mainly of people with depression and/or anxiety syndromes.

The analysis has also confirmed the general importance of the common mental disorders in contributing to disability in working age adults. As predicted by the WHO Global Burden of Disease estimates[1] neurotic disorder made a large contribution to all reported disability in the survey: for example, 38% of those with more severe disabilities (difficulties with three or more activities of daily living) had a limiting neurotic disorder.

In initial statistical analyses, all the available markers of less privileged social position (including education, occupation, and material circumstances) were individually associated with higher prevalence rates of the common mental disorders.

In statistical analyses designed to identify the best markers of social inequality in the prevalence of neurotic disorder (adjusted for gender and age group only), the following factors emerged:

- markers of poorer material circumstances (housing tenure and lack of car ownership);
- having less education (having left full-time schooling before age 16);
- being unemployed or economically inactive.

The Registrar General's occupationally based Social Class classification (a marker designed to give more weight to social status) does not emerge as a significant factor in the multivariate model, perhaps suggesting that material circumstances and education are more important than status in inequalities in the distribution of the common mental disorders.

In comprehensive statistical analyses, markers of less privileged material circumstances and having less education remained important and independent risk factors for neurotic disorder. Additional significant factors were:

- having physical illnesses, especially having two or more ICD "disease systems" involved;
- being a lone parent;
- having had recent stressful life events;
- lacking social support.

The size of the risks associated with these factors tends to increase as the definition identifies more disabling disorder.

Interestingly, women have a greater risk of neurotic disorder than men, but risks were equal for disabling neurotic disorder. This finding is in line with previous work on the gender difference[24] and may reflect illness behaviour, in which men are less willing to report milder symptoms of psychological distress. As the severity of the condition increases, gender differences then disappear.

2.9.4 High-risk groups

The analyses presented above suggest that certain high-risk subgroups for neurotic disorder exist. The size and prevalence of neurotic disorder in each (overlapping) high-risk group is presented graphically in Figure 2.1.

In addition to the groups identified in the logistic regression analysis, a further category is implicit in the analysis. Disability was used in the analysis as part of the definition of neurotic disorder categories, and people

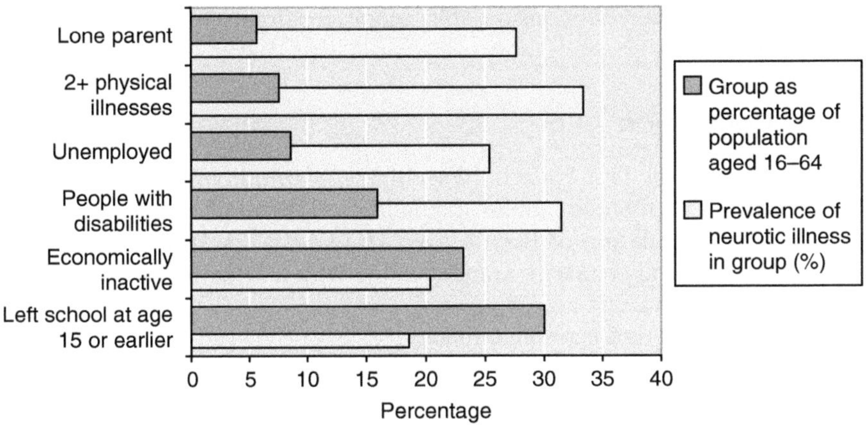

Figure 2.1. High-risk subgroups as a percentage of the general population aged 16–64, and the prevalence of neurotic disorder in each group (note: group membership overlaps).

with disabilities form a further group with high prevalence of neurotic disorder.

Specific policy initiatives to reduce mental health inequalities in these "target groups" could be justified, within a comprehensive policy for dealing with the common mental disorders. For example, lone parents, those with physical diseases involving two or more ICD-10 disease systems, and those who are unemployed together make up 20% of the population, but have a prevalence of neurotic disorder more than double that in the general population (27%). Perhaps more importantly from a disease control perspective, these three groups contributed:

- 36% of all those with neurotic disorder;
- 39% of those with limiting disorder; and
- 51% of those with disabling neurotic disorder.

The lone parent group raises concern not only for the adult suffering from a common mental disorder, but also because the children of lone parents suffering from a common mental disorder can be adversely affected. In the survey, 3% of children were in this category, although this may be an underestimate. There was a sizeable increase during the 1990s in the percentage of households headed by lone parents.

Levels of treatment overall were low, with only 35% of all those with neurotic disorder having spoken to their general practitioner about mental health problems during the previous year. In the high-risk groups identified above, between 44% and 56% had spoken to a GP about such problems, suggesting that there is considerable scope for improving utilisation of professional care.

2.9.5 Conclusion

This analysis of the first National Psychiatric Morbidity household survey shows clearly that there are major inequalities in mental health status in the general adult population of Britain aged 16 to 64 years. It also shows that the common mental disorders are associated with a large proportion of the disability present in this age group.

Unemployment and economic inactivity, less privileged material circumstances, and less education are all important markers of risk of neurotic disorder. Specific high-risk groups exist, including those with physical illness, lone parents, unemployed people, people with disabilities, and economically inactive people. This pattern of distribution of disorder, especially disabling neurotic disorder, may be somewhat different from the stepwise trends in risk with decreasing social position, identified with most physical conditions.

This analysis suggests that specific policy initiatives are needed to reduce the burden of the common mental disorders in high-prevalence sub-groups, to supplement a comprehensive policy aimed at reducing the burden of mental ill health.

2.10 NOTES

1. Murray C, Lopez AD. *The Global Burden of Disease*. Harvard: Harvard School of Public Health, 1996.
2. Meltzer H, Gill B, Petticrew M. *The Office of Population Censuses and Surveys: Survey of Psychiatric Morbidity in Great Britain. Report No 1, The Prevalence of Psychiatric Morbidity Among Adults Aged 16–64 Living in Private Households in Great Britain*. London: HMSO, 1995.
3. Jenkins R, Lewis G, Bebbington P, Brugha T, Farrell M, Gill B et al. The National Psychiatric Morbidity Surveys of Great Britain: Initial findings from the household survey. *Psychological Medicine* 1997;**27**:775–89.
4. Meltzer H, Gill B, Petticrew M, Hinds K. *The Prevalence of Psychiatric Morbidity Among Adults Living in Private Households. 1*. London: ONS, 1995.
5. Meltzer H, Gill B, Petticrew M, Hinds K. *Economic Activity and Social Functioning of Adults with Psychiatric Disorders. 3*. London: HMSO, 1995.
6. Meltzer H, Gill B, Petticrew M, Hinds K. *Physical Complaints, Service Use, and Treatment of Adults with Psychiatric Disorder*. London: OPCS, 2000.
7. Lewis G, Pelosi AJ, Araya R, Dunn G. Measuring psychiatric disorder in the community: A standardized assessment for use by lay interviewers. *Psychological Medicine* 1992;**22**:465–86.
8. Lewis G, Bebbington P, Brugha T, Farrell M, Gill B, Jenkins R et al. Socioeconomic status, standard of living, and neurotic disorder. *Lancet* 1998;**352**:605–9.

9. Cooper B, Singh B. Population research and mental health policy: Bridging the gap. *British Journal of Psychiatry* 2000;**176**:407–11.
10. Kish L. *Survey Sampling*. London: Wiley, 1965.
11. Lewis G, Pelosi AJ. *Manual of the Revised Clinical Interview Schedule (CIS-R)*. London: Institute of Psychiatry, 1990.
12. World Health Organisation. *The ICD-10 Classification of Mental and Behavioural Disorders: Diagnostic Criteria for Research*. Geneva: World Health Organization, 1993.
13. Bebbington P, Nayani T. The Psychosis Screening Questionnaire. *International Journal of Methods in Psychiatric Research* 1995;**5**:11–9.
14. World Health Organization Mental Health Division. *Schedules for Clinical Assessment in Neuropsychiatry*. Geneva: World Health Organization, 1992.
15. Wing K, Babor T, Brugha T, Burke J, Cooper JE, Giel R et al. SCAN. Schedules for Clinical Assessment in Neuropsychiatry. *Archives of General Psychiatry* 1990;**47**:589–93.
16. Norusis M. *SPSS for Windows Version 9*. Chicago: SPSS Inc, 1998.
17. SPSS/WESTAT. *WesVar Complex Samples 3.0*. Chicago: SPSS Inc, 1998.
18. Korn E, Graubard B. *Analysis of Health Surveys*. New York: John Wiley and Sons Inc, 1999.
19. Brugha TS, Bebbington PE, Jenkins R, Meltzer H, Taub NA, Janas M et al. Cross validation of a general population survey diagnostic interview: A comparison of CIS-R with SCAN ICD-10 diagnostic categories. *Psychological Medicine* 1999;**29**:1029–42.
20. Henderson S. Conclusion: The central issues. In G Andrews, S Henderson (Eds), *Unmet Need in Psychiatry: Problems, Resources, Responses*, pp. 422–8. Cambridge: Cambridge University Press, 2000.
21. Andrews G. Meeting the unmet need for disease management. In G Andrews, S Henderson (Eds), *Unmet Need in Psychiatry: Problems, Resources, Responses*, pp. 11–38. Cambridge: Cambridge University Press, 2000.
22. Bebbington P. The need for psychiatric treatment in the general population. In G Andrews, S Henderson (Eds), *Unmet Need in Psychiatry: Problems, Resources, Responses*, pp. 85–96. Cambridge: Cambridge University Press, 2000.
23. Office for National Statistics. *Social Trends 30*. London: The Stationery Office, 2000.
24. Jenkins R. Sex differences in minor psychiatric morbidity. *Psychological Medicine* 1985;**15**:1–53.

REPORT THREE

Ethnicity and the common mental disorders

Ajit Shah

This work was undertaken by the University of Cambridge who received funding from the Department of Health; the views expressed in this publication are those of the authors and not necessarily those of the Department of Health.
Address for correspondence: Dr Ajit Shah, West London Mental Health NHS Trust, Uxbridge Road, Southall, Middlesex UB1 3EU, UK. Email: a.k.shah@ic.ac.uk

Contents: Report three

List of tables: Report three

3.1 INTRODUCTION

3.1.1 Scope of the review

Inequalities in prevalence rates of common mental disorders within ethnic minority groups have been relatively little studied in the United Kingdom in spite of the increase in the size of these groups in recent decades. What research has been done has often appeared to be based on two broad assumptions: (i) there is greater morbidity in ethnic minority groups compared to the indigenous white group; and (ii) ethnic minority groups under-utilise services. The chief aim of the present review was to establish whether or not common mental disorders are more prevalent in ethnic minority groups than the white indigenous population of the UK. It also examines associated risk factors and the use of treatment and services, although this is not a review of service utility. The review does not deal with the most serious but less frequent psychotic disorders, but is confined to the far more frequent neurotic disorders, now generally called the common mental disorders, and mostly comprising anxiety and depression, from which arise the major population burden.

The review encompasses the following aspects:

- the definitions of ethnicity;
- population demography;
- methodological issues in cross-cultural research;
- development of instruments for use in ethnic groups;
- the strategy and methods of review;
- the studies meeting inclusion criteria and additional relevant studies;
- discussion of the findings;
- policy implications of the findings.

3.2 BACKGROUND

3.2.1 Definition of ethnicity

The terms race, culture, and ethnicity are often used interchangeably. Guidelines on the use of these terms for research, audit, and publication are emerging.[1;2] Race is a phenomenological description based on physical characteristics;[3] it can also be considered a social and a political construct. Culture describes shared features that bind individuals together into a community. It is possible to be racially different but culturally similar or vice versa. The definition of ethnicity is difficult[4–6] because it incorporates aspects of both race and culture, often including such related characteristics as language, religion, upbringing, nationality, cultural traditions, and ancestral place of origin.[3;7] In the UK, ethnic categories were used for the first time in the 1991 census in which respondents classified themselves. Self-assigned ethnicity is influenced by life experience and domicile, and can change over time.[3;8] This dynamic and contextual nature of ethnicity should be acknowledged in research.[9]

Many recent studies have used self-assignment into the pre-determined categories of the 1991 census.[11–18] Others have supplemented these definitions with data on country of birth,[20;21] country of birth plus race and religion combined,[19] country of birth and country of residence in combination,[13] or country of family origin.[22] However, even within these approaches, ethnic grouping may be heterogeneous because of cultural variations within country of birth, self-perceived ethnicity, and socio-economic status. Others have defined ethnicity on the basis of a common language or religious affiliation,[24;25] or simply as those individuals with a cultural heritage distinct from the majority population.[10] These are problematic as they take no account of most of the factors discussed above. Furthermore, because of the problem of small numbers, many studies have variably combined obviously different small groups into a large, heterogeneous and not very useful group.[3;14–18;22] Sadly, many studies fail to define ethnicity at all.[3;23]

3.2.2 Population demography

Over 3 million (5.5%) people were from ethnic minority groups according to the 1991 census,[26] a substantial increase from the 1% reported in the 1961 census.[27] Table 3.1 shows the proportions of particular groups in the 1991 UK population. The demographic detail given below in this section was derived from the 1991 census data.[26]

TABLE 3.1
Ethnic minority groups in the general population in Great Britain in 1991[26]

*Group**	%
Indian	1.5
Pakistani	0.9
Black Caribbean	0.9
Black African	0.4
Black Other	0.3
Bangladeshi	0.3
Chinese	0.3
Other	0.9

* These were some of the ethnic categories. They are self-assigned and not defined formally in OPCS work.

All ethnic groups were generally younger than the white indigenous population, and were concentrated in metropolitan and industrial areas.

More than 25% of the ethnic minority groups combined lived in nine London boroughs and two other urban districts (Leicester and Slough). Almost half (47%) of ethnic minority individuals had been born in the UK, with the highest proportions among young people.

Table 3.2 shows the proportion of those over 16 years of age that was married. Table 3.3 shows the proportion that was economically active: 68% of the ethnic minority population compared with 77% of the indigenous population. The social class distribution is shown in Table 3.4.

TABLE 3.2
Ethnic group and marital status in 1991[26]

Group	*% Married*
Indian	69
Pakistani	70
Bangladeshi	68
Chinese	59
Black Caribbean	39
Black African	47
Black Other	29
Whole Population	58

TABLE 3.3
Ethnic group and economic activity in 1991[26]

Group	*% Economically active*
Indian	72
Pakistani	53
Chinese	65
Black Caribbean	80
Black African	66
Black Others	63

TABLE 3.4
Ethnic group and social class[26]

	Social class (%)					
Group	*I*	*II*	*IIIN*	*IIIM*	*IV*	*V*
White	5	28	23	21	15	6
Black Caribbean	2	25	22	22	19	8
Black African	8	27	22	13	16	9
Black Other	3	26	27	17	15	5
Indian	9	27	22	16	21	3
Pakistani	6	23	18	23	22	4
Bangladeshi	5	13	19	26	23	10
Chinese	12	25	25	23	10	3

3.2.3 Methodological issues

Population-based studies of common mental disorders in ethnic minority groups in the UK are fraught with difficulties, not least of language (Table 3.5). Definition of groups has already been discussed; inappropriate groups, especially large heterogeneous groups, prejudice interpretation of analysis.[14–18;22] However defined, identification of the sample is never easy; the practice of using surnames assumed to originate from specific ethnic groups can be problematic,[25;28–31] and general practice lists are not always accurate and up-to-date.

Instruments used in psychiatric surveys may be culturally inappropriate. Questions used to detect symptoms are derived from Western concepts of mental illness and may mean different things to people with different cultural backgrounds.[22;32] Such instruments may not detect symptoms or syndromes not bound to Western cultures, and symptomatic expression of illness characteristic of non-Western cultures.[22;33] Cultural barriers include communication difficulties,[27;34] taboo topics, differential stigma attached to mental illness,[32] bias and prejudice of clinicians,[32] institutional racism,[35] and unfamiliarity of symptoms of mental illness to subjects and relatives.

TABLE 3.5
Methodological issues

Language difficulties and literacy levels[22;36]
Small sample size[25;36]
Inappropriate sampling method[27;36]
Non-response and refusal to participate[36]
Reluctance to answer the door to unexpected callers[36]
Pessimism that local services will change[36]
Indigenous subjects feeling surveys for benefit of ethnic groups[36]
Lack of screening and diagnostic instruments[22;34;37]
Lack of indigenous comparison group[25]
Unrepresentative indigenous comparison group[20;21]
Lack of comparison with country of origin

3.2.4 Development of instruments for use in ethnic groups

Thus instruments developed in one culture may not be equally valid across all cultures. Ideally we need instruments that allow ethnic minority subjects to perform at their best without the influence of extraneous factors discussed above. Modifying existing instruments makes empirical and economic sense and most research with well-developed techniques has adopted this method.[22;34;38;39] Detailed knowledge of relevant cultural factors and their influence on presentation and development of symptoms is needed.[40] A "Delphi" panel of experts from the culture of interest using structured interviews, semi-structured interviews, questions or vignettes, or wider consultation with professionals and/or lay people, has been used to examine each item for cultural relevance and to assist translation and modification. The aim is to develop instruments that are culture-fair, education-free, and analogous (that is having comparable meaning, difficulty, familiarity, and salience).

Translation and back-translation by separate groups of bilingual translators are necessary to ensure accuracy of both meaning and significance of questionnaire items; content, semantic, technical, criterion, and conceptual equivalence with the parent version for every item should be maintained.[41] Ideally, comprehensive field pre-testing should identify variations in dialect, concepts, and practical difficulties, and the scoring system and discriminating power of the instrument should be re-validated. There is no "gold standard" for validating diagnosis, but a semi-structured diagnostic interview has been used in some studies despite the observation that diagnostic instruments have not themselves been thoroughly evaluated. Important properties of instruments measuring common mental disorders are listed in Table 3.6. Such rigorous evaluation has the scope to incorporate essential somatic symptoms (often considered to be important in ethnic minority

TABLE 3.6
Characteristics of scales measuring common mental disorders in ethnic groups[42;43]

Subject characteristics
User characteristics
Type of instruments
Setting of administration of instruments
Source of data
Output of instrument
Psychometric properties
Reliability
Validity
Sensitivity to change
Floor and ceiling effects
Practical features
Timeframe of symptoms
Training needs
Duration of administration
Availability of operational manual with glossary and definitions
Qualification of users
Costs

groups), syndromal nature of psychiatric diagnosis, and concepts of distress and its implications for the definition of ill health in the measurement instrument, while maintaining all the above properties.

Scales evaluated in clinical settings such as primary care cannot be assumed to work effectively in population-based studies as their psychometric characteristics may be different in the community.

The administration for self-rating scales should be modified for illiterate respondents.[34] Questions may need to be read out[27] (e.g. with the SRQ in Manchester[34]). For bilingual respondents clear rules need to be developed as to choice of language, usually the respondent's choice or what he or she considers to be their first language.[39]

Very few instruments have been evaluated as rigorously as indicated above, but there are examples of well-established, partially evaluated instruments. The Clinical Interview Schedule, revised version (CIS-R) has been extensively used in primary care, occupational, and community studies.[44] It has been evaluated in Punjabi, Gujarati, Bengali, Hindi, Urdu, and Chinese dialect languages[22] and provides a partial validation for survey instruments. The 12-item General Health Questionnaire (GHQ-12), standardised in India[45] and validated against the CIS-R developed in Hindi for the Fourth National Survey of Ethnic Minorities,[22] was evaluated in ethnic Indian women attending primary care clinics in the UK.[39]

The Self-Reporting Questionnaire (SRQ) is a 20-item scale measuring "minor psychiatric morbidity" (assumed to equate with "common mental disorders") in primary healthcare settings, and contains most items of the GHQ-12.[46] It has been evaluated in Asian mothers attending well baby clinics in the UK (Manchester)[34] against a clinical interview providing DSM-III diagnostic criteria. This study reported a different threshold on the SRQ for probable psychiatric morbidity than reported in previous studies in other groups, indicating a need for validation in each separate ethnic group. The GHQ and SRQ have both been evaluated in India[45;48;49] and Brazil,[50] but the application of instruments evaluated in the country of family origin to ethnic minority individuals in their new country is problematic, as it does not take into account acculturation, effects of migration, new life circumstances, and country of birth (e.g., "Indians" born in Kenya).

The Langner Scale,[47] which measures undifferentiated psychiatric symptoms, has been evaluated among Indian and Pakistani migrants to the UK, and apparently discriminates well between psychiatric patients and community subjects, shows good test–retest reliability, and concurrent validity against the GHQ-12, but does not provide information on "case-ness". The Edinburgh Post-Natal Depression Scale (EPND) was evaluated in Punjabi mothers after childbirth[38] but only against an un-standardised clinical interview by community psychiatric nurses.

3.2.5 Background literature as a prelude to critically examining population-based studies

Early studies suggested higher rates of psychiatric morbidity among people who migrated.[51;52] There are several possible explanations: first, those with mental illness or a propensity to developing mental illness may selectively migrate. This could be facilitated if immigration is easy; the higher rate of mental hospital admission in England and Wales for patients from Scotland and Ireland has been cited as an example of this.[53] But if barriers to immigration are strong then there could be a "healthy migrant selection effect" producing lower prevalence of mental illness in migrants.[54] Second, the process and reasons for migration may influence the development of mental illness. Migration may be enforced (for political reasons or natural disaster) or voluntary (for economic, career, or family reasons), and migrants may or may not remain segregated or adopt the host culture and life-style to varying degrees. Third, migrants may be subject to a variety of stresses associated with migration. These stresses include adaptation to a new environment, culture, society, and language, reduced support from family networks, and experience of racism and discrimination.[27;54] Fourth, there may genuinely be a different prevalence of mental illness in the migrant's community of origin.

Early general-practice studies in the UK reported higher rates of mental illness in West Indians[55;56] compared to their indigenous counterparts, although in one study this was confined to women[55] and in the other to men.[56] A study reporting total general-practice (GP) consultation rates for South Asians to be similar to the indigenous population[57] suggested that GPs may have difficulty in recognising mental illness in South Asians, also reported (as for Black patients) by two inner city GPs.[11;12;60] This was reinforced by another GP study in London reporting equal rates of non-psychotic psychiatric morbidity in South Asians and whites consulting their GP,[58] which also reported that South Asians with psychiatric morbidity were more likely to say that the consultation was for physical problems. There is other evidence that South Asians are more likely to report somatic symptoms in depression.[59] Clearly there are important factors relating to how patients from particular cultures experience and communicate psychological distress and how GPs respond.[58]

Age- and sex-standardised admission rates to mental hospitals in 1971 and 1981 suggest that overall rates for Irish and West Indian immigrants were higher than people born in England and Wales.[53;61] Admission rates for South Asians were consistently lower than the indigenous population.[53;61] Irish people showed high admission rates,[61] but West Indians and South Asians had consistently lower admission rates than indigenous people for affective and neurotic disorders.[53;61] However, Carpenter and

Brockington[62] reported higher first admission rates in younger, but not older, West Indian and South Asian immigrants, a pattern confirmed for West Indians by a more recent study in London.[63] The prevalence of all affective disorders and neurosis of subjects on the Camberwell Psychiatric Register was lower for West Indians of both sexes, and higher for the Irish of both sexes, when compared to the indigenous population.[54]

In a comprehensive study of all pathways into care (see Goldberg & Huxley[64]) in Birmingham, West Indians were over-represented and South Asians under-represented in the psychiatric services including admissions.[12] South Asians may also be under-represented in psychology services.[67] Black psychiatric out-patients have been reported to show a pattern of self-referral and non-attendance, and to be more likely to receive physical treatments like major tranquillisers and electroconvulsive therapy, and to be seen by the most junior members of the team.[66] These findings could be explained by differences in phenomenology or stereotyped attitudes of mental health professionals.[66]

Most research has examined differences in rates of treatment or case-identification among treated populations.[22] Such studies give us no data on untreated populations or aetiological factors.[20] They may simply reflect differences in pathways to care rather than true differences in prevalence rates, and barely address the effects of culture on the experience and expression of mental illness.[22;33;68] Thus, the first step towards unravelling these conflicting findings requires population-based studies of common mental disorders in well-defined ethnic minority groups.

3.2.6 Policy context

Psychiatric morbidity is a major source of ill health and disability, and use of health and social services. Effective policy requires up-to-date knowledge of the descriptive epidemiology, risk factors, and social and economic consequences of psychiatric morbidity, and need for and use of services. Large-scale population surveys can provide this information, with time-trends if they are repeated. More specifically for ethnic minority groups, surveys can ascertain:

(1) The prevalence of mental illness in ethnic groups and their geographical location.
(2) The resultant physical and social disabilities and consequent needs.
(3) Potential aetiological risk factors, including recent life events, social support, and socio-economic circumstances.
(4) Natural history, outcome, long-term prognosis, and treatment response.

(5) Current access to treatment, primary and secondary health services, social services, and voluntary services.
(6) Perception of health, social, and voluntary services.

This can guide appropriate development of health and social services, and public education as to risk factors, use of services, and general acculturation of migrants. It can inform targeting of particular ethnic and geographical communities, training of health and social service staff in respect of the specific needs of members of ethnic minorities, and setting priorities for preventive programmes and research.

3.3 METHODOLOGY FOR LITERATURE SEARCH

The review focuses on population-based studies of common mental disorders in ethnic minority groups.

3.3.1 Inclusion criteria

- Community-based studies in the UK including an ethnic minority population.
- Age group to include 16–64 years.
- A diagnostic range encompassing common mental disorders.
- Use of standardised screening and diagnostic instruments to identify common mental disorders.
- Clear definition of ethnicity.
- Published data on the common mental disorders by ethnicity.
- Studies conducted in the last 15 years (so they are of current relevance).

Common mental disorders consisted of neurotic disorders, including anxiety and depression. Studies were included if they used a clear definition of the ethnic groups studied, independent of the exact definition used. Similarly, studies using any instruments with some degree of validation were included, as long as they had undergone translation and back-translation. With so few studies available, none with a large sample of ethnic groups, the sample size was not restricted, or some groups would have been completely unrepresented, and new and pioneering data might have been neglected. This review must be seen as a beginning and a possible stimulus for more sophisticated studies in the future.

The review was confined to studies of UK ethnic minority groups because they and their experiences are peculiar to the recent UK context, and only these have relevance for UK policy and planning. Most studies providing evidence for differences in prevalence in ethnic minorities, associated with socio-economic status and other important variables, were conducted in the United States. It is unlikely that their findings can validly be translated into the UK context, although principles and generalities might be.

3.3.2 Issues not included in the review

The literature on "stress" has not been included; the complexities of definition and measurement render interpretation very difficult and there is no direct or clear relationship to the common mental disorders. Severe mental illness, psychosis, has not been reviewed as numbers are very small, and different research strategies are required. Studies of treated populations raise important issues of availability of services, variation in professional practice, and illness behaviour, but cannot be interpreted in terms of population prevalence.

3.3.3 Search methodology

The literature search strategy adopted was broad because this field is generally poorly defined and key words are not well standardised. EMBASE and MEDLINE databases were searched for medical, psychological, and social journals in English.

To maximise the studies identified, a range of search terms was used:

- psychiatry, psychiatric symptoms/disorder/illness, mental disorder/illness, emotional disorder/illness, mental health;
- epidemiology, prevalence, incidence, community/population surveys;
- ethnicity (combined with the first two categories).

This search produced a large number of published reports, most with an abstract that permitted studies potentially meeting the inclusion criteria to be identified for further consideration. Additional studies were suggested by known researchers in the field, and cross-references in published work were rigorously followed-up. Identified studies were systematically and critically examined for validity and reliability of their methods, definitions of ethnicity, data relevant to ethnic differentials in the prevalence of common mental disorders, and potential risk factors. Where available, from the original publication, confidence intervals are reported in the next section.

3.4 FINDINGS

Seven studies fulfilling the inclusion criteria were identified. Their basic characteristics are listed in Table 3.7, in rank order of methodological rigour. Two studies used the same data set (22 and 71).

TABLE 3.7
Summary of the studies identified

Authors	*Ethnic groups*	*Randomisation*	*National or local*	*Comparison group*	*Instruments used*	*Validation interview*	*Year*	*Sample size*
Nazroo, 1997[22]	Caribbean Indian African Asian Pakistani Bangladeshi Chinese	Yes	National	White	CIS-R	PSE-9	1993–94	5196
Halpern & Nazroo, 1999[71]	As above	Yes	As above	As above	As above	As above	1993–94	5196
Meltzer et al., 1995a,b,c[14–16]	Asian & Oriental West Indian & African	Yes	National	White	CIS-R	Nil	1993	447
Williams, 1993[28]	South	Yes	Local	White	GHQ	Nil	?1987–92*	319
Williams et al., 1993, 1997[29,30]	Asian				PSS			
William & Hunt, 1999[28–31]						Self-assessed distress		
Creed et al., 1999[25]	South Asian	Yes	Local	South Asian	SRQ	Nil	?1991–95*	485
MacCarthy & Craissati, 1989[36]	Bangladeshi	Yes	Local	White	SRQ	Nil	?1981–89*	26
Commander et al., 1999[13]	Irish	Yes	Local	White	Nil	Standardised Clinical Interview	1992	24

* The date of the study was not specified in the paper and was established to be between date of publication and the latest year of referenced papers.

3.4.1 The Fourth National Survey of Ethnic Minorities 1993–94[22;32;69]

3.4.1.1 *Summary of methods*

A large population-based study in 1993–94 of 5196 people from ethnic minorities, with a comparative sample of 2867 white "indigenous" people, was conducted by the Policy Studies Institute across the UK. Ethnicity was assigned by researchers according to the subjects' family origins to avoid the instability of self-perceived ethnicity.[3;8] White respondents were divided into "British" and "Other White" groups. Only the "British" were used for comparison. The category "African-Asian" was people of Indian origin whose parents were born in Africa. The "Black Caribbean" group mostly had grandparents and parents of Caribbean origin. The Bangladeshi and Pakistani groups were amalgamated because of small numbers, and on the basis that they share a common religion and socio-economic characteristics.

The 1991 census was used to identify enumeration districts and electoral wards with a high, medium, and low density of ethnic minority. Households were then selected randomly using the Postcode Address File. The technique of focused enumeration was used to identify the sample.[70] This involves researchers visiting every *n*th (e.g., every 5th) address and asking about ethnicity at that address and addresses on either side. The white sample was selected first, from a random sample of wards; second, a random sample of households in each selected ward, using the Postcode Address File; third, random selection of one eligible subject from each selected household.

The initial assessment, by lay interviewers, used the CIS-R.[44] This standardised interview is based on 14 groups of symptoms but, due to time constraints, it was applied to only half of the ethnic minority sample and the only questions asked were those on depression and depressive ideas, anxiety, phobias, panic, and introductory questions on sleep and fatigue. Respondents meeting pre-set responses to any of the eight depression questions on the CIS-R received a second interview by a doctor or a nurse trained in psychiatric diagnosis, using the Present State Examination version 9 (PSE-9), a detailed diagnostic instrument.[72] The survey also recorded measures of socio-economic disadvantage.

Interviewers were from the same ethnic group and spoke the same language as each respondent. The CIS-R items were translated into six Asian languages (Hindi, Urdu, Gujarati, Bengali, Chinese dialects, and Punjabi). The accuracy of translation was checked by independent back-translation. If translated PSE-9 versions were available, they were used; otherwise bilingual psychiatrists translated the PSE-9, but there was no back-translation. The

CATEGO computer program for the PSE-9 can provide syndromes, categories, types, and 50 hierarchical diagnostic classes.

3.4.1.2 Discussion of methods

There are a number of methodological issues that require consideration before interpreting the findings. The definition of ethnicity was assigned by the researchers on the basis of family origin, an approach unique in mental health research. However, the ethnic minority sample was identified using data on population density from the 1991 census, in which respondents assigned their own ethnic status from a list of predetermined categories. The implication of these differing definitions on the findings is unclear. Because of small numbers, researchers variably amalgamated ethnic categories for analysis, a procedure of doubtful validity as ethnic groups are heterogeneous; some findings may, therefore, be spurious.

Although the CIS-R was translated and back-translated into appropriate languages, the translations and their psychometric properties were not systematically evaluated (see Section 3.2.4 above). The same applies to the PSE-9, although using ethnically matched interviewers may have helped reduce any bias arising from this. No data are given for inter-rater reliability for the large number of interviewers used. Not all CIS-R items were used, which may have resulted in missing cases of psychiatric morbidity, particularly as items on somatic symptoms were excluded, and mental illness in some ethnic groups may present more commonly with somatic symptoms.[59]

Despite concern that the sample for each ethnic group was small, only half of the original sample received the CIS-R, which may have further reduced the power of the study to detect differences between various groups. Only half of the CIS-R-positive white group received the PSE-9 diagnostic interview. For all groups, people who were CIS-R-negative did not receive a diagnostic interview, leaving the false negative rate for the CIS-R in doubt. It was also not possible to calculate sensitivity, specificity, and predictive values of CIS-R in identifying the common mental disorders.

The significant inconsistency between the initial and second interview in the South Asian group (people of Indian/African Asian, Pakistani or Bangladeshi origin) suggests that one or both interviews may not be identifying depression accurately. The instruments may perform differently in different groups[69] and lack of psychometric data makes it difficult to resolve this issue. The interviewers reported difficulty in translating concepts such as depression into South Asian languages. The association between fluency in English and higher prevalence of depression in South Asians suggests that they may be closer to Western culture than some other groups, and may respond more appropriately to instruments developed for

Western cultures.[69;82] Confidence intervals were not always described and this also makes interpretation of data difficult.

3.4.1.3 Results

The sample included 5196 individuals from ethnic minority groups including 1205 Caribbean, 1273 Indian, 728 African Asian, 1185 Pakistani, 591 Bangladeshi, and 214 Chinese adults. The comparison group of 2867 white individuals included 119 with Irish family origins and 94 with neither Irish nor British family origins ("Other White"). The proportions of respondents completing the CIS-R screening interview were: White, 71%; Caribbean, 61%; South Asian, 75%. Of those interviewed, the following proportions were selected for follow-up diagnostic interview: White, 13% (n = 188); Caribbean, 21% (n = 74); South Asian, 8% (n = 113); Indian/African Asian, 5% (n = 66); Pakistani and Bangladeshi, 3% (n = 47). The proportions of respondents completing the second interview were: White, 69%; Caribbean, 62%; South Asians, 65%.

The age- and gender-standardised prevalences of neurotic depression and anxiety (respondents reported as "anxious", with two or more autonomic symptoms, or had panic attacks) are given in Table 3.8. Lower prevalence of depression in Indian, Pakistani, and Bangladeshi groups for both sexes did not reach statistical significance. The "Other White" group and the Caribbean group had significantly higher rates. Women had higher rates in all groups except Pakistani, where they had lower rates. Rates of anxiety among women were uniformly high, the highest being in the white groups, especially the "Irish and Other White" group. The difference between the "White" group and each other group was statistically significant.

TABLE 3.8
Age- and gender-standardised prevalence rates of neurotic depression (PSE-9/CATEGO)[22]

Ethnic group	*Depression % (95% CI)*	*Anxiety %*
White	3.8 (2.6–5.0)	18
Irish and Other White	6.3 (4.5–8.1)	28
Caribbean	6.0 (4.0–7.9)	13
Indian/African Asian	2.8 (2.0–3.7)	9
Pakistani	3.4 (2.3–4.4)	11
Bangladeshi	1.9 (1.3–2.5)	5
Chinese	1.6 (1.0–2.3)	7

Anxiety and neurotic depression in men revealed no association with marital status in the White, Caribbean, and South Asian groups. In White women, rates were highest in lone parents with children aged under 11, followed by single and then married women. Findings in the South Asian group were similar, but the difference between single and married women did not reach statistical significance. Single Caribbean women had the lowest rate, lower than single White women. When social class of household was considered (three categories: "no full-time worker", "manual", and "non-manual workers"), non-manual households had the lowest prevalence of both anxiety and neurotic depression in White, Caribbean, and South Asian groups. However, there was no difference between manual and non-manual Caribbeans for depression, and there was no association between prevalence and social class in the combined Pakistani and Bangladeshi group.

Age at migration was used to test two alternate hypotheses: (i) those with the highest risk of mental illness selectively migrate; or (ii) those who are healthy selectively migrate. Fluency in English and ability to answer questions based on Western concepts of mental illness were used for South Asians as proxy measures of the degree of acculturation. Migrants were dichotomised into two groups: (i) those born in the UK or migrating before age 11; and (ii) those migrating after age 11. Those migrating after age 11 had lower rates for anxiety in all three ethnic groups (Caribbean, combined Indian and African Asian, and combined Pakistani and Bangladeshi groups), but these were significant only for the Indian/African-Asian groups. The amalgamated category of all South Asians with good fluency in English also had lower rates, but this was not of statistical significance.

For neurotic depression, South Asians migrating after age 11 had a lower prevalence rate than those migrating earlier; the difference in prevalence of depression between the South Asian and White group was mainly accounted for by those who migrated after age 11. For Caribbeans there was no difference according to migration, and both groups had higher prevalence than the White groups. The prevalence of depression in South Asians fluent in English was closer to the rate in Whites. Multivariate logistic regression was performed to examine the interaction between age at migration and fluency in English. The odds ratios (ORs) for those migrating before age 11, fluency in English, and the interaction term (i.e., being fluent and migrating before the age of 11) were 2.3, 1.0, and 1.9 respectively.

Multivariate analysis, using logistic regression for presence or absence of two or more symptoms of depression on the CIS-R showed that for the White group the ORs for contributory factors were: female, 1.2; one parent, 2.5; single, 1.5; manual worker, 1.7; no full-time employment in the household, 2.5; age 25–34, 1.7; age 35–54, 1.9. In the Caribbean group increased rates were found with no full-time worker in the household (1.8) and reduced rates in those who were single (0.5) or lone parents (0.4). In the South Asian group increased rates were found in lone parents (3.7), those with no full-time worker in the household (2.0), and those who migrated before the age of 11 (2.2); a reduced rate was observed in the 16–24 age group (0.2).

Caribbeans, compared with Whites, were 1.8 times more likely to have two symptoms of depression, controlling for age and gender. This was reduced to 1.6 if social class was also considered. The OR remained the same if marital status and age at migration were added. South Asians, compared with Whites, had a reduced risk, with an OR of 0.7, not affected by age, sex, marital status, or social class. The OR was modified by migration after the age of 11 years (0.9), but not significantly.

Respondents from all ethnic groups were more likely to have visited their GP regardless of their CIS-R score than the White group. Those in all ethnic groups scoring 2 or more on the CIS-R depression items were more likely to have visited their GP in the last month, and were more likely to have consulted their GP in the preceding year "about being anxious or depressed or having a mental, nervous or emotional problem". For White, combined Indian and African Asian, and combined Pakistani and Bangladeshi groups, those scoring 2 or more on the CIS-R were more likely to have received anti-depressants or minor tranquillisers, which was not true for Caribbeans, hardly any of whom received medication. South Asians (especially the combined Pakistani and Bangladeshi group) were less likely to receive medication than their White counterparts. In White, combined Indian and African Asian, and combined Pakistani and Bangladeshi groups, those with a CIS-R depression score of 2 or more were associated with greater use of therapists, alternative practitioners, and social workers in the preceding year; there was no such association in the Caribbean group.

3.4.1.4 Summary and discussion

This landmark study, the first national study of psychiatric morbidity among ethnic minority groups in the UK, had the largest sample of all extant studies, included several ethnic groups, had a white comparison group, and used standardised measurement instruments. The prevalence of depression was significantly higher in the Caribbean group and similar to the White group in other ethnic groups. The prevalence of anxiety was higher in the Irish and Other White groups than the White group and lower than the White group in all other ethnic groups. Absence of a full-time worker in the household was significantly associated with depression in the South Asian and Caribbean groups. In the South Asian group migration before the age of 11, being older, and being a lone parent were associated with depression. These associations were absent or reversed in the Caribbean group. Ethnic groups had a higher GP consultation rate. However,

Caribbeans with common mental disorder tended not to be prescribed anti-depressants or minor tranquillisers or to receive help from therapists, social workers, or alternative therapists. All ethnic group respondents with common mental disorder received less medication than their white counterparts.

3.4.2 The Fourth National Survey of Ethnic Minorities; Ethnic Density Study 1993–94[71]

3.4.2.1 Summary of methods

In the UK, Cochrane and Bal[61] found a weak, non-significant within-group effect and no between-groups effect for psychiatric admissions among foreign-born individuals. However, their geographical areas were very large for evaluating the effects of ethnic density, and psychiatric admissions are a poor proxy for population frequency. The current study used much smaller geographical areas and was population-based.

The basic survey methodology is described above (Section 3.4.1.1). The density of an ethnic minority was expressed as the percentage of residents in the respondent's ward who were of the same ethnic group. Several indicators of social disadvantage were recorded, including absence of central heating, shared kitchen, mortgage arrears, rent arrears, no car access in household, and being unemployed and on benefits. Two indirect measures of acculturation were used: fluency in English and age at migration. Two indicators of victimisation experience were also included: physical attacks in the past 12 months, and having property deliberately damaged in the past 12 months. Multivariate regression models were used to explore the relationship of density to other factors. Ethnic groups were analysed separately and combined, to examine both between-groups and within-group effects.

3.4.2.2 Results

For all ethnic minority groups combined, and for the White group, there were significant associations between high own-group density and low frequencies of neurotic symptoms. Controlling for age, sex, and hardship, this association became non-significant for the White group, but was strengthened for the combined ethnic groups. Fluency in English attenuated the association between group density and symptoms, but did not eliminate it. Age at migration had no independent effect. The hypothesis that own-group concentration can help reduce victimisation was confirmed in respect of property damage, which was less in areas of high own-group density. Because they were rare events, similar results in respect of personal attacks did not reach statistical significance. The correlation between group density and symptom score was examined for each ethnic group and controlled for age, sex, hardship, fluency in English, and age at migration. The association between high group density and low neurotic scores reached significance for the Indian and Caribbean groups, but for the African Asian, Bangladeshi, and Chinese groups similar results did not reach statistical significance. An opposite, but non-significant association was observed for Pakistanis.

3.4.2.3 Discussion

The ethnic density effect in this study was very small, explaining only 1% of the variance. The authors argue that this cannot be explained by socio-economic selection because individuals living in areas of high density of their own ethnic group, but with poor socio-economic conditions, were less likely to have psychiatric morbidity, although this was not so for Whites. Indeed, individuals living in more prosperous areas of low density of their ethnic group (usually with greater density of Whites) had higher rates of mental illness. Moreover, when economic hardship was controlled for in ethnic groups, the association between psychiatric morbidity and ethnic density was strengthened. These findings taken together supported a social causation hypothesis for the mental illness. The various South Asian groups, with similar densities of clustering, consistently reported lower levels of symptoms than the Caribbean and Chinese groups who had less dense clustering. However, there are difficulties in interpretation because the density measure from the census is biased by overall group size. For example, the White group is dominant in the population and such simple density measures may be inappropriate for between-groups comparisons. Furthermore, sampling and selection bias may also have influenced the findings. The authors suggest alternative measures for future research.

3.4.3 The first national Survey of Psychiatric Morbidity in Great Britain, 1993[14–18]

3.4.3.1 Summary of methods

Using the Postcode Address File (PAF) as the sampling frame, postal sectors were stratified by Health Authority region and by proportion of manual socio-economic groups. Ninety delivery points in 200 postal districts were selected to yield a sample of 18,000 delivery points with the aim of yielding 10,000 subjects. One person was randomly selected from each household. The age of the subjects was 16–64 years.

The main assessment instrument for neurotic disorder was the CIS-R[44] from which ICD-10 diagnoses can be derived. Brief questions about stressful life events, social support, social disability, activities of daily living (ADLs), education, and employment were also asked of all respondents, who were also asked about long-term illness and medication. Those scoring

12 or more on the CIS-R were asked for more detail on treatment, use of health, social, and voluntary services, activities of daily living, and informal care. Ethnicity was defined using the 1991 census categories and was self-assigned. The study was not specifically designed to examine ethnic minorities, but to represent all groups according to their proportion in the total population, and so there was no over-sampling of ethnic minorities. To overcome the problem of small numbers for analysis, two categories were created: Asian/Oriental, consisting of Indian, Pakistani, Bangladeshi, and Chinese groups; and West Indian/African, consisting of Black Caribbean, Black African, and Black Other categories.

3.4.3.2 Discussion of methods

Because there was no over-sampling of areas of greater density of ethnic minorities to improve sample size, the study lacked power to examine critically the prevalence and associations in ethnic minorities. The two large, heterogeneous groups created for analysis have no obvious validity, and results may thus be very limited and possibly spurious. Data were collected systematically on ethnicity according to 1991 census definitions, and used as one variable in the multivariate logistic regression analyses, but within-group analyses were not performed, so it is impossible to draw conclusions about the associations of socio-demographic and socio-economic variables with neurotic illness within individual ethnic minority groups.

The CIS-R was administered to ethnic minority individuals who could speak English and it was not translated or back-translated. It was not possible to administer CIS-R in this manner to about 50 individuals who could not speak English. This study did not report on age of migration, fluency in English, or duration in the UK, variables that can be used as proxy for acculturation and which may affect rates of psychiatric morbidity.

3.4.3.3 Results

The overall sample size was 12,730. Interviews were completed by 10,108 (79%) subjects. Neurotic disorders in the whole sample were more common in women than men (OR 1.72; 95% CI 1.57–1.97) adjusted for age, household size, and social class.

The White sample was of 9179 subjects. Ethnic minorities made up 5% of the whole sample, 4.1% being contained within the two main combined ethnic categories, 299 Asian and Oriental, and 148 West Indian and African. Table 3.9 summarises the prevalence of neurotic disorders in men and women by ethnic category. The prevalence of neurotic disorders, and symptom scores, were higher in women in all ethnic groups. The overall 1-week prevalence of neurotic disorders in these categories is given in Table 3.10. The prevalence appeared higher in the West Indian and African group

TABLE 3.9
Ethnicity and prevalence of neurotic disorders per 1000 population

	Ethnicity		
Disorder	*White*	*African/Caribbean African*	*Asian and Oriental*
Women			
Mixed anxiety and depression	96	36	160
Generalised anxiety disorder	35	22	8
Depressive episode	24	6	51
All phobias	14	18	29
Obsessive-compulsive disorder	9	0	3
Panic disorder	9	7	7
All neurotic disorders	194	190	258
Men			
Mixed anxiety and depression	54	58	68
Generalised anxiety disorder	28	62	10
Depressive episode	17	21	19
All phobias	7	7	18
Obsessive-compulsive disorder	10	0	0
Panic disorder	8	7	0
All neurotic disorders	124	155	115

TABLE 3.10
The overall prevalence of neurotic disorders (%)

Ethnicity	*Prevalence (95% CI)*	*Odds ratio (95% CI)*	*Adjusted odds ratio (95% CI)*
White	15.9 (14.9–16.9)	1	1
Asian and Oriental	18.2 (11.8–24.6)	1.12 (0.79–1.58)	1.14 (0.79-1.65)
Caribbean/African	17.3 (12.9–22.7)	1.43 (0.98–2.08)	1.02 (0.68-1.52)

Adjusted for age, sex, social class, family type, urban/rural residence, and employment status.

than the White group and the difference approached significance ($p = 0.07$), which disappeared after adjusting for age, social class, and family type. On multiple logistic regression with nine personal, family, and household characteristics as independent variables, ethnicity was not associated with CIS-R scores as the dependent variable. The prevalence of phobias was higher in the Asian and Oriental (OR 2.34; 95% CI 1.07–5.12) categories, compared to the White group. There was no other significant relationship between any specific neurotic disorders and ethnicity.

Multiple logistic regression was used to quantify the association between neurotic disorder and employment (as the dependent variable). Neurotic disorders were associated with not working (adjusted OR 1.52; 95% CI 1.34–1.74) and being Asian and Oriental significantly increased the risk of not working (adjusted OR 2.23; 95% CI 1.68–2.99). No data are currently reported on ethnicity in relation to ADLs and stressful life events. Using multiple logistic regression, and controlling for various socio-demographic factors, the presence of neurotic disorder was significantly associated with having a small primary social support group of 0–3 persons). Both neurotic disorder and small primary social support group were independently associated with perceiving a severe lack of social support, controlling for socio-demographic factors. Being Asian and Oriental was significantly associated with having a small primary social support group (adjusted OR 1.75; 95% CI 1.18–2.60), and with a perceived severe lack of social support (adjusted OR 1.51; 95% CI 1.17–1.93).

Multiple logistic regression analysis was performed for respondents with neurotic disorders to identify factors associated with those receiving treatment and those not receiving treatment in six categories: taking anti-depressants; taking hypnotics or anxiolytics; taking any anti-depressant, hypnotic, or analgesic; having therapy; having counselling; and having therapy or counselling. Factors examined included age, sex, ethnicity, family unit type, employment status, tenure and locality, number of neurotic symptoms, presence of long-standing limiting physical illness, number of stressful life events, and perceived social support. Ethnicity did not independently predict any of the treatments. In general, treatment with medication was predicted by having two or more neurotic disorders, older age, physical illness, and being economically inactive. Treatment category of therapy was associated with being economically inactive or unemployed. Counselling was associated with two or more neurotic disorders, being unemployed, and reporting perceived lack of social support.

Report 2 of this volume (Melzer et al., Table 2.15) describes how, on further analysis of data from the National Survey, three categories of disorder were introduced: "disorder" (any diagnosis of neurosis on CIS-R), "limiting disorder" (neurosis in a respondent reporting that the symptoms had stopped them doing things), and "disabling disorder" (limiting disorder plus at least one difficulty with ADLs). From multiple logistic regression analysis, being Asian and Oriental significantly increased the likelihood of limiting disorder (OR 1.49; 95% CI 1.01–2.21). Other associations were not significant.

The National Survey also recorded use of health and social services including GP consultations, in-patient episodes, out-patient visits, and home visiting by a social or voluntary worker. All GP consultations in the previous 2 weeks, and in the past year, separately for physical complaints or mental or emotional problems, were recorded. These were also separately recorded for the past 2 weeks for respondents with a neurotic disorder. Multiple logistic regression analyses encompassed a wide range of personal, social, and illness-related variables to relate to GP consultations.

GP consultations in the previous 2 weeks were associated with neurotic disorder, physical illness, female gender, and being economically inactive; ethnicity was not associated. GP consultations for physical illness in the last year were associated with neurotic disorder, physical illness, older age, female gender, being economically inactive, and being in the Asian and Oriental category (OR 1.39; 95% CI 1.09–1.79). GP consultations for a mental problem in the last year were significantly associated with neurotic disorder, physical illness, female gender, every employment status other than full-time work, presence of drug dependence, age groups between 25 and 54, and being in the Asian or Oriental category (OR 2.53; 95% CI 1.49–4.35). GP consultation for any reason in the last 2 weeks was not linked to ethnicity. There are no similar analyses in respect of the other service use categories.

3.4.3.4 Summary and discussion

This study provided one of the largest samples of UK ethnic minority groups. After adjusting for a number of socio-economic and demographic variables there was no significant difference in the overall prevalence of neurotic disorders between the Asian and Oriental category and the White group, but the prevalence appeared higher in the Caribbean and African category. The prevalence of phobias was significantly higher in both ethnic minority categories. In the whole sample, neurotic disorders were significantly associated with not working, small social support group, and perceived lack of social support. Being Asian and Oriental was also associated with not working, small support group, and perceived lack of social support. Asian and Oriental people with neurosis also had significantly more limiting illness, and consulted their GPs more frequently than the White group for physical complaints in the previous 2 weeks and for mental health in the previous year.

3.4.4 The second national Survey of Psychiatric Morbidity in Great Britain, 2000[86]

3.4.4.1 Summary of methods

The methodology was similar to the First National Psychiatric Morbidity Household Survey[14–18] as described in Section 3.4.3.1 above. There were some differences, and of relevance is the extension of the upper age limit to 74 years for inclusion in the study sample. Because of small numbers, ethnic minority groups were collapsed into three groups in this survey compared to two in the first survey. Black Caribbean, Black African, and Black Other groups were collapsed into a single Black group. The Indian, Bangladeshi, and Pakistani groups were collapsed into a single South Asian group. All other groups, except the White group, were collapsed into the Other group. Ethnicity was defined as in the 1991 census. The study utilised 438 postal sectors and this eventually resulted in 15,804 delivery points with 8450 full interviews. The numbers for ethnic minority groups were: Black group, 185; South Asian group, 142; Other group, 156.

3.4.4.2 Discussion of methods

The methodological issues raised in Section 3.4.3.1 above apply to this study.

3.4.4.3 Results

In all ethnic groups, women had higher CIS-R scores than men. Moreover, women were more likely to score more than 18 on the CIS-R than men, particularly in the South Asian group. South Asian adults and those in the Other group appeared to have a higher prevalence for most neurotic disorders than the White group. The Black group appeared to have a lower prevalence than the other groups. However, these differences did not reach statistical significance. Table 3.11 illustrates the prevalence of various neurotic disorders in the four groups.

TABLE 3.11
Prevalence of neurotic disorders[86] (rates per 1000 population)

	Ethnicity			
Disorder	*White*	*Black*	*South Asian*	*Other*
Women				
Mixed anxiety and depressive disorder	107	82	96	19
Generalised anxiety disorder	46	42	70	27
Depressive episode	27	28	41	13
All phobias	22	37	23	6
Obsessive-compulsive disorder	12	44	56	0
Panic disorder	7	0	0	21
All neurotic disorders	192	178	229	249
Men				
Mixed anxiety and depressive disorders	67	69	104	87
Generalised anxiety disorder	44	35	14	5
Depressive episode	22	26	33	48
All phobias	13	7	14	17
Obsessive-compulsive disorder	9	0	24	0
Panic disorder	7	5	0	13
All neurotic disorders	134	117	156	135

In this initial report no other correlates or treatment data have been published and no doubt future publications on this survey will contain them.

3.4.4.4 *Summary and discussion*

The findings of this survey are limited by small numbers of ethnic minority individuals, and also the full results have not yet been published. Furthermore, the ethnic grouping was different from the first national survey and thus comparison between the surveys is problematic. The available published data from this survey have added little to the first survey.

3.4.5 The West of Scotland Twenty-07 Study (1986–87)[28–32]

3.4.5.1 *Summary of methods*

This Glasgow study of psychological distress in South Asians recruited 319 adult subjects from the general population aged 30–40 years, and 159 South Asians from the same population. The median age was 35 years. They were identified using a stratified random cluster design of 22 postcode sectors. The electoral register (1986) and district valuation register (1987) were scanned for South Asian first and second names, further stratified into Muslim and non-Muslim names. Half of each group were selected for the study.

The GHQ-12, a self-assessment distress scale,[73] and a psycho-somatic scale (PSS) based on that used by Dressler,[74] with 12 items and similar to that used by Mumford et al.[75] among South Asians in Bradford and Pakistan, were used, and questions were asked about stressful life events. The PSS correlates closely (0.89) with the Mumford scale.[75]. All the scales were translated into Urdu, Hindi, and Punjabi by an educational psychologist fluent in these languages. The quality of the translation was assessed by another multi-lingual assessor, a bilingual doctor, and other bilingual interviewers, and were also back-translated. Subjects received two interviews: one by a trained bilingual social survey interviewer and the other by a nurse. The nurse was involved in taking physical measurements for another part of the study. For those not speaking English a pre-assigned interpreter helped the research interviewer.

3.4.5.2 *Discussion of methods*

There was no evidence provided of the validity of using Asian names as identifiers of cultural/ethnic group and no data were provided to allow critical evaluation of the accuracy of this sampling strategy. The data analyses were of groups defined by religion as a proxy for ethnicity;

ethnicity and religion were used interchangeably without a clear rationale. It is unclear from the reports whether the general population sample excluded South Asians, as some by chance would have been selected. All South Asians were included in the same category, ignoring their heterogeneity and diversity. The impact of these strategies on the findings is unclear.

The confinement of the study to the age-range 30–40 years limits the applicability of the findings to other age-groups. All scales were translated and back-translated into several South Asian languages and examined for accuracy of translation, but further validation was apparently not undertaken, and the psychometric properties of the new versions were only partially evaluated. This prejudices interpretation, as does the lack of data on inter-rater reliability of the large number of interviewers used. The sample size was small, although the authors provide a power calculation detecting distress between the general population and South Asian groups and the figures were consistent with the sample size of the study. Although the impact of length of stay in the UK on the GHQ-12 scores was examined, its effect on the other two instruments was not reported. The impact of fluency in English on the results of all three instruments was examined, but not the age at migration. It is unclear if the study was adequately powered to examine differences.

3.4.5.3 Results

The prevalence of psychiatric morbidity on the GHQ-12 (a score of 3 or more), PSS (a score of 4 or more), and distress scale ("often sad or depressed") for men and women in the South Asian and White group is shown in Table 3.12. Women in both groups generally had a higher prevalence of psychiatric morbidity. South Asian women on the PSS and the distress questionnaire, but not the GHQ-12, had higher prevalences than women in the general population. There was no difference in the GHQ scores in men and women of South Asian origin according to their length of residence in the UK. Similar data for the PSS and distress scale were not reported.

TABLE 3.12
The prevalence of common mental disorders

	White (%)		*South Asian (%)*	
Scale	*Men*	*Women*	*Men*	*Women*
GHQ-12	21	29	22	25
PSS	22	29	24	45
Self-rated distress	11	20	25	39

The absence of parents or in-laws increased scores on all three measures among South Asians, but not the general population. Being mugged or assaulted in the area of current residence increased scores in South Asians only, and only on the PSS.

Multivariate log-linear analyses were performed using different models. Women and limited English speakers showed higher levels of distress on the PSS (OR 1.66; 95% CI 1.06–2.6 and OR 2.59; 95% CI 1.33–5.05). However, when six stressful situations (mugged or assaulted, stress in work around the house, low standard of living, low satisfaction in work, absence of parents and in-laws, and lack of a confidante) were included, the ORs declined to 1.5 and 1.15 and were not significant. Individually, stress in work around the house and low standard of living were significant (OR 2.73; 95% CI 1.27–5.86 and OR 1.41; 95% CI 1.07–1.87).

Women and Muslims were shown to have higher levels of self-assessed distress (OR 4.44; 95% CI 2.44–8.08 and OR 1.93; 95% CI 1.16–3.19), but including the above six stressful situations reduced the ORs to non-significant levels, while low standard of living, absence of parents and in-laws, and lack of a confidante became significant (OR 1.72; 95% CI 1.25–2.38, OR 2.03; 95% CI 1.08–3.80, and OR 3.30; 95% CI 1.52–7.17), respectively.

3.4.5.4 Summary and discussion

The prevalence of common mental disorders appeared to be higher in both sexes in the combined (Muslim and non-Muslim) ethnic minority category compared to the White group. This appeared to be linked to low standard of living, absence of parents and in-laws, lack of a confidante, and stress in work around the house.

3.4.6 A study of non-psychotic disorders in people from the Indian sub-continent living in the UK and India (unspecified date between 1991 and 1995)[25]

3.4.6.1 Summary of methods

This study was conducted in one electoral ward in Southall, London as part of a larger study of heart disease risk factors.[76] Of 12,858 individuals on the electoral register, 8764 people had Indian surnames, and 485 of these subjects were randomly selected for study. Respondents' siblings living in Punjab, India were interviewed over the same period, but this aspect will not be presented here. The Self-Reporting Questionnaire (SRQ)[46] was administered to all subjects. This has been validated in mothers attending a well-baby clinic in Manchester[34] and primary care attenders in Calcutta.[49]

Based on these studies a cut-off score of 7 or more was used to define psychiatric morbidity and was assumed to reflect depressive illness. Recent life events were recorded using the brief "List of Threatening Life Events".

3.4.6.2 Discussion of methods

The definition of ethnicity was clear; the ethnic sample was chosen from South Asian names on the electoral register, but there is no evidence to validate this method. The method of random selection of ethnic minority subjects was not reported.

The SRQ has been validated in South Asian mothers in Manchester, UK[34] and in Bengali primary care attenders in Calcutta,[49] but there is no evidence that this will transfer to a London community sample. In the well-baby clinic study many subjects were illiterate and the SRQ questions were read out to them in their mother tongue; in the current study there is no information on how the SRQ was administered and the literacy rate of the sample is not given. Other evaluations are not reported, nor are data on psychometric properties. There were no second interviews to evaluate and justify the chosen SRQ cut-off score used to define a case.

There was no indigenous comparison group and the comparison group of siblings in India was a biased convenience sample. The impact of these methodological inadequacies on the results is unclear, but interpretation is problematic. Generalisation from a London sample is also limited. Age at migration, duration in the UK, and fluency in English, or other measures of acculturation, were not used, and no multivariate analysis was undertaken.

3.4.6.3 Results

Complete psycho-social datasets were available for 376 participants. The religious distribution was: Sikhs, 223 (59.3%); Hindus, 100 (26.6%); Muslims, 49 (13%); Christians, 4 (1.1%). The mean age for men and women was 46 (SD 10.6) and 45.6 (SD 9.4) respectively. The country of birth was: India and Pakistan, 309; UK, 5; elsewhere, 62. Almost all the men (94.8%) and women (89.4%) were married. The prevalence of depression in Sikh, Muslim, and Hindu men was 5%, 23%, and 13% respectively; the corresponding figures in women were 16%, 57%, and 27%. Depression was more common in older men, but not in older women.

In men, marital status was not associated with high SRQ scores, but in women, high SRQ scores were significantly raised in widowed, single, and separated women. The SRQ score was significantly raised in unemployed and retired men; this did not apply to women. There were significant differences in the distribution of SRQ scores in the three religious groups, but adjusting for unemployment using analysis of co-variance rendered the differences non-significant in men. In women the difference in SRQ scores between religions (Muslims had the highest scores) persisted after adjustment for unemployment. There were no significant effects of occupational social class or education on these differences between religious groups. Unemployment was more common among Muslims. One or more threatening life events in the preceding 6 months were observed in 35 of the 62 respondents with a score of 8 or more on the SRQ, and this was statistically significant compared to the remainder of the subjects.

3.4.6.4 Summary and discussion

This study managed to secure one of the largest samples of all UK ethnic minority studies of common mental disorders. Unemployment and older age was associated with depression in men. Not-married marital status was associated with depression in women. Unemployment and financial difficulties were the most important life events. The authors speculate that the higher SRQ scores in Muslims may be due to increased distress because they experienced a greater number of threatening life events.

3.4.7 Community study of Bangladeshi adults in East London (unspecified date between 1981 and 1988)[36]

3.4.7.1 Summary of methods

All residents over age 18 years in three representative blocks on a council estate in East London were asked to complete two self-rating scales. The SRQ[46] has been validated in Calcutta[49] where Bengali is spoken. The List of Threatening Experiences[77] has 12 categories of life event, to which were added 5 items considered to be of particular relevance to this study, after consultation with local professionals: racial discrimination, harassment, poor housing, feelings of isolation, and fears for safety outside the home. Both questionnaires were translated into Bengali by a Bengali-speaking psychiatrist and back-translated by a Bangladeshi community worker. Some words were amended to be consistent with the local dialect.

Questionnaires were posted to 150 Bengalis and 150 Whites. It is unclear how they were selected. Only 12 Bengali and 22 Whites initially responded. Two weeks later non-responders were visited at home by either a local Bangladeshi worker (known to the community) for the Bangladeshis, or a research worker for the Whites. In total, 28 (19%) of the Bangladeshi sample and 77 (52%) of the White sample were interviewed, but only 26 (17%) Bangladeshis and 44 (29%) Whites completed questionnaires.

3.4.7.2 *Discussion of methods*

A strength of this study is ethnic homogeneity, but the authors do not adequately describe how Bangladeshi subjects were identified or how the three council blocks were selected. The sample size was small, and the extremely high non-response rate renders the findings very weak and interpretation almost impossible. The high refusal rate in the Bangladeshi sample was considered to be due to: working long and unsociable hours; reluctance to answer the door to unexpected callers; an unsettling effect on this community of recent changes in immigration law; and poor literacy rates in their mother tongue. The high refusal rate in the White sample was considered due to pessimism about positive change arising from surveys, and the perception that surveys were only for the benefit of Bangladeshis.

Although the SRQ was translated and back-translated, further validation was not undertaken, and psychometric properties were not given. It has previously been used in primary care, but its validity in community populations is yet to be established. The authors argue that in other populations it has been shown to have predictive validity similar to the GHQ.[50] In Calcutta, where Bengali is the main language, Sen and Williams[49] showed that a higher cut-off score was needed for a largely illiterate population recently migrated from rural areas. They speculate that the same might apply to Bangladeshis in this study, and this might explain the apparently high prevalence of psychiatric morbidity using the conventional cut-off score of 8 or more. The single small-scale location of the study also prejudices generalisation to other areas and communities. Given the very low response rate, the apparently high prevalence might represent selective response by those who were ill.

3.4.7.3 *Results*

There were equal numbers of men ($n = 13$) and women ($n = 13$) in the Bangladeshi sample. There were more women ($n = 26$: 59%) than men ($n = 18$: 41%) in the White group. The mean ages of the Bangladeshi and White groups were 42 years (SD 13.8) and 44.5 years (SD 18.7) respectively. All Bangladeshis were born in Bangladesh. The mean years in the UK was 12.45 years (range 1–33). Only one (5%) of the Bangladeshi sample spoke English fluently. Almost all Bangladeshis were married, compared to only 15% of Whites.

Using a cut-off score of 8 or more on the SRQ, the prevalence of common mental disorder was 50% in the Bangladeshi group ($n = 13$) and 29% ($n = 13$) in the White group. Bangladeshis reported significantly more chronic adversity than Whites, and more life events ($p = 0.06$). Bangladeshis reported more serious money problems, problems with police, racially motivated attacks, discrimination in work and housing, and feeling socially isolated. SRQ scores in the Bangladeshi group correlated with life events, chronic adversity, and combined scores. In the White group this correlation was evident only for life events and the combined score.

3.4.7.4 Summary and discussion

Prevalence of common mental disorder was higher in these Bangladeshi respondents than the white respondents. Levels of adversity were high for both groups, but higher in the Bangladeshi group, particularly chronic adversity, and this may have been the most important association with mental disorder. However, small numbers and an extremely low response rate make any conclusions of doubtful utility.

3.4.8 Psychiatric morbidity in Irish immigrants to the UK (1992)[13]

3.4.8.1 Summary of methods

A community sample of 508 individuals was randomly selected from those aged 16–64 years from general-practitioner lists. Subjects were interviewed by researchers trained in using the Structured Clinical Interview for DSM-III-R.[78] Diagnostic categories relevant to this review included major depression, dysthymia, panic disorder, agoraphobia, and generalised anxiety. In both samples ethnicity was defined using the 1991 census framework. People born in Ireland (Eire, Northern Ireland, and Ireland—part not stated) formed the Irish-born group. The remainder of the white group, of whom 99% were born in the UK, formed the comparison group and will be referred to as "Other White".

3.4.8.2 Discussion of methods

There are several problems with using the definition of ethnicity in the 1991 census to compare those born in Ireland with Other Whites. First, the comparison group of "Other White" may include people of Irish origin, so that the significance of being Irish-born is unclear. Second, there are doubts over the accuracy of the 1991 census in identifying Irish-born people, thus prejudicing the denominator for calculations. Third, the comparison group of "Other White" included about 1% born outside the UK. Fourth, there are doubts about the validity of combining all Irish-born people into one group.

The rationale for the sample size being 500 was not given and it appears that the study was not specifically designed to examine psychiatric morbidity in Irish-born people. The community sample was very small with resultant wide confidence intervals. The difficulties in defining ethnicity and the small sample are likely to have biased the findings, although it is not possible to say in which direction. Prevalence rates were provided only for all affective disorders combined rather than for individual disorders. The study was restricted to one geographical area and it is unclear how far its findings may be generalised to other areas of the UK.

3.4.8.3 Results

In the community, to attain a target sample of 500, 1500 people were sampled, providing 508 subjects for interview, of whom 24 were Irish-born and 286 were "Other White" (the remainder came from other ethnic groups). There were no gender differences, but the Irish-born were significantly older. The prevalence rate for affective disorder in the Irish-born was 16.7% compared to 14.9% in the "Other White" group (OR 1; 95% CI 0.3–3.1). The wide confidence intervals are due to a small number of cases of psychiatric morbidity

3.4.8.4 Summary and discussion

Although prevalence rates in Irish-born people were higher, when age and sex were taken into account the difference was not significant. It is difficult to draw firm conclusions from this study due to small numbers.

3.4.9 Other relevant studies

Some studies not fulfilling the inclusion criteria, but which may be of relevance, particularly from a methodological viewpoint, are described in Section 3.6, Appendix A.

3.5 DISCUSSION

3.5.1 General discussion

From the literature, seven studies fulfilling the inclusion criteria (although two share the same dataset) were identified, and four other relevant studies. Individual studies and their characteristics have been described above. Comparisons between different studies were problematic. Definitions of ethnicity and methods of ascertaining ethnicity varied, and ethnic groups were amalgamated into heterogeneous categories without any clear rationale other than small numbers. Sample size ranged from 28 to over 1200, and many results had wide confidence intervals. Comparison groups within the indigenous population were inadequately defined or absent, or were unrepresentative of the population due to the sampling method used. Some sampling methods such as postal surveys were inappropriate in populations with high levels of illiteracy, leading to low response rates.

Instruments used to detect common mental disorders were only partially evaluated and were often based on unwarranted assumptions that instruments effective in one ethnic group or one setting (e.g., primary care or hospitals), will be effective in other groups or settings (e.g., community). Inter-rater reliability was not reported even where a large number of interviewers was used. Odds ratios and confidence intervals were not always given, nor was multivariate analysis always applied. Studies reporting data on ethnic minorities had not always been designed for that purpose, and the effects of ethnic density, age at migration, duration in the UK, degree of acculturation, fluency in English, and difficulties associated with migration were often ignored.

Although this review was confined to 15 years, it is likely that there have been substantial demographic, cultural, and environmental changes during this period and thus the studies should not be viewed as one block. Different cohorts of migration and acculturation may have influenced the findings.

3.5.2 Summary of findings

However, there were some findings that can be summarised. Overall, there was no clear evidence that the prevalence of the common mental disorders in any ethnic minority group studied was lower than in the population in general. The available evidence suggests that prevalence is at least similar to that in the population in general, and in some cases may be higher. There were indications from particular studies that the prevalence of neurotic disorders, particularly depression, might be higher in Caribbeans and Africans, that the prevalence of anxiety might be higher in Irish-born and non-British "Other White" groups, and that phobias might be more common in Asian and Oriental people than in the indigenous British white population. The prevalence figures can be influenced by the type of measurement instrument used and the relative weighting given to psychological and to somatic symptoms.

A number of risk factors for common mental disorders in ethnic minority groups were identified and are listed in Table 3.13. These need to be interpreted cautiously because different studies with differing methodologies have identified different risk factors and no one risk factor is robust across most studies. One study suggested that the prevalence of psychiatric morbidity is higher in ethnic minority groups who lived in areas of own-group "low density", perhaps implying that living in areas of own-group "high-density" has a protective effect.

Although not the principal focus of this review, there is evidence from these studies, particularly the Fourth National Survey of Ethnic Minorities, that ethnic minority groups with common mental disorders tend to have

TABLE 3.13
Risk factors for common mental disorders in ethnic minority groups

Absence of full-time worker in the household[22;32;69]
Unemployed[14–18;25]
Lower standard of living[28–32]
Financial difficulties[36]
Migration before the age of 11 years[22;32;69]
Older age-group[14–18;25]
Lone parents[22;32;69]
Victimisation[36;71]
Personal attacks[28–32;71]
Racial discrimination[36]
Problems with the police[36]
Discrimination in housing and employment[36]
Absence of confidante[28–32]
Absence of parent in laws[28–32]
Social isolation[36]
Small primary group[14–18]
Perceived lack of social support[14–18]

lower rates of treatment, receiving fewer anti-depressants and minor tranquillisers. This was particularly so for the Caribbean and African group, which also appeared to use therapists, social workers, and "alternative healers" much less frequently than the White and South Asian groups. All ethnic minority groups had higher GP consultation rates than Whites. There were similar findings in the National Household Psychiatric Survey of 1993, in which Asians and Orientals with neurosis were found to have consulted their GPs more frequently for physical problems and mental problems in the preceding year.

3.5.3 Policy implications

In spite of the serious inadequacies in the methods used in the studies reviewed, they do suggest that the common mental disorders, often associated with functional disability, are at least as common in ethnic minority groups as in the general population, and may be more common in some groups. As ethnic minority populations are increasing, the absolute number of individuals with common mental disorders will also tend to rise. It is therefore important that strategies are developed to promote primary prevention, early identification, secondary prevention, and tertiary prevention.

Most suggested risk factors for common mental disorders in ethnic minority groups are the same as for the general population, including unemployment, absence of anyone employed in the household, financial insecurity, low standard of living, social isolation, small social network, and perceived lack of social support. But others are more specific to ethnic minorities, including racial victimisation and discrimination in housing and employment. National and local social policy should address these in an effort to reduce the development of common mental disorders. This may require better co-ordination between health, social service, education, judicial, and social security sectors with innovative developments.

The available evidence suggests that GP treatment rates for common mental disorders in ethnic minority groups may be low despite high GP consultation rates. There are several possible explanations. Clinical presentation with physical symptoms may be more common, patients may have limited ability to communicate psychological distress, and the GPs may have limited ability to recognise mental illness. Better information and in-service training for health, social service, and voluntary sector staff, in the identification and management of common mental disorders, especially related to ethnic minority groups in particular communities, could improve this situation. Basic medical and other health and social service training also needs to address these issues. We also need to improve awareness of common mental disorders in ethnic minority groups themselves and the general public through a public education campaign.

Although there is evidence that Caribbean and Africans may have more depression and that Irish-born and non-British "Other White" people may have more anxiety, on the whole the prevalence of common mental disorder is similar in ethnic minority and indigenous white groups. Services, therefore, should be targeted at all ethnic minority groups in the same manner as for the indigenous white population.

However, there are clearly some additional difficulties in ethnic minority populations with very different cultures, especially where there are low levels of literacy in English. In areas with significant minorities, core catchment area primary healthcare, social service, and psychiatric services need to become ethnically informed and sensitive, and to develop special skills to meet the needs of their particular ethnic minority populations. Separate services should be avoided as they can reinforce marginalisation and compete for resources with mainstream services. The principle of improving ethnic sensitivity and understanding in mainstream services applies both to situations where individuals from ethnic minorities are uncommon in the population (in whom the common mental disorders might be more common), and to situations where particular ethnic groups are a significant or large proportion of the population.

Improving the ethnic sensitivity of existing services needs to recognise the perceptions of ethnic minority groups of existing services and their views on how services should meet their needs. Very few hard data are available from population-based studies to inform this, and there is a clear and urgent need for local studies (based on health authority or social service areas).

Service developments should be underpinned by quality assurance and audit, and more research is needed. This is discussed in the next section. One important point needs to be made here. There is an urgent need to encourage further analysis and publication of relevant unpublished data from existing studies. For example, the National Psychiatric Morbidity Survey did not report on any within-group analysis for particular ethnic minority groups; there are many other examples from the studies reviewed. Such refined data would help inform many of the issues discussed in this section.

3.5.4 Implications for research

New research studies should take account of the methodological pitfalls of earlier studies. Epidemiological studies should have clear objectives from the outset: for example, planning services in a district with high density of one specific ethnic group may require a locally based epidemiological study, but identifying potential risk factors for a disorder may require a national sample.

Most previous research has relied on differences in rates of treatment or case-identification among treated populations.[69] Such studies provide no data on untreated populations or associated possible aetiological factors.[20] They may simply reflect differences in pathways to care rather than differences in prevalence rates and may ignore the effect of culture on the experience and expression of mental illness.[33;68;69] Understanding these issues requires population-based studies of common mental disorders in well-defined ethnic minority groups.

All studies should use a clear definition of ethnicity, ideally a consistent definition to facilitate comparison. This could only be achieved if researchers and central organisations such as the Department of Health and research funding bodies were to agree a common definition. The common practice of amalgamating all ethnic minority groups into one category should be discouraged; such heterogeneous categories are unlikely to provide useful information. However, the implication of this is that sample sizes of each ethnic group being studied must be much larger, with implications for both cost and logistics of research.

Studies should only use instruments that have been appropriately evaluated in the relevant ethnic groups (see Section 3.2.4). Considerable effort and funding needs to be dedicated to rigorous evaluation of instruments before undertaking large-scale epidemiological studies, for the findings to be worthwhile. Clear rules need to be agreed on the administration of instruments (especially self-rating) to illiterate subjects, those not fluent in

English, those fluent in both English and their mother tongue, and those who only speak English. Ideally, case-identification should follow a two-stage procedure: a screening instrument followed-up with a formal diagnostic instrument. There is now enough information available to allow estimation of sample size for any field study.

Many previous studies compared ethnic minority and indigenous groups, but did not undertake within-group analysis to examine socio-demographic and socio-economic associations with psychiatric morbidity within each group. There is a need for both between-groups and within-group analysis.

As well as conventional epidemiological studies,[79;80] we need methods designed to identify the barriers on pathways into all levels of care up to inpatient care,[64] and to identify presenting clinical features at different "filters", for different ethnic groups. Possible risk factors at each filter should include not only conventional socio-demographic and socio-economic factors, but also age at migration, difficulties associated with migration, duration in the UK, degree of acculturation, and experience of victimisation and racism. Also needed are studies of adverse life events, and ethnic density.

Prevalence rates are influenced by incidence rates, duration of illness, and survival after onset, but the course, outcome, and natural history of common mental disorders among ethnic minority groups in the UK has not been studied. Incidence studies may also identify more potential risk factors. This requires longitudinal population-based studies, but these are time-consuming and expensive, and need large samples that are very difficult to achieve for most ethnic minorities.

If differences in population frequency are confidently established after several well-conducted studies, cross-national and cross-cultural studies would allow investigation of underlying genetic and environmental risk factors and interaction between them. If genetic factors dominate, migrants would tend to show similar frequencies to the same ethnic group in the country of origin, but if environmental factors dominate, different frequencies should be revealed. Comparisons of genetically homogeneous ethnic groups in different communities, at different stages of economic development and in different environments, may reveal the importance of particular environmental risk factors such as changes in diet, occupation, education, and physical environment, experience of victimisation and racism, disengagement from culture of origin, and general acculturation.

Knowledge of environmental and genetic risk may lead to better understanding of causal processes, and improved treatments and preventive strategies. Well-conducted cross-national and cross-cultural studies using appropriate screening and diagnostic instruments can help this. Thus far, only two studies of common mental disorders have attempted to examine cross-national prevalence rates and correlates,[25;81] although such cross-national and cross-cultural approaches are well established in the epidemiological study of dementias.[43]

3.6 APPENDIX A: SOME OTHER RELEVANT STUDIES

3.6.1 Psychiatric morbidity among people of Irish Catholic descent in Britain (1987–88)[24]

3.6.1.1 *Summary of methods*

This was a longitudinal population-based study of everyday life and health among three cohorts aged 15, 35, and 55 at inception into the study in 1987–88. This study is referred to as the "West of Scotland 20–07" study and was conducted in a large urban area of Glasgow. In 1990–91, 908, 852, and 858 subjects in the three cohorts were followed up. Depression was measured using the self-rating Hospital Anxiety and Depression Scale (HADS)[83] to detect possible and probable depression. A conservative cut-off score of 9 or more on the HADS was used to define depression. In this community, those of Catholic religion are considered mostly to be of Irish descent. The authors argue that although recent Irish migrants are uncommon, Catholic inter-marriage maintains a strong Irish heritage. Subjects were classified as of Catholic heritage in the youngest and eldest cohort if one parent was of Irish descent and in the middle cohort if they responded as being born in the Catholic heritage. Reasons for this approach were not specified.

3.6.1.2 *Results*

The study reported only data on depression in the oldest cohort, then aged 58 years. The sample size of Catholics of Irish heritage was not given. The prevalence of depression in this group was 18%; no confidence intervals were given, nor was the prevalence of depression in non-Catholics reported, but the odds ratio was said to be not significant.

3.6.1.3 *Summary and discussion*

The prevalence of depression was reported only in one cohort although the study had three cohorts and a large sample size (though the exact sample size of the Catholic group was not reported). The study assumed that the ethnic classification of all cohorts were similar, without good evidence. The HADS is essentially a screening instrument for use in hospital settings, where it has been rigorously evaluated; here it was used as a diagnostic instrument in community settings. Lack of any second-stage validation interview to confirm the diagnosis makes interpretation difficult. The focus of the study was health-related behaviours; it was not designed to examine depression, which was barely discussed. Relevant data are sparsely reported. It is difficult to draw any conclusions.

3.6.2 A comparative population-based study of "psychological disturbance" in Irish immigrants to England, English, and Irish samples (unspecified date before 1979)[81]

3.6.2.1 *Summary of methods*

The Immigrant Irish group was defined as those born in Ireland but resident in England; the Irish group was those born and resident in Ireland; the English group was those born and resident in England. The 1971 UK census was used to identify the age and sex distribution of Irish-born residents in England, to select towns and districts with a relatively high concentration of immigrant Irish, including London, Birmingham, Coventry, and Manchester. The "random walk" technique (this method involves a random selection of dwelling, rather than individuals, by having the interviewer follow a pre-designed random walk) was used to identify a sample of 200 Immigrant Irish in these communities and 200 English matched for age, sex, and area of residence. Similarly 200 Irish were selected from 17 districts of Dublin, also matched with the Immigrant Irish group.

Psychological symptoms were assessed using two scales: the Symptom Rating Test (SRT),[84] and the Langner Scale of Distress.[47] The SRT has a total score and sub-scale scores for four conditions: depression, anxiety, somatic, and inadequacy. Both scales measure symptoms consistent with common mental disorders and provide an overall score, rather than a measure of "case-ness". They were administered by trained research interviewers. Additionally data on socio-demographic factors and several newly created, though not fully validated, indices were gathered. These indices included family contact index, social isolation index, migration difficulty index, and acculturation index.

3.6.2.2 *Results*

In the three samples of 200, the refusal rate ranged from 13% to 19% but differences were not significant. The three groups were similar on most demographic variables including mean age (40 years). The notable differences were religion, social class (more Dublin Irish in social classes I and II), type of community of birth (fewer Immigrant Irish-born in urban areas), and home ownership (fewer English owned their own houses). On the SRT the Immigrant Irish group had lower total and sub-scale scores than both other groups, but there were no differences between the other two groups. The highest scores were in women and older respondents. Greater number of years of education was associated with lower SRT scores in Irish men, Immigrant Irish women, and native English women. Longer duration in England in Immigrant Irish women was associated with higher SRT scores. Greater degree of acculturation was associated with higher SRT scores in Immigrant Irish men. Older age at migration was associated with lower SRT scores in Immigrant Irish women. Greater social isolation was associated with higher SRT scores in Irish men, Immigrant Irish men, and women, and English women. Similar findings were observed for the Langner scale. Sadly no multivariate analysis was undertaken to separate out independent effects of the various factors.

3.6.2.3 Summary and discussion

Ethnicity was clearly defined using a combination of country of birth and country of residence. Although clear, the inclusion of people of Irish origin, but born and living in England, in the English group may have reduced observed differences. Although better than many studies, the sample size is still relatively small, and no rationale for restricting it to 200 in each group is given. Identification of ethnicity is not possible from the electoral register and private censuses of the areas were considered too expensive. Random walk sampling may then have been the best choice. Only the Immigrant Irish group can be considered to be representative of the Irish immigrant population from which it was drawn, as the other groups were age and sex matched to them; the impact of this on the findings is difficult to estimate.

The SRT and the Langner scales had both been validated in England and their psychometric properties, including reliability, evaluated. The Langner scale has been validated for use in immigration studies[37] but in Asian groups, and its applicability to both Dublin Irish and Irish immigrant groups can be questioned. The authors provided no data on this issue and appear to have assumed that evaluation in English and American samples was adequate. Although there were different interviewers in England and Ireland, information on inter-rater reliability was not given. Because there was no measure of "case-ness", there could be no prevalence estimates of psychiatric disorders. The various socio-economic indices specifically developed were not fully validated, which may be a source of bias, and without multivariate analysis interpretation of the socio-economic and demographic associations was problematic, as independent effects were not teased out.

This was a landmark study as it was one of first population-based studies of psychiatric morbidity in a UK ethnic minority group and with one of the largest sample sizes up to that time. The findings did not show high psychiatric admission rates for Irish immigrants, and it is possible that the scales used were measuring different morbidity than that normally leading to psychiatric admission; for example alcohol-related disorders significantly contributed to admission rates but the questionnaires did not screen for alcohol. Migrants may under-report symptoms to outsiders if they think they raise issues of social undesirability. Interestingly, a greater degree of acculturation was associated with higher scores on both scales. This was a cross-sectional study so that causality cannot be inferred from the associations identified.

3.6.3 A community survey of psychological adjustment of Asian immigrants to Britain (unspecified date before 1977)[20]

3.6.3.1 *Summary of methods*

Ethnicity for the Indian and Pakistani group was not clearly defined: the study selected those who were born in India or Pakistan and "were of appropriate ethnic origin". The comparison group was defined as being born in England, Scotland, or Wales, having parents from these countries, and being white. In total, 50 Indians and 50 Pakistanis were selected in age and sex categories to reflect population demography using quota sampling techniques in a high-density immigrant area of Birmingham. The comparison group was selected by individual matching for age, sex, and area of residence of both Asian groups. They were administered a questionnaire with three components: a psychological disturbance scale; a life events inventory; and specific questions on demography, personal and family relations, and satisfaction with living conditions. Psychological disturbance was measured using the 22-item Langner Scale.[47] which in 1977 was considered to be as good as the GHQ.[37] The Life Events Inventory[85] measures a list of possible disruptions in ordinary daily life, and asks questions about housing and employment history. The entire questionnaire was translated into Gujarati, Bengali, Urdu, Hindi, and Punjabi by professional translators. Only the Gujarati version was back-translated for a check on accuracy. All interviews were conducted in the respondent's mother tongue in their home.

3.6.3.2 *Results*

Indian and Pakistani samples of 50 each had their comparison group of 50 Whites. Response rates in Indian, Pakistani, and White samples were 94%, 90%, and 78%, respectively. Asians were more likely to be married and more poorly educated than Whites. Indians and Pakistanis had been in the UK for an average of 11 and 11.6 years, respectively. There were no differences in Langner Scale scores between the Indian sample and their White matched group for either sex. Pakistani men, but not women, had lower Langner scale scores than their White matched group. Indians and Pakistanis both had significantly lower Life Events Inventory scores than Whites. Indians were more likely to be employed than Whites but there was no difference between the Pakistani and White groups. Indians were more likely than Whites to be owner-occupiers, but there was no difference between the Pakistani and White groups. Both Indians and Pakistanis lived in significantly more crowded conditions than Whites.

In Indian males, higher Langner scale scores were associated with higher life event scores, lower length of residence in the UK, and lower length of residence in the UK for spouse. In Indian women, higher Langner Scale scores were associated with greater crowding. In Pakistani men, higher Langner Scale scores were associated with increased age, higher social class, and upward social mobility. In Pakistani women, higher Langner Scale scores were associated with higher life event scores. In White men and women, higher Langner Scale scores were associated only with higher life event scores.

3.6.3.3 Summary and discussion

This study was confined to one geographical area of high ethnic density, so its generalisability to other areas can be questioned, especially as ethnic density effects on psychiatric morbidity[71] may be important. Ethnicity for the Indian and Pakistani groups was poorly defined. The sampling techniques and methods of identifying ethnic groups were not fully described. The rationale for the small sample size of 50 in each group was not explained. The Indian and Pakistani groups were chosen to reflect their age and sex distribution in the community, but native White samples were matched to them and were therefore not representative of the white population. Differences may therefore have been masked or results biased. Although all scales were translated into appropriate languages, only the Gujarati version was back-translated. Furthermore, the detailed procedure for developing instruments across cultures was not followed (see Section 3.2.4) and no data on psychometric properties were provided. The Langner scale only provides a score and does not measure "case-ness", which limits the results. There was no multivariate analysis to separate out independent effects of significant variables which may have themselves been intercorrelated.

This was one of the first community studies of psychiatric morbidity among Asians in the UK and it set the agenda for this type of research, but the methodological inadequacies make it impossible adequately to interpret the findings.

3.6.4 A community study of psychological symptom level in Indian immigrants to England (unspecified date before 1981)[21]

3.6.4.1 *Summary of methods*

Using 1971 census data, Indian immigrants were chosen from four areas with a high density of this ethnic group: Slough, London, Birmingham, and Coventry. The study excluded ethnic Indians from East Africa. All Indian subjects were born in India; this was the sole criterion for the definition of the group. The comparison group of native-born English was also defined solely by place of birth. The Indian sample was selected using a random walk technique. The indigenous sample was obtained from comparable working-class residential areas of other large towns.

Psychological symptoms were assessed using the Langner 22-Item Scale of Distress,[47] which had previously been validated in both the original form and in a translation for Asian immigrant populations.[37] Psychometric evaluation had shown it to be a reliable indicator of mild, undifferentiated psychological symptom levels. These might loosely be considered to equate with common mental disorders; there was evidence for this from a favourable comparison with the 12-item GHQ in Indian immigrants.[37] A "migration difficulty index" and an "acculturation index" were also completed, together with data on demography, social mobility, housing, and employment. All interviews were conducted in the subject's home in their mother tongue (English, Gujarati, Punjabi, Urdu, Hindi, and Bengali).

3.6.4.2 *Results*

There were 110 men and 90 women in each sample, with a mean age of 36 years. The refusal rate was 5% for Indians and 13% for Whites. The Indian group consisted mainly of Sikhs who predominantly spoke Hindi and Punjabi. Indians were more likely to be employed, be in unskilled or semi-skilled jobs, come originally from rural areas, and own their homes. Marital status, paid employment in women and education were similar in both groups. Indians had significantly lower scores on the Langner Scale compared to Whites for both sexes at any of the three cut-off scores (4, 7, 10). Women had higher scores than men in both groups. There was no interaction between ethnicity and sex.

At the lowest cut-off score (4), 16.3% of Indian men and 22.9% of Indian women were identified; the corresponding figure for White men was 27.1%, and for White women 46.6%. At the highest cut-off score (10), 2.7% of Indian men and 0% of Indian women were identified; the corresponding figure for White men was 4.5%, and for White women 13.3%.

Higher Langner scale scores were associated with lower social class in Whites, but with higher social class in Indians, largely accounted for by Indian women. Unemployment was associated with higher scores in men of both groups, but in women only among Whites. Women in both groups had high scores if their spouse was unemployed; in men this was seen only in Whites as Indian males had high scores if their spouse was employed. Unmarried Indian women had higher scores. Social mobility was a predictor for high scores in Indians but not Whites, but, within the Indian group, higher scores were associated with upward mobility in women and lower scores with downward mobility in men. In Indian men and women, the greater the degree of acculturation the lower the scores, but the older people were at migration, the higher the scores. However, these analyses were not controlled for degree of acculturation, chronological age, and duration in the UK. Length of residence in the UK was negatively correlated with scores. There was no association with difficulties associated with migration.

3.6.4.3 Summary and discussion

Ethnicity was not clearly defined other than by country of birth and the method of ascertaining ethnicity was not specified. All Indian ethnic groups were combined, although they are heterogeneous. The Langner scale was available in several Indian languages, but it is unclear to what extent the Langner scale can be said to capture common mental disorders, and it was not designed to establish "case-ness". It has not been rigorously evaluated (see Section 3.2.4) and data on psychometric properties are few (Table 3.6). Selecting areas of high ethnic density raises the issue of bias introduced by the ethnic density effect on psychiatric morbidity.[71] This study had one of the largest sample sizes of all UK ethnic group studies, but multivariate analysis was not conducted to separate out independent effects of the various correlates of psychological disturbance.

Indian immigrants of both sexes had lower levels of psychological disturbance than native Whites. Higher social class was associated with higher scores in Indians, due to women in non-manual jobs, a finding that is difficult to explain—the authors propose various speculative hypotheses. The effects of unemployment were in the expected direction in both groups. Longer residence in the UK, greater acculturation, and a lower age of migration were all associated with lower levels of psychological disturbance. However, as these three variables are inter-related, and also interact with chronological age and difficulties associated with migration, the findings were difficult to interpret as multivariate analysis was not undertaken.

3.7 APPENDIX B: POSTSCRIPT. AN ADDITIONAL STUDY

A study missed by the search strategy and pointed out by one of the reviewers is described below.[87]

3.7.1 Summary of methods

Subjects were randomly drawn from four Manchester general-practice lists. They were initially contacted by letter, phone, or home visits. All available and consenting subjects were administered the GHQ-12. All those scoring 3 or more on the GHQ-12 and one in four of those scoring less than 3 were selected for a second-stage interview with Schedules for Clinical Assessment in Neuropsychiatry (SCAN)[88] by a trained psychiatrist. They were all provided with an ICD-10 diagnosis. Those taking part in the second-stage interview were also given a short explanatory model questionnaire. Ethnicity was defined using the 1991 census categories. Although the paper does not make this explicit, it implies that these were self-assigned.

3.7.2 Discussion of methods

The authors provide no data on the power of the study to detect differences, although it has one of the largest samples in the literature in this area. Ethnicity was essentially self-assigned and has been criticised by other authors.[89] Also, comparison with the white group amalgamated is problematic as it includes other ethnic minority groups such as the Irish (which in this review have been designated an ethnic minority grouping). Although GHQ-12 has previously been used in African Caribbeans in primary care, there are no clear data on the psychometric and the other properties of the GHQ-12 and the SCAN interview in this ethnic minority population.

3.7.3 Results

Of the 1467 subjects randomly selected from GP lists, only 864 were resident at the designated address. Moreover, 131 refused consent and 121 were persistently unavailable. Thus, 337 African Caribbeans and 275 white Europeans completed the first stage of the study. The sex ratio was in favour of women with 55% and 51% being women in the African Caribbean and White European groups, respectively. The mean age in these two ethnic groups was 49.5 and 51.3 years, respectively. Moreover, 71% of African Caribbeans were born abroad (mainly in Jamaica) and 23% of White Europeans were born abroad (mainly in Ireland). Second-stage interview was completed by 92 (88% response rate) African Caribbeans scoring 3 or more on the GHQ-12 and 35 (71% response rate) scoring 2 or less on the

GHQ-12. The corresponding figures for White Europeans were 62 (79% response rate) and 41 (82% response rate).

The overall 1-month prevalences of all common mental disorders were 13% (95% CI 10%–16%) and 14% (10%–18%) in the African Caribbean and White European groups. The prevalences of depressive disorders in all African Caribbeans, their men, and their women were 13% (10%–16%), 4% (1%–7%), and 19% (14%–25%), respectively; the corresponding figures in the White European group were 9% (6%–12%), 7% (3%–11%), and 11% (6%–16%), respectively. The prevalences of anxiety disorders in all African Caribbeans, their men, and their women were 3% (1%–5%), 0%, and 5% (2%–8%), respectively. The corresponding figures for White Europeans were 9% (6%–12%), 7% (3%–11%), and 10% (5%–15%), respectively. Anxiety disorders were significantly less common in the African Caribbean group (difference 6%, 2%–10%). Depressive disorders were significantly higher in African Caribbean women (difference 8%, 1%–15%).

3.7.4 Discussion and summary

This study utilised one of the largest samples of a relatively homogeneous ethnic minority group. The findings are consistent with some of the studies described earlier in this report.

3.8 NOTES

1. Anonymous. Ethnicity, race, culture: Guidelines for research, audit and publication. *British Medical Journal* 1996;**312**:1094.
2. Singh SP. Ethnicity in psychiatric epidemiology: The need for precision. *British Journal of Psychiatry* 1997;**171**:305–8.
3. Bhopal R. Is research into ethnicity and health racist, unsound or unimportant science? *British Medical Journal* 1997;**314**:1751–56.
4. Lloyd K. Ethnicity, primary care and non-psychotic disorders. *International Review of Psychiatry* 1992;**4**:257–62.
5. McKenzie K, Crowcroft NS. Describing race, ethnicity and culture in medical research: Describing the groups is better than trying to find a catch all name. *British Medical Journal* 1996;**312**:1051.
6. Pringle M, Rothera I. Practicality of recording patient ethnicity in general practice: Descriptive intervention study and attitude survey. *British Medical Journal* 1996;**312**:1080–2.
7. Rait G, Burns A. Appreciating background and culture: The south Asian elderly and mental health. *International Journal of Geriatric Psychiatry* 1997;**12**:973–7.
8. Senior PA, Bhopal R. Ethnicity as a variable in epidemiological research. *British Medical Journal* 1984;**309**:327–30.
9. Ahmad W. Race and health. *Sociology of Health and Illness* 1995;**17**:418–29.
10. Manthorpe J, Hettiaratchy P. Ethnic minority elders in Britain. *International Review of Psychiatry* 1993;**5**:173–80.
11. Commander MJ, Sashidharan SP, Odell SM, Surtees PG. Access to mental

health care in an inner-city health district. I: Pathways into and within specialist psychiatric services. *British Journal of Psychiatry* 1997;**170**:312–16.
12. Commander MJ, Sashidharan SP, Odell SM, Surtees PG. Access to mental health care in an inner-city health district. II: Association with demographic factors. *British Journal of Psychiatry* 1997;**170**:317–20.
13. Commander MJ, Odell S, Sashidharan SP. Psychiatric morbidity in people born in Ireland. *Social Psychiatry and Psychiatric Epidemiology* 1999;**34**:565–9.
14. Meltzer H, Gill B, Petticrew M, Hinds K. *The Prevalence of Psychiatric Morbidity Among Adults Living in Private Households*. London: OPCS, 1995.
15. Meltzer H, Gill B, Petticrew M, Hinds K. *Physical Complaints, Service Use and Treatment of Adult Psychiatric Disorders*. London: OPCS, 1995.
16. Meltzer H, Gill B, Petticrew M, Hinds K. *Economic Activity and Social Functioning of Adults with Psychiatric Disorders*. London: OPCS, 1995.
17. Jenkins R, Bebbington P, Brugha T, Farrell M, Gill B, Lewis G et al. The National Psychiatric Surveys of Great Britain—strategies and methods. *Psychological Medicine* 1997;**27**:765–74.
18. Jenkins R, Lewis G, Bebbington P, Brugha T, Farrell M, Gill B et al. The National Psychiatric Morbidity Surveys of Great Britain—initial findings from the household survey. *Psychological Medicine* 1997;**27**;775–89.
19. Davies S, Thornicroft G, Leese M, Higgingbotham A, Phelan M. Ethnic differences in risk of compulsory psychiatric admission among representative cases of psychosis in London. *British Medical Journal* 1996;**312**:533–7.
20. Cochrane R, Stopes-Roe M. Psychological and social adjustment of Asian immigrants to Britain: A community survey. *Social Psychiatry* 1977;**12**:195–206.
21. Cochrane R, Stopes-Roe M. Psychological symptom level in Indian immigrants to England—comparison to native English. *Psychological Medicine* 1981;**11**:319–27.
22. Nazroo JY. *Ethnicity and Mental Health. Findings from a National Community Survey. PSI Report No. 842*. London: Policy Studies Institute, 1997.
23. Rwegellera GGC. Differential use of psychiatric services by West Indians, West Africans and English in London. *British Journal of Psychiatry* 1980;**137**:428–32.
24. Abbott J, Williams R, Ford G, Hunt K, West P. Morbidity and Irish Catholic descent in Britain relating to disadvantage in behaviour. *Ethnicity and Health* 1999;**4**:221–30.
25. Creed F, Winterbottom M, Tomenson B, Britt R, Anand IS, Wander GS. Preliminary study of non-psychotic disorders in people from the Indian subcontinent living in the UK and India. *Acta Psychiatric Scandinavica* 1999;**99**:257–60.
26. Office of Population Censuses and Surveys. *1991 Census: Ethnic Group and Country of Birth. Great Britain*. London: OPCS, 1993.
27. Bhui K. Epidemiology and social issues. In D Bhugra, R Cochrane (Eds), *Psychiatry in Multicultural Britain*, pp. 49–74. London: Gaskill, 2000.
28. Williams R. Health and length of residence among South Asians in Glasgow: A study controlling for age. *Journal of Public Health Medicine* 1993;**15**:52–60.
29. Williams R, Bhopal R, Hunt K. Health of a Punjabi ethnic minority in Glasgow: A comparison with the general population. *Journal of Epidemiology and Community Health* 1993;**47**:96–102.
30. Williams R, Eley S, Hunt K, Bhatt S. Has psychological distress among British south Asians been underestimated: A comparison of three measures in the West of Scotland population. *Ethnicity and Health* 1997;**2**:21–9.

31. Williams R, Hunt K. Psychological distress among British South Asians: The contribution of stressful situations and subcultural differences in the West of Scotland Twenty-07 Study. *Psychological Medicine* 1997;**27**:1173–81.
32. Berthoud R, Nazroo J. The mental health of ethnic minorities. *New Community* 1997;**23**:309–24.
33. Kleinman A. Anthropology and psychiatry: The role of culture in cross-cultural research on illness. *British Journal of Psychiatry* 1987;**151**:447–54.
34. Upadhyaya A, Creed F, Upadhyaya M. Psychiatric morbidity among mothers attending well-baby clinic: A cross-cultural comparison. *Acta Psychiatrica Scandinavica* 1989;**81**:148–51.
35. Soloman A. Clinical diagnosis among diverse populations: A multicultural perspective. *Family in Society: The Journal of Contemporary Human Service* 1992;**June**:371–377.
36. McCarthy B, Craissati J. Ethnic differences in response to adversity. *Social Psychiatry and Psychiatric Epidemiology* 1989;**24**:196–201.
37. Cochrane R, Hashmi F, Stopes-Roe M. Measuring psychological disturbance in Asian immigrants to Britain. *Social Science and Medicine* 1977;**11**;157–64.
38. Clifford C, Day A, Cox J, Werrett J. A cross-cultural analysis of the use of the Edinburgh post-natal depression scale (EPDS) in health visiting practice. *Journal of Advanced Nursing* 1999;**30**:655–64.
39. Jacob KS, Bhugra D, Mann AH. The validation of the 12-item General Health Questionnaire among ethnic Indian women living in the United Kingdom. *Psychological Medicine* 1997;**27**:1215–17.
40. Dien S, Huline-Dickens S. Cultural aspects of ageing and psychopathology. *Ageing and Mental Health* 1997;**1**:112–120.
41. Flaherty JA, Gavira FM, Pathak D et al. Developing instruments for cross-cultural psychiatric research. *Journal of Nervous and Mental Disorders* 1988;**176**:257–63.
42. Zaudig M. Assessing behavioural symptoms of dementia of Alzheimer's type: Categorical and quantitative approaches. *International Psychogeriatrics* 1996;**8**(Suppl 2):183–200.
43. Shah AK, Lindesay J. Cross-cultural issues in the assessment of cognitive impairment. In J O'Brien, D Ames & A Burns (Eds), *Dementia* pp. 217–31. London: Arnold, 2000.
44. Lewis G, Pelosi A, Araya R, Dunn G. Measuring psychiatric disorder in the community: A standard assessment for use by lay interviewers. *Psychological Medicine* 1992;**22**:465–86.
45. Gautam S, Nijhawan M, Kamal P. Standardisation of the Hindi version of Goldberg's General Health Questionnaire. *Indian Journal of Psychiatry* 1987;**29**:63–6.
46. Harding TW, De Arango MV, Baltazar J et al. Mental disorders in primary health care: A study of frequency and diagnosis in four developing countries. *Psychological Medicine* 1980;**10**:231–41.
47. Langner TS. A twenty-two item screening score of psychiatric symptoms indicating impairment. *Journal of Health and Social Behaviour* 1962;**3**:269–75.
48. Shamsunder C, Murthy SK, Prakash O, Prabhakar N, Subbakrisna DK. Psychiatric morbidity in general practice in an Indian city. *British Medical Journal* 1986;**292**:1713–15.
49. Sen B, Williams P. The extent and nature of depressive phenomena in primary health care: A study of Calcutta. *British Journal of Psychiatry* 1987;**151**:486–93.
50. Mari JJ, Williams P. A comparison of the validity of two psychiatric screening

questionnaires (GHQ-12 and SRQ-20) in Brazil using receiver operating characteristic (ROC) analysis. *Psychological Medicine* 1985;**15**:651–9.
51. Odegard O. Emigration and insanity: A study of mental disease among the Norwegian-born population of Minnesota. *Acta Psychiatrica Scandinavica* 1932;**Suppl. 4**.
52. Krupinski J. Sociological aspects of mental ill-health in immigrants. *Social Science and Medicine* 1967;**1**:267–81.
53. Cochranc R. Mental illness in immigrants to England and Wales: An analysis of mental hospital admissions, 1971. *Social Psychiatry* 1977;**12**:25–35.
54. Bebbington P, Hurray J, Tennant C. Psychiatric disorders in selected immigrant groups in Camberwell. *Social Psychiatry* 1981;**16**:43–51.
55. Pincent RJFH. Morbidity in an immigrant population. *Lancet* 1963;**I**:437–8.
56. Kiev A. Psychiatric morbidity of West Indian immigrants in an urban group practice. *British Journal of Psychiatry* 1965;**109**:356–63.
57. Brewin C. Explaining the lower rates of psychiatric treatment among Asian immigrants to the United Kingdom: A preliminary study. *Social Psychiatry* 1980;**15**:17–19.
58. Wilson M, MacCarthy B. GP consultation as a factor in the low rate of mental health service use by Asians. *Psychological Medicine* 1994;**24**:113–19.
59. Husain N, Creed F, Tomenson B. Adverse social circumstances and depression in people of Pakistani origin in the UK. *British Journal of Psychiatry* 1997;**171**:434–8.
60. Odell SM, Surtees PG, Wainwright NWJ, Commander MJ, Sashidharan SP. Determinants of general practitioner recognition of psychological problems in a multi-ethnic inner city health district. *British Journal of Psychiatry* 1997;**171**:537–41.
61. Cochrane R, Bal SS. Mental hospital admission rates for immigrants to England: A comparison for 1971 and 1981. *Social Psychiatry and Psychiatric Epidemiology* 1989;**24**:2–11.
62. Carpenter L, Brockington IF. A study of mental illness in Asians, West Indians and Africans living in Manchester. *British Journal of Psychiatry* 1980;**137**:201–5.
63. Glover G. The pattern of psychiatric admissions of Caribbean-born immigrants to London. *Social Psychiatry and Psychiatric Epidemiology* 1989;**24**:49–56.
64. Goldberg D, Huxley P. *Common Mental Disorders: A Biosocial Model*. London and New York: Tavistock and Routledge, 1991.
66. Littlewood R, Cross S. Ethnic minority and psychiatric services. *Sociology of Health and Illness* 1980;**2**:194–200.
67. Goodwin A, Power R. Clinical psychology service for ethnic minority groups. *Clinical Psychology Forum* 1986;**5**:24–8.
68. Sashidharan SP. Afro-Caribbeans and schizophrenia: The ethnic vulnerability hypothesis re-examined. *International Review of Psychiatry* 1993;**5**:129–44.
69. Nazroo JY. Rethinking the relationship between ethnicity and mental health: The British Fourth National Survey of Ethnic Minorities. *Social Psychiatry and Psychiatric Epidemiology* 1998;**33**:145–8.
70. Smith P. Methodological aspects of research amongst ethnic minorities. *Survey Methods Centre Newsletter* 1986;**16**(1):20–1.
71. Halpern D, Nazroo J. The ethnic density effect: Results from a national community survey of England and Wales. *International Journal of Social Psychiatry* 1999;**46**:34–46.

72. Wing JK, Cooper JE, Sartorius N. *Measurement and Classification of Psychiatric Symptoms*. Cambridge: Cambridge University Press, 1974.
73. Fenton S, Sadiq-Sangster A. Culture, relativism and expression of mental illness. South Asian women in Britain. *Sociology of Health and Illness* 1996;**18**:66–85.
74. Dressler WW. Psychosomatic symptoms, stress, and modernisation: A model. *Culture, Medicine and Psychiatry* 1985;**9**:257–86.
75. Mumford DB, Tareen IAK, Bajwa MAZ, Bhatti MR, Pervaiz T, Ayub M. An investigation of functional somatic symptoms among patients attending hospital medical clinics in Pakistan—1. Characteristics of non-organic patients. *Journal of Psychosomatics Research* 1991;**35**:245–64.
76. Bhatnagar D, Anand IS, Durrington PN, Patel DJ, Wander GS, Mackness MI et al. Coronary risk factors in people from the Indian subcontinent living in West London and their siblings in India. *Lancet* 1995;**345**:405–9.
77. Brugha T, Bebbington P, Tennant C, Hurry J. The list of threatening experiences: A subset of 12 life event categories with considerable longterm contextual threat. *Psychological Medicine* 1985;**15**:189–94.
78. Spitzer RL, Williams JBW, Gibbon M, First MB. The Structured Clinical interview for DSM-III-R (SCID) 1. History, rationale and description. *Archive of General Psychiatry* 1992;**49**:624–9.
79. Shepherd M. Epidemiology and clinical psychiatry. *British Journal of Psychiatry* 1978;**133**:289–98.
80. Shepherd M. The contribution of epidemiology to clinical psychiatry. *American Journal of Psychiatry* 1984;**141**:12.
81. Cochrane R, Stopes-Roe M. Psychological disturbance in Ireland, in England and in Irish immigrants to Britain: A comparative study. *Economic and Social Review* 1979;**10**:301–20.
82. Jadhav S. The cultural origins of western depression. *International Journal of Social Psychiatry* 1996;**42**:269–86.
83. Zigmond AS, Snaith RP. The Hospital Anxiety and Depression Scale. *Acta Psychiatrica Scandinavica* 1983;**67**:361–70.
84. Kellener R, Sheffield BF. A self-rating scale of distress. *Psychological Medicine* 1973;**3**:88–100.
85. Cochrane R, Robertson A. The life events inventory: A measure of the relative severity of psychosocial stressors. *Journal of Psychosomatic Research* 1973;**17**:135.
86. Singleton N, Bumpstead R, O'Brien M, Lee A, Meltzer H. *Psychiatric Morbidity Among Adults Living in Private Households, 2000*. London: The Stationery Office, 2001.
87. Shaw CM, Creed F, Tomenson B, Riste L, Cruickshank JK. Prevalence of anxiety and depressive illness and help seeking behaviour in African Caribbeans and white Europeans: Two phase population survey. *British Medical Journal* 1999;**318**:302–6.
88. World Health Organisation. *SCAN Schedules for Clinical Assessment in Neuropsychiatry*. Geneva: WHO Division of Mental Health, 1992.
89. Rait G. Commentary: Counting heads may mask cultural and social factors. *British Medical Journal* 1999;**318**:305–6.

Index

Page numbers in *italic* indicate tables.

For Product Safety Concerns and Information please contact our EU representative GPSR@taylorandfrancis.com
Taylor & Francis Verlag GmbH, Kaufingerstraße 24, 80331 München, Germany

www.ingramcontent.com/pod-product-compliance
Ingram Content Group UK Ltd.
Pitfield, Milton Keynes, MK11 3LW, UK
UKHW022133190926
475702UK00013B/1790

9781138871960